TEACHING THE NATIVE AMERICAN

Second Edition

Hap Gilliland
Professor, Eastern Montana College

KENDALL/HUNT PUBLISHING COMPANY
2460 Kerper Boulevard   P.O. Box 539   Dubuque, Iowa 52004-0539

Edited by **Rachel Schaffer**

Artwork by **Lori Sargent**

Dedicated to the many excellent teachers whose skill and efforts are daily inspiring Native American children, and who have willingly shared their creative ideas for providing a more relevant education for these students.

My sincere appreciation to the professional people who have willingly shared their experience and their expertise in teaching Native American students by contributing chapters to make this book complete. They are identified with their chapters, in the contents, and in the authors' biographies at the back of the book. Thanks also to the many teachers who have sent ideas and suggestions for this second edition. My gratitude also to my wife, Erma Gilliland, for her patience, suggestions, and her willing assistance in proofreading.

We also appreciate the assistance of the nonprofit Council for Indian Education, without whose help this book would not have been completed. The members of their Intertribal Editorial Board are listed below.

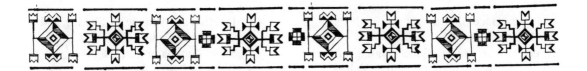

Contents

Introduction

A great deal has been written about what is wrong with Indian education, but too little emphasis has been placed on positive ideas for making that education better and more relevant to the needs of these students. This book was written to help fill that gap.

Teaching the Native American is a book of ideas—not abstract, theoretical concerns, but practical information and suggestions for educators working with Native American students. The book's central focus is on how the cultural differences between white and Native American societies affect the educational progress and development of Native American students. While it is intended to be an enlightening, thought-provoking, and above all helpful reference work for teachers and teachers-in-training from Head Start to High School, the issues discussed by the individual chapter authors also provide valuable insights for parents, teacher aides, administrators, and college faculty teaching Native American students or teaching courses in Native American Studies, Bilingual Education, or cross-cultural studies.

The first chapters of *Teaching the Native American* deal with specific areas of Native American culture that affect the education of Native American students: self-image, learning styles, discipline, and others. The rest of the book discusses cultural concerns and cultural relevance in a wide variety of academic areas: the language arts, social studies, mathematics, science, computers, art, and physical education. Each chapter suggests references for further reading and other types of resource materials. The authors of these chapters come from a wide variety of backgrounds, and all have experience with teaching Native American students at different grade levels. The editors have worked extensively with several different North American and South American tribes, and bring special insight to a book which is personal, practical, and immediately relevant to all concerned educators of Native American students.

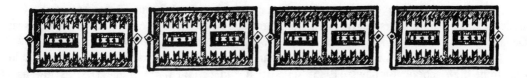

Chapter 1
A Culturally Relevant Education
by Hap Gilliland

> *"The task challenging Native communities is to retain their distinct cultural identities while preparing members for successful participation in a world of rapidly changing technology and diverse cultures."*
>
> —Indian Nations at Risk Task Force

Will our Native American students use their full potential in our classrooms? Will they reach their own individual goals and grow into adults who believe in themselves, who consider themselves successful? There are classrooms in which Native Americans are at the bottom of the line academically, socially, and emotionally; where neither the students nor the teacher expect anything but failure. Fortunately, there are many other classrooms in which Native American youth are happy, highly successful students who are growing into beneficial, contributing members of society. Which we have depends largely upon how well we learn to understand our students' backgrounds and values, their ways of learning, and whether or not we can adapt to their needs.

The emphasis in teaching must be on the positive, the good things that can be done to help the student. That is what we will emphasize in this manual. However, we cannot remedy a problem until we look it squarely in the face, see that the problem exists, and know why. An alcoholic cannot recover from his drinking problem until he recognizes that he has a problem; a school will not change its approach to Indian education until the teachers recognize a need for change.

The Need for a Culturally Relevant Education

> *"Our schools have failed to nurture the intellectual development and academic performance of many Native children, as is evident from their high dropout rates and negative attitudes toward school."*
>
> —Indian Nations at Risk Task Force

Educational statistics indicate underachievement, absenteeism, and overage students. More subjective evaluations add negative educational goals, low levels of aspiration, and low socio-economic status.

In an educational survey of the Crow Indian Reservation, I found 50 percent of the Crow students two or more years below the national average in reading. The high school students in a Denáina Indian village in Alaska with whom I worked averaged 5th grade reading level.

Tierney (1991) found that in 1984, less than 60 percent of American Indians were graduating from high school. Mohawk (1985) stated that "in certain parts of the U.S. as few as 26 percent of the Indian children who enter the seventh grade graduate from high school." Armstrong (1990) reports that it was only 25 percent in 1986 in Canada.

As W. S. Johnson (1984) said, in describing Eskimo and Alaskan Indian education, "The native student who aspires to success is faced with the difficult and often dissonant task of marching to more than one drum. The dilemma of not rejecting one's own rich cultural heritage, while preparing to be successful in a context which at best ignores or at worst contradicts such a heritage along with its inherent values and ethics is not a simple one. It is little wonder that the native and non-native student [or teacher] find it difficult to recognize, least of all appreciate, each other's orientation, efforts, purpose and values."

The Indian Nations at Risk Task Force (1991) wrote: "When the demand for new work skills is compounded by rapid social, cultural, and political changes, it is easy to understand the significant increase in individual apathy, use of alcohol, suicide, and loss of purpose and pride. Unless greater attention is paid to strengthening the physical, mental, and spiritual health of Natives, these problems will continue to multiply in tribal groups and families."

They list among the barriers to be overcome: "An unfriendly school climate that fails to promote appropriate academic, social, cultural, and spiritual development among many Native students"; "extremely high dropout rates, especially in urban schools, where Natives are in the minority and where the school climate does not support Native students"; "Teachers with inadequate skills and training to teach Native children effectively"; and "Economic and social problems in families and communities—poverty, single-parent homes, family violence, suicide, substance abuse, and physical and psychological problems—that act as direct barriers to the education of Native children."

I could go on and cite volumes of research and evidence that proves the need for change, but to those of you who are in the classrooms teaching Indian children, the need is obvious. You see it in the eyes of the student who doesn't understand your explanation because his experiences are different. You see it in the lack of effort of the student who is convinced that he cannot achieve and that even the teachers are against him. You see it in the silence of the student who does not believe you will accept his kind of reasoning or who won't speak up because he would be putting down his friend who already gave the wrong answer.

Too much of the literature on Indian education is devoted to enumerating the problems. We have recognized the problems; let us look for solutions.

Recommendations for Action

"To find harmony in diversity, teachers must wade through the rhetoric to glean the best research on multicultural education and, as usual, rely on their own best instincts."

—Sara Bullard (1992)

There are no easy answers, no simple changes that would give all Native Americans an equal opportunity for the success that others achieve. Each tribe is different, and each individual student is different. But there are teachers who have been innovative and understanding enough to succeed. Throughout this chapter and the chapters that follow are suggestions—ideas that have proven effective for individual teachers. It is up to each of you to select and adapt from them, to meet the needs of the *individual students* in *your* classroom.

1. Provide a Multicultural Education for All Children

"To fully participate in our democratic society . . . all students need the skills a multicultural education can give them to understand others and to thrive in a rapidly changing, diverse world."

—James A. Banks (1992)

Each person becomes culturally oriented during childhood. We accept our family's and our community's view of the world; we internalize their values, their concepts, and their stereotypes.

Children living in the Indian, the Inuit, the Chicano, or any other minority culture are forced early to confront, examine, and question the cultural assumptions of their home environments. If the school recognizes the values of each of the cultures represented in the classroom as equally valid and valuable, these minority children retain their self-esteem, their confidence in themselves and their people, and they learn to adapt to and live in both their own and the dominant society. If their own culture is rejected by the school, they may be forced to reject either their own or the mainstream culture. Whichever they choose, they are handicapped, not only academically but in all of life.

As was stated by Kirkness and Bainhardt (1991), the desire of Native American people is an education that will bring them "not just empowerment as individuals but empowerment as bands, as tribes, as nations, and as people. For the institutions to which they must turn to obtain that education, the challenge is clear. What First Nations people are seeking is not a lesser education, and not even an equal education, but rather a better education—an education that respects them for who they are, that is relevant to their view of the world, that offers reciprocity in their relationships with others, and that helps them exercise responsibility over their own lives."

A multicultural education is, therefore, not only essential to the Native American child, but just as essential to the child of the dominant society. Urban children who attend the typical school find all the assumptions and stereotypes of their home environments reinforced in the school and feel secure in their value. They therefore have little opportunity to challenge, to evaluate thoughtfully, to become free of cultural biases that devalue other cultures, the poor, and the victims of prejudice. If these children are not challenged by a multicultural education, and given an opportunity to understand the values and motivations of their Indian neighbors or those of other cultures, they are handicapped by a lack of both the understanding and the motivation to benefit from cross-cultural relationships. They will lack the ability to function effectively and work cooperatively within the multitude of other American cultures which they will confront throughout life.

James Banks (1989) offers three goals that should be taken to heart by all those concerned with multicultural education. He recommends that we: 1. "Transform the school so that male and female students, exceptional students, as well as students from diverse cultural, social, racial, and ethnic groups, will experience an equal opportunity to learn in school." 2. "Help all students develop more positive attitudes toward different cultural, racial, ethnic, and religious groups." 3. "Empower students from victimized groups by teaching them decision-making and social action skills."

2. Become Familiar With and Accept Native American Ways

"Respect for diversity is the hallmark of democracy."
—Asa G. Hilliard III (1992)

To be effective teachers of culturally diverse students we must be prepared to understand, and accept as equally valid, values and ways of life very different from our own. If we become aware of the differences, then learn to know and understand the child's culture well enough to accept it as equally good and equally valid, then neither teacher nor child will be pressured to adopt the other's culture, and mutual respect and understanding can develop.

Educators sometimes speak of Native American students as being "disadvantaged." In reality, these Native people have the double advantage of knowing and living in two cultures. The teacher, on the other hand, may know only one culture, and may have accepted that culture as being superior without any real thought or study. *It is the teacher, then, who is disadvantaged!* However, if the teacher does not know, understand, and respect the culture of the students, then the students *are* at a disadvantage *in that teacher's class*.

If you, as the teacher, are to be respected by your students, then you must first demonstrate your respect for the children and their culture. However rich and worthwhile the culture of a people, if you, the teacher, do not know and understand the cultural background of your students, you not only will fail to adapt to their experiential background, their motivations, and their values, but whether or not you are aware of it, you will be exerting pressure for change, and giving the students the feeling that you do not respect either them or their culture.

The need for mutual respect seems obvious, yet in actual practice it is rare. Throughout the world, wherever the Native people have become the minority, they have found themselves under great pressure to adopt the culture, values, and ways of life of the dominant society. In most cases there has been very little respect for mores and values of the Native culture. Nowhere is this more evident than in the schools. In the classroom, the Native culture is seldom used, valued, or even understood.

We have all heard unknowing people speak of Native students as being "culturally deprived." The very use of the term indicates the speaker's lack of understanding of their very rich cultures. A Blackfeet Indian told me, "A man stood on the top of the pass in Glacier National Park and said, 'I've heard there is some really fantastic scenery around here. Where is it?' The person who lives on an Indian reservation and calls his neighbors culturally deprived is as unseeing as that man."

Don't let your actions or attitudes imply that one culture is superior to another. Don't fall for the rhetoric of either type of extremist, those who would turn all children into middle-class urban whites, or those who would teach contempt for everything European. We must teach respect for all people and all groups in our society and prepare each student to live in a multicultural society. For this, the student needs to gain enough knowledge of various people and cultures to be independent, to choose from each culture that which is *best for him,* so that he can be successful in his own way.

As an Aboriginal once told me, "You can't expect a person to see eye to eye with you if you are looking down on him."

One Navajo told his daughter's teacher, "Don't try to make every child over like you. One like you is enough!"

Tierney quotes an American Indian college student: "I think White people think education is good, but Indian people often have a different view. I know what you're going to say—that education provides jobs and skills. It's true. That's why I'm here. But a lot of these kids, their parents, they see education as something that draws students away from who they are. . . . I would like to tell them at the university that education shouldn't try to make me into something I'm not."

Fortunately, in spite of all the pressures to change, many Native people have been able to retain their essential values, and some of the more important aspects of their old cultures. American Indians, Chicanos, Eskimos, Aleuts, Hawaiians, New Zealand Maoris, Aboriginal Australians, Camorros of Guam, Lapps of Norway, the Tribal people of the Philippines, the Natives of American Samoa, and the Gaelic speaking people of Ireland all have very rich and beautiful cultures. It would be a great loss to them, and to the world, if these cultures were to disappear. Yet the children of all of these cultures are often disrespected by people from the dominant culture and are pressured to change.

How well do you really know and accept the culture in which your students were raised? Most of us assume that the Indian child will find that some of the ways of the non-Indian have value for him, and that he will want to adopt them for himself. Then we must also assume that the non-Indian child will see and want to adopt some of the values and ways of his Indian neighbors. Until we really believe that this is good, so that we make it plain in our daily attitudes in the classroom, we will not give every student an equal opportunity; we are not ready to teach Indian students. Until you know the culture, you will have prejudices even if you are not aware of them, for *"prejudice is being down on something you are not up on!"*

3. Value the Student's Background and Provide Additional Experience

> *"Do not do unto others as you would want that they should do unto you. Their tastes may not be the same."*
>
> —Bernard Shaw

Clarence Wesley, Chairman of the San Carlos Apache Tribe in Arizona, says: "The School curriculum is geared to a whole set of concepts and literary background too often totally unfamiliar to an Indian child. Few teachers have the time . . . or know how to go back and supply that deficiency or to teach the reading skills necessary to catch up. So the Indian child becomes confused and lost, and sits unchallenged while the non-Indian part of the class moves eagerly ahead."

As you study, observe, and become acquainted with the people of the community, learn how your students' background of experiences differs from your own. Where students need additional background to understand specific subject matter, you have to help them build that background. Develop instructional materials which are related to student experiences, and present to the students problem assignments which relate to their backgrounds. Choose culturally related reading material for the majority of your instruction in reading and comprehension skills.

4. Identify and Emphasize Positive Indian Values

> *"Indian culture has not been wiped out. This culture has been greatly modified since 1942 but those cultural essences which have filtered down to the present are still integral, shaping forces in Indian society, and these essences must be included in Indian education programs if they are to be relevant.*
>
> —Dick Little Bear, Northern Cheyenne

As Harriet Light (1986) says, "Children reflect their families' strengths, weaknesses, attitudes, and values. In order for teachers to meet their students' needs, they must understand and appreciate the values and relationships within the student's family."

You cannot assume that any student believes in or follows all the values of what some might consider the "typical Indian culture," or that he follows the patterns of the non-Indian society. Each student is somewhere in between, though he is usually nearer one end of the scale than the other. Even the Native American student who appears to have lost contact with the old culture of his people will usually vary from the student from the dominant society in his background of experience, the vocabulary he uses and understands, his ways of communicating, his willingness to talk and express ideas, his concept of time, his willingness to compete with his classmates, and his attitudes toward property, future and success.

If you are observant you will find many valuable and useful ideas and values that are integral parts of the traditional culture. Then be creative and you will find many ways of incorporating these into your classroom activities. Honor the good in both societies; recognize that two opposite approaches can both be right, that either can be best, depending upon the individual and the circumstances. Teach students to think for themselves, to know the alternatives, and to *make their own choices.*

5. Develop the Student's Self-Concept

"How glorious it is—and also how painful—to be an exception."
—Alfred DeMusse

The importance of developing a good self-concept cannot be overemphasized. To do well in school or in life, each person must know who he is and be proud of his background. He must have a positive self-image. Much of the curriculum and reading material of the typical school are designed to build this positive self-image on the part of the middle-class white student. The Native American may not get any of this positive reinforcement.

The high incident of teenage suicide in tribal groups in which suicide was, in the past, completely unknown indicates that school is not leading to satisfaction and happy lives. Whereas the suicide rate for most teenagers is highest in mid-winter, for Native American students it is highest at the beginning and end of the school term. Suicide and poor achievement are both indicators of poor self-concept.

Since the self-image of the students is such an important factor in the success of education, the entire second chapter of this manual will be devoted to its development.

6. Promote Relaxed Communication

"Oh, the comfort, the inexpressible comfort of feeling safe with a person; having neither to weigh thoughts nor measure words. . . ."
—George Eliot

Communication, real communication, between teacher and student is essential to effective teaching. Misunderstandings, discipline problems, dislike for school, and lack of effort can all be caused by lack of understanding. If children feel that they can communicate with the teacher, that they can ask questions without hesitation, that they and the teacher can discuss their problems freely without emotional upset, that they can be relaxed with the teacher, then many of these problems will not arise.

With some Native students, this will be our most difficult job. Many of them have been trained not to express an opinion; not to make a statement unless they are positive that they are correct. They have been taught that silence in the company of an adult denotes respect. Others have already been in several classrooms in which their ideas were not respected or used, but were criticized by the teacher or ridiculed by other children.

How good a listener are you? To develop communication with your students you have to listen—really listen, both to their ideas and their questions. In group discussions and individually, in and out of class, let them see that you are really listening, that you are really interested in their ideas. You will never do this with one hand on the door knob and your eyes on the clock.

Explain to students that much of learning is trial and error. Demonstrate to them that errors are a good way of learning. Instead of criticizing the mistakes and failures of your students, congratulate them on a good learning experience. Let them see that you, too, learn by experience. Don't try to conceal your own errors, weaknesses, and faults. Admit that you, too, can be wrong, that you make mistakes. Students need to hear a teacher say, "I'm sorry that I . . ." or "I was wrong about that," or "It was unkind of me to say that." Teachers gain, not lose, standing when they admit being human.

Listen to students' questions too. As Muesig says: "A student's request for help—almost any kind of assistance, however unimportant it may appear on the surface—is a genuine compliment and an unusual opportunity. It says, 'I am reaching out to you, and I trust you.' The pupil's appeal for aid can open future possibilities for a deeper relationship and more significant, enduring service. A teacher should, therefore, think twice before ignoring any plea that comes his way."

Part of listening is giving help when it is needed. "Few people ever get dizzy from doing too many good turns." This doesn't mean jumping in and giving final answers. Sometimes, as Erica Jong says, "Advice is what we ask for when we already know the answer but wish we didn't." More often, talking is a way of clarifying a question and the alternatives, and/or making a decision. Whenever a student can come to a conclusion for himself, he should have the opportunity to do so.

Eventually, if you listen well enough, students will share their feelings with you. Then you will know that you have developed real communication. Remember the Swedish proverb: "Shared joy is double joy and shared sorrow is half sorrow."

7. Develop a Culturally Relevant Curriculum

> *"If we cannot now end our differences, at least we can help make the world safe for diversity."*
>
> —John F. Kennedy

The Indian culture should become an integral part of basic instruction. Bring the Indian heritage, Indian values, Indian contributions to thought and knowledge into the discussions in every subject whenever possible. Show the students that you value their heritage. Impress upon the students that they have a great heritage and that their values are important. Help them to put their values into words that they can use to defend these values. Give them assurance that they can learn to live in the dominant society without rejecting the culture and heritage of their families and their community. Make the Native American culture a visible part of your instructional program. Give it a place of honor.

Too often teachers think they have given their Native American students a relevant curriculum by emphasizing Indian history in their social studies class, or by using some cultural material in the reading program. To really make your instruction relevant to the children's lives you need to use Native American values and examples in all of your instruction, and show how they apply to whatever subject you are studying, and to life in the community and the nation.

We must teach children the skills and the knowledge they need for good citizenship, for continued education, and for work; but we must also show them how the values of their own culture can help them maintain peace and happiness within themselves as they learn to participate in society as a whole.

8. Adapt Instruction to Students' Learning Styles

> *"The Indian educational enterprise is peculiarly in need of the kind of approach that . . . is less concerned with a conventional school system and more with the understanding of human beings."*
>
> —William Byler (then Executive Director, Association on American Indian Affairs)

Every child has his own learning style, the way in which he learns most easily. Some are auditory learners, others visual. Some find kinesthetic experience most effective. Some of these differences are differences in innate ability. Others are caused by a learning disability in one area. For most children, however, the differences are cultural. That is, they are caused by a difference in early learning experience.

Consider carefully the learning styles of each student. Present new learnings through as many different modes as possible, and thus give your Native American student a fair chance. Much information on Native American learning styles will be found in Chapter 6 of this manual.

9. Work with Parents and the Community

> *"Only by being true to the full growth of all who make it up, can society by any chance be true to itself"*
>
> —John Dewey

Know the homes from which your students come. Understand that there may be no place where a student can sit down and do homework, isolated from the extended family and from the TV. Meet the parents. Let them know what you are doing in the classroom. Show them how it relates to daily life in the community. Help them to see the connection between what the students learn in school and what they must know to live in and contribute to their own society. Many Indian parents make little effort to motivate their children's school work because the schools have not found ways of involving them in the school curriculum or of keeping them informed.

Attend community functions, especially pow-wows or other cultural activities, so children and their parents know that you are interested. Then in the classroom, help the students see how the material you are teaching relates to life in their community—that it has meaning in life outside of school. Make your instruction relevant to their immediate needs.

There is a clear relationship between students' understanding of their culture and its role in society and their academic success and later success in the community. As the Indian Nations at Risk Task Force (1991) has stated:

"Often schools have failed to make clear to students the connection between what they learn in school and what they must know to live comfortably and contribute to society. . . . Problems can be overcome through partnerships between schools and organizations that prepare individuals for careers and promote economic security. Partnership organizations can send specialists to help in the schools, offer services for students to participate in meaningful work, provide training, and promote a work ethic. Partnerships can also demonstrate the relationship between what is learned in school and what knowledge and skills are needed by adults.

Parents, schools, and communities together can show young children that school and learning are important. Partnerships can reinforce the idea that every student is expected to complete school and to develop the skills and knowledge to become self-sufficient and to contribute to the development of independent communities."

Summary

There is much evidence of a need for improvement in the educational experience of Native children. Low levels of achievement, teenage suicide, and adult unemployment all indicate a need for better education.

There are many causes for this lack of achievement. Poor self-concept and lack of motivation on the part of the students may be largely responsible. However these are brought about by many other factors inside and outside the school. Alcoholism and lack of community support are problems in many communities. But an education that is not relevant to the needs of the community is equally to blame.

There is no quick cure for the problems. You have to learn to understand your students and their culture before you can adapt to their needs. This takes hard work and a willingness to be flexible in both your thinking and your instructional procedures.

Start by learning about the culture, the backgrounds, and the learning styles of your students; learn them well enough so you can treasure them and use them in developing relevant instruction and in building effective communication and the self-esteem that will motivate your students to learn. Knowledge and understanding will help you to accept language differences and new ways of thinking. By meeting parents and taking part in community activities you can continue to learn and grow in the understandings needed to teach in your community.

Each of the chapters that follow will discuss some of the problems and will recommend ways in which positive changes can make instruction more relevant to the needs of Native students. Implementation of these suggestions will depend upon your ability to adapt these ideas to the needs of individual students.

The fact that many Native American students are not reaching their potential should not be a cause for discouragement, but a challenge: a challenge to every teacher to find ways of adapting to the needs of each student, to give every student an equal opportunity to succeed.

References for Further Reading

Armstrong, R., J. Kennedy, and P. R. Oberle. *University Education and Economic Well-Being: Indian Achievement and Prospectus.* Indian and Northern Affairs, Ottawa, Canada. 1990.

Banks, James A. "Multicultural Education: For Freedom's Sake." *Educational Leadership.* Vol. 29, 4. Jan. 1992. pp 32–36.

Banks, James A. *Multiethnic Education: Issues and Perspectives.* Allyn & Bacon. 1989.

Bullard, Sarah. "Sorting Through the Multicultural Rhetoric." *Educational Leadership.* Vol. 49, 4. Jan. 1992. pp 4–7.

Gilliland, Hap. "A Fable for Americans." *Chant of the Red Man*. Council for Indian Education. 1976. pp 24–36 & 74–83.

Hilliard, Asa G. III. "Why We Must Pluralize the Curriculum." *Educational Leadership*. Jan. 1992. pp 12–16.

Indian Nations at Risk Task Force. "Part I: Why the Native Peoples Are at Risk" and "Part III: Task Force Recommendations." *Indian Nations at Risk: An Educational Strategy for Action*. U. S. Dept of Education. Oct. 1991. pp 1–9 & 19–26.

Johnson, W. S., and R. N. Suetopka-Duerre. "Contributory Factors in Alaska Native Educational Success: A Research Strategy." *Educational Research Quarterly*. Vol. 8, 4. 1984. pp 47–51.

Kirkness, Verna J., and Ray Barnhardt. "First Nations and Higher Education: The Four R's— Respect, Relevance, Reciprocity, Responsibility." *Journal of American Indian Education*. Vol. 30, 3. May 1991.

Light, Harriet K., and Ruth E. Martin. "American Indian Families." *Journal of American Indian Education*. Vol. 26, 1. Oct. 1986. pp 1–5.

Little Bear, Dick. "Teachers and Parents Working Together." In Jon Reyhner (Ed.), *Teaching the Indian Child: A Bilingual/Multicultural Approach*. Eastern Montana College Bilingual Education. 1986.

Mohawk, John. "Seeking a Language of Understanding." *Social Education*. Feb. 1985. pp 104–105.

Muesig, Raymond. *Aphorisms on Education*. Phi Delta Kappa.

The author, Hap Gilliland with Indian students

Chapter 2
Promoting a Positive Self-Image
by Hap Gilliland

> *"Self-esteem is an aspect of human dignity—and schools have a moral obligation to seek its enhancement."*
>
> —James A. Beane

Are your students happy with themselves? Do they have a high self-esteem? This is the real measure of the success of any teacher. Achievement in school is more highly related to self-concept than to mental ability or any other factor. Give students self-esteem, show them that they have the ability to succeed, let them believe that they are worthwhile people who have and deserve your respect and the respect of their fellow students, and they will work, they will cooperate, they will succeed. Take away this self-esteem, leave them without hope, and they have no reason to try. To every student in any culture, self-respect is essential to success and a good life.

The Need for Improved Self-Concept

> *"The greatest need among Native Americans today is having positive attitudes toward themselves."*
>
> —Carol Black Eagle (Crow Indian)

Children's concept of their own worth is the most significant factor in the development of personality and the ability to work and play with others. Academic performance is also directly related to self-esteem.

Father John Bryde once said, "Practically all educators will agree that, basically, the overall purpose of education is to turn out happy and socially contributing human beings. This means that as a result of his education, the student feels that he is on top of his environment, is contributing to its development, and has a joyful sense of achievement according to his ability."

Children with self-esteem like themselves. They have good feelings about their own personal worth. Self-esteem is not only the key to motivation; it is necessary to clear thinking and to concentrated effort. Yet as Floy Pepper (1985) says, "Many discouraged Indian children believe that they have little possibility of solving their problems, or even of moving toward a solution. They lack confidence and approach each challenge with the anticipation that they will perform poorly or fail.''

Indian students are ahead of other students on self-concept before they begin first grade, but they fall far behind later (Bruneau, 1985).

Suicide is now the second most common cause of teenage death in the United States, and suicide is several times as prevalent among reservation Indian students as in the general population. Each year as many as one out of every 200 Indian students attempts suicide. This is sure evidence of the great need for the students to build the self-concept of the Native students. Yet as Edward Wynne, Professor of Education at the University of Illinois in Chicago, stated in U.S. News and World Report, ''When Scholastic Aptitude Test scores drop 5%, people hit the roof. But when the suicide rate of youth goes up almost 250%, you barely get a nod.''

It is of critical importance that we, as teachers, recognize that if we are to be successful in teaching Native American students, we must, first and foremost, find ways to raise the self-esteem of the students.

Eleven Ways of Building a Positive Self-Image

Although many Native students are lacking in self-esteem, there are many others who are excellent students and who attack their work with confidence. What are the reasons for the differences? Can some of the following suggestions help you to build the self-confidence and self-image of your students?

1. Start with a Happy, Accepting Classroom Climate

> "I saw a child today who didn't have a smile—so I gave him one of mine!"
>
> —Unknown

Students' feelings about the teacher, the school, and about other children are determined to a large extent by how well they feel they are accepted. Therefore, it is essential that all students feel accepted by their teachers and that every possible effort be made to see that they are accepted by their peers.

The climate you set in the morning may be the most important thing you do all day. Let your students learn from experience that when they walk into the classroom in the morning they will be greeted by a smile, a touch, the body language that says, ''I'm glad you are here.'' This means you must go to the classroom as a happy, loving, caring adult. It means controlling your own life so that it includes recreation and self-fulfillment, so that you can be the caring, cheerful, confident, and compassionate person your students deserve for a teacher. And it means starting the day with some social activity to set the climate. It means letting your students know, through actions as well as words, that they are important to you.

Meet your students in the morning with a cheerful, positive greeting that says that this day will be good. Follow this by seeing that every single day, you give your students a comment that lets them know of your interest in them, and your acceptance of them. As Sara Bullard (1992) says, ''Most teachers, after all, have a pretty good understanding of what they need to do: Care about their children. Teach them to care about each other. Show them that hatred hurts. Show them how to think critically. Open up new worlds for them to discover. Offer them the tools of change. Create a small caring community in the classroom.''

Just remember that a smile produces a smile in return. Your attitude is more contagious than chicken pox or measles.

2. Expect Every Student to Succeed

> *Give me the benefit of your convictions, if you have any; but keep*
> *your doubts to yourself, for I have enough of my own.''*
>
> —Goethe

Your curriculum must be academically challenging, but that challenge must be accompanied by high expectations. The students must see your high expectations and your confidence in them. They also need to see high expectations from their parents, the community, and the other students. The more you can help to develop these, the higher will be the students' expectations of themselves.

Students gain an opinion of themselves through "reflected appraisals"; their idea of what others think of them; their concept of the opinions of friends, parents, peers, teachers, and other individuals who are significant to them. What concept of themselves will the Native students have when they reflect your opinions? Our attitudes and feelings are expressed in every action when our pupils are present. Native American students are exceptionally skilled in reading these actions, especially if there is any indication that they are being rejected.

Students will believe that they can succeed if they can see that *you* believe that they will. Let your approach to all students reflect your confidence that they will succeed. When teachers like their students and expect the best from them, those students just naturally expect more of themselves.

3. Recognize Students' Strengths

> *"The dream begins most of the time with a teacher who believes in*
> *you, who tugs and pushes and leads you on to the next plateau, some-*
> *times even poking you with a sharp stick called truth.''*
>
> —Dan Rather, *The Camera Never Blinks* (Ballantine)

One of the ways in which we can lead students to believe in themselves is to identify and recognize their strengths. All children have strengths. It is up to us to find them, to help the students see their own strengths, and how they can use them in learning.

We must make sure that all students have success every single day. Call the students' attention to their successes. Make sure they are aware of them. Every person *must* have the memory of a series of successes to build self-confidence necessary to sustain effort when difficulties arise.

If you want to be respected by your students, remember that the pupils' opinions of you depend not on what they see in you, but what you help them see in themselves.

You can produce more gains in a week by proving to your students how much *they* know than you can in a year by showing them how much *you* know.

A mother asked, "You say you think Miss Timber is a better teacher than Miss Jones. Why?'' Her son answered, "When I'm in Miss Jones's class I think she is the smartest person I know, but when I'm in Miss Timber's class I think *I* am.''

One teacher, in order to help her second graders see their own strengths, had each student write a statement beginning with, "I like myself because . . .'' The statements she got were simple but revealing, and they helped her to find good things to emphasize. Extra-curricular activities also provide a channel through which students can exhibit those strengths that do not show up in the classroom. Perhaps you can find ways that they can apply those strengths to aid their academic performance as well as their self-image.

As Bennett Cerf says, "A pat on the back, though only a few vertebrae removed from a kick in the pants, is miles ahead in results."

4. Compliment Instead of Criticizing

> "If a child lives with criticism, He learns to condemn. . . .
> If a child lives with encouragement, He learns confidence.
> If a child lives with praise, He learns to appreciate. . . .
> If a child lives with approval, He learns to like himself.
> If a child lives with acceptance and friendship, He learns to find love
> in the world."
>
> —author unknown

Your attitude toward your students is mirrored in the students' thinking. They can build the self-respect that is necessary to a happy life and to success in school only if they live in a school atmosphere that is warm and supportive, where each child is recognized by himself and others as a worthy individual who is wanted, respected, and liked.

Children look to others to confirm or deny that they are important or significant. Let your actions tell each child that he, as an individual, has your respect, that you respect those qualities that make him special and different. Let all the children know that what they do or say is special to you.

"Praise is like Seven-up; it should be served while it is still bubbling." Praise given to Native students for a job well done should be given immediately but unobtrusively. Don't wait until afternoon to praise students for what they did in the morning. Speak to the students individually, unobtrusively, and let them know your approval, but don't hold them up before the class in a way that will separate them from their classmates. This not only can be humiliating to them but may cause other students to react negatively and thereby force them to quit trying. Remember that to Native students, the approval of friends is more important than the approval of the teacher. Don't force them to choose between you and their friends. If you do, you are the one who will lose.

You seldom need to criticize your students' work. Telling them what is good about it teaches them much more, and they listen much more closely. When you absolutely must criticize, make sure that they understand that you are helping them see how the story, or whatever, can be improved, that this is not criticism of the writer.

Gary Herman, editor of *The Love Letter*, says that there is a "language of encouragement" that we should all learn to speak. He lists the following basic phrases of "the second language that with careful practice we can learn to use like a real expert":

> "I like the way you handled that."
> "I have confidence in your judgment."
> "If anyone can figure it out I'm sure you can."
> "What do you think would be the best way to . . .?"
> "I like the way you tackle a problem."
> "I can tell that you really worked hard on this project."
> "Thanks, that was very thoughtful of you."
> "I need your help on . . ."

Herman also points out that "effective phrases of encouragement seldom focus on judging or evaluating performance, but instead they are aimed at recognized effort put forth, designed to build confidence, used to demonstrate acceptance, focus on contributions or assets, and show appreciation."

A calm atmosphere in which students are respected will also do much to help Native students get over their natural shyness. The hesitant feeling where we don't quite belong is natural for Native students in the environment of the classroom. To pressure the children only increases it. "Feelings are everywhere—be gentle."

If your Native students are unsure of themselves and of your attitude toward them, they will "retreat into whispers and hide their lack of confidence behind impassive faces."

Along with giving your students understanding, don't be afraid to show affection for them. Will Rogers said, "What constitutes a life well spent? Love and admiration from our fellow men is all that anyone could ask." Be sure, of course, that they *all* feel it, not just the good students. As one teacher said, "To love the world is no big chore. It's that miserable student in the corner of my room who is the problem."

In a study of Indian dropouts, a third of them mentioned that their teachers didn't care about them or give them sufficient help (Coladarci, 1983). Might your students feel that the only time they get any feedback from you is when they do the wrong thing? Why not ignore the mistakes and have fun trying to catch them doing something right!

5. Give Your Students Respect. Show Them That You Need Their Help

Too many teachers and other well-intentioned individuals look at the physical surroundings in which children live, the prejudice they face, or their problems in school, and they sympathize. They feel sorry for them. They do not need sympathy; they need something to be proud of. Pity and pride do not go together. Building sympathy for a group of people may be a good way to raise money for a mission or a school, but it has no place in the work within the school or mission.

Chief Dan George (1970) expressed the idea much more clearly than I can:

"Do you know what it is like to be without pride in your race, pride in your family, pride and confidence in yourself? You don't know, for you never tasted its bitterness.

. . . You hold out your hand and you beckon me to come over. Come and integrate you say. But how can I come? . . . How can I come in dignity? I have no presents. I have no gifts. What is there in my culture you value? My poor treasure you can only scorn.

Am I to come as beggar and receive all from your omnipotent hand? Somehow, I must wait. I must delay. I must wait until you want something of me . . . until you need something that is me. Then I can raise my head and say to my wife and family: Listen. . . . They are calling. They need me. I must go. Then I can walk across the street and I will hold my head high for I will meet you as an equal . . . you will not receive me in pity. Pity I can do without. My manhood I cannot do without!"

How do we show our students that they have our respect—that we need them? We must develop our powers of observation and learn to see and assess each student correctly and fully. All students have good points of which they can be proud. *We* have to learn to see their strengths before we can help the students to see their own. Bring out each student's strengths and talk about what each does well.

The language experience method of teaching reading is one way of showing children that you respect their ideas and of giving them something to be proud of. It helps them see that you consider their ideas worth listening to, recording, and using as reading material.

It hardly seems necessary to mention that helping students to become good readers, to solve math problems well, and to achieve academically is an important means of building self-esteem. This can be enhanced even further if students can also share their knowledge and help each other to achieve.

We must *believe in* our students. We must *know* that they can make a contribution. Then we can ask students for help and for suggestions. We can use their ideas. We can learn from them. They are a source of knowledge that we should recognize, especially knowledge of the Indian culture and of the community in which they live. An emphasis on making teaching and learning a two-way process, in which there is give and take between faculty and students, not only builds the self-esteem of the students but makes learning more meaningful.

One teacher I know can always identify students who don't believe in their own ability, and she can identify the things those students can do well. She asks the students for help. She takes them to other students who are having difficulty and asks them to help those students. All of the students are benefited. Helping each other is an important part of Indian culture; why not use it more?

Ideas on helping students help each other will be discussed more thoroughly in the chapter on "Learning Through Cooperation and Sharing."

6. Give Students a Voice in Decision Making

One important way in which the self-esteem of any group of students can be improved is by showing them how to assume responsibility for their actions, then trusting them to be responsible. Many Native students have not learned to take this responsibility in the school room because they have not been given the opportunity.

Giving students opportunities to make decisions and choices is an effective way of showing respect for each of them. Students must learn to see the consequences of their actions, not only to themselves, but also to others. They need to see themselves as responsible people. They can learn this only if we, their teachers, give them an opportunity to learn early how to solve their problems and give them experience in making their own decisions. They need to be asked their opinions, to have their questions answered, and to see their ideas put to use so they can learn to see the consequences, good or bad. Only in this way can they learn to make decisions based upon reasoning and thinking and develop the self-confidence necessary to be willing to make their own decisions.

Students will be afraid to make decisions until they trust their teacher, and our Native American students will hesitate to trust us unless we trust them.

The teaching of decision making skills will be discussed in the chapter on discipline.

7. Help the Students Develop Their Own Realistic Goals

If Indian students have no personal goals, they have little reason for effort. The tribe or community may enforce compulsory education laws and keep the child in the classroom, but they cannot force anyone to learn. The student needs a goal, an immediate goal, not vague talk about the future.

When you have recognized the students' strengths and shown them that they can succeed, then they will be ready to sit down with you individually and discuss where they have been, how far they have advanced, and where *they* want to go from here. Encourage the students to set goals that fit their talents and way of life, not those that fit your dreams. The goals must be *short range,* specific, measurable, attainable, and they must be *the students'* goals. *They* must see a reason for them and want to attain them. Otherwise the goals are yours, not theirs.

8. Include Native American Literature in the Curriculum

How can Indian children believe that you really respect them, that you respect their culture, their ideas, and their people, unless you include Native American literature as an essential part of the literature that you read, that you study, and that you make available for free reading? There is enough high quality literature by and about Indian people so you can give it equal status with the best white American and European literatures.

Of course, we all know there is also a great deal of reading material that includes Indian characters, written by authors who have no understanding of Indian people or Indian culture, so this material should have no place in the education of Indian children, or any other children. The selection of literature to be used in the classroom will be discussed at length in Chapter 10 of this guide.

9. Accept the Language of the Community

> *"The vast majority of Indian children find themselves under attack in the school systems because they are constantly reminded of their English 'deficiencies.'"*
>
> —John C. Mohawk

All children must learn to speak and to write "standard English" when it is appropriate. But whether their language, the language of their people and community, is an Indian language, or a variation of English, they should not be made to feel that it is an inferior language, that it is the "wrong" way to speak. They should be fluent in the local language and should understand that it is the "right" language to speak among their family and friends.

If you teach children that they should only speak "good" English at all times and if they try to do so, they may be laughed at by their families and called a snob by their friends. But if you try to learn a little of their language while they learn yours, you will each be able to speak the appropriate language at the appropriate times. And you will not be dragging down students' self-esteem by implying that their people don't know what is "right." Many children resist learning standard English because it is less painful to be rejected by the school than to lose identity within their own group. Children who are made to feel inferior because of criticism of their language may also learn never to express their ideas in the classroom.

There are many "Englishes" and each of us must learn which variety of English to speak in our homes and at our place of work, so that we can have pride in our ability to communicate wherever we are.

10. Understand Community and Individual Problems and Seek Solutions

No matter how positive your approach or how great your desire to help your students, there will be problems within your school and your community that will interfere with student progress and will drag down the self-concept of some students.

The Indian Nations at Risk Taskforce (1992, p. 21) states that one of the most important priorities of the school should be "to resolve the social problems that limit students' ability to concentrate on learning. Family violence, alcohol and drug abuse, suicide, and the breakdown of family structures all hinder students' performance in school. Health and social agencies must work with families and schools to help students achieve their potential."

On some reservations, the number of residents over 14 who are alcoholics is as high as 80% (Curley, 1984). High dropout rates, poor achievement, and behavior problems are all correlated with alcoholism in the home. There are few, if any, Native American students who are not affected by alcoholism.

The school must be a comfortable and safe place, free of alcohol and drugs. It must also include preventative programs to insure that today's children do not become the next generation of alcoholics. Cultural education and the development of self-esteem must be an essential part of those programs. At the same time, if the children, the members of their extended families, or their close friends are being physically or emotionally abused as a result of alcoholism, their self-esteem will be damaged.

You need to really understand the disease of alcoholism to understand what is going on in the lives of your students. And you need to teach the children about it, to help them understand it as a disease, along with the destructive behavior that goes with it. But you must teach for understanding, without condemnation of the victims. If the students understand it as a disease, they can learn to cope better, and alcoholism in their families will have less effect on their self-esteem. If both you and your students understand the problem, the students can discuss it openly, along with the individual problems that accompany it.

Some teachers have looked at all the problems and said, "What's the use?" Don't let this happen to you. Regardless of where you teach, some of your students will have serious problems, and some will be the victims of drugs, alcohol, or abuse.

It is essential that you learn to understand the problems affecting your students, whatever they are, that you be willing to discuss them openly in a non-condemning way, and that you help your students to adapt. Part of the students' self-esteem is in realizing that they must not hold themselves responsible for their relatives, but that they can take charge of their own lives.

11. Give Your Students Pride in Their People and Their Heritage

> "Too many teachers, unfortunately, seem to see their role as rescuer. My child does not need to be rescued; he does not consider being Indian a misfortune. He has a culture, probably older than yours; he has meaningful values and a rich and varied experiential background. However strange or incomprehensible it may seem to you, you have no right to do or say anything that implies to him that it is less than satisfactory."
>
> —an Indian mother*

To develop self-esteem, students must have pride in their people and know that they are worthy of respect. For students to develop this pride, you must show in your actions, and develop within your class as a whole, a respect for Indian culture and for Indian people as a group.

---

*An excerpt from a letter written by an Indian mother to teachers of Indian children, published in the *Powell River News* of British Columbia. Reprinted in the *Navajo Times,* April, 1974.

Give your students pride in their heritage by using the values of the culture in your classroom. Emphasize the positive aspects of the culture in your discussions. This is so important that Chapters 3, 4, and 5 will be devoted to learning the culture and using its positive forces in the classroom.

Show your respect for the language by learning and using at least some important words or phrases.

Teach about Native history and culture. Use ideas from the culture in teaching other subjects. Use cultural objects as prominent parts of the classroom environment. Make the crafts, games, and music an integral part of your instruction.

Provide acceptable reading materials. Your students will quickly identify prejudice and stereotypical expressions. If you give them biased material to read, they will assume you agree with what is said, unless you precede the reading with adequate discussion of the author's bias.

Summary

Self-esteem is the most important factor in achievement. Since many Native students have become convinced that they will not succeed, this must be a major concern of every teacher of Native students.

We must expect success and ignore weaknesses. In place of criticism we must recognize and emphasize the individual's strengths. Help the students develop their own goals—goals in which they *can* succeed; then *expect* success. Teach with encouragement, humor, and enthusiasm.

We must have respect for the students and show it in our actions. We have to treat them with the same kind of respect that we would like from them. Give them understanding and help preserve their identity, their self-fulfillment as worthwhile individuals.

We must teach students to face and understand the problems in their own lives and in their communities. Teach them decision making skills, and then give them a voice in decision making and responsibility for their own actions.

We must develop good communication. *Listen* to the students. Show them respect and let them know they are worthwhile as individuals, regardless of their academic achievement.

We must respect the students' people and their way of life, see the good things in the culture, learn its values, then show our respect for these values in the way we teach.

References for Further Reading

Baird, Clifford G. *The Power of a Positive Self-Image.* Victor Books, 1985.

Brown, Violet H. *The Integration of Self-Identity and Self-Esteem Through Curriculum Development.* Native American Educational Services Inc., Chicago. 1986. 52p.

Bruneau, Odette J. "Self Concept." *Psychology in the Schools.* Oct. 1985. pp. 378–379.

Bullard, Sara. "Sorting Through the Multicultural Rhetoric." *Educational Leadership.* Vol. 49–4, Jan. 1992. pp. 4–7.

Coladarci, Theodore. "High School Dropout among Native Americans." *Journal of American Indian Education.* Oct. 1983. pp. 15–21.

Curley, Georgia. *Self-Esteem and Northern Cheyenne Children of Alcoholics.* Native American Educational Services Inc., Chicago. 1984. 32p.

Erlandson, Ray, et al. *Character Education Curriculum.* American Institute for Character Education. 1985.

George, Chief Dan. "What Will You Teach My Children? Excerpts from a speech at the conference of the Canadian Association of Indian and Eskimo Education, Banff, May 1970." In Hap Gilliland, *Chant of the Red Man.* Council for Indian Education. 1976.

Gilliland, Hap. "Building Self Confidence." *A Practical Guide to Remedial Reading.* Charles E. Merrill. 1978. pp. 164–168.

Gilliland, Hap, and Harriet Mauritsen. "Humor in the Classroom." *The Reading Teacher, 24–8. May 1971. pp. 753–756+.*

Herman, Gary. *The Love Letter.* Published monthly by Schoolmaster Educational Services, 412 South Second Street, Olivia, MN 56277.

Indian Nations at Risk Taskforce. "Task Force Priorities, a Strategic Framework and Recommendations." pp. 19–36.

McGinnis, Alan Loy. *Bringing out the Best in People.* Augsburg Publishing House, 1985.

Mohawk, John C. "Seeking a Language of Understanding." *Social Education,* Vol. 49–2, Feb. 1985, pp. 104–5.

Pepper, Floy C. *Effective Practices in Indian Education: A Teacher's Monograph.* Northwest Regional Educational Laboratory. 1985.

Rampaul, Winston E., and others. "The Relationship between Academic Achievement, Self-Concept, Creativity, and Teacher Expectations among Native Children in a Northern Manitoba School." *Alberta Journal of Educational Research.* Vol. 30–3, Sept. 1984. pp. 213–25.

Sanders, Danielle. "Cultural Conflicts: An Important Factor in the Academic Failures of American Indian Students." *Journal of Multicultural Counseling and Development.* Vol. 15–2, Apr. 1987. pp. 81–90. (Reviews the literature showing how clash of values contributes to the development of a negative self-concept, and shows how failure to achieve academically is a function of this negative self-image.)

Indian children arrive at a pow-wow.

Chapter 3
Recognizing the Students' Backgrounds in Culture and Experience

"We must learn to appreciate diversity, not suppress it. How devastating to think of a world in which everyone is the same!"

—Janice LaFountain, Crow Indian

Cultural diversity is like an orchestra. Each cultural group, like each instrument, retains its identity, making its own kind of music. But it becomes part of the whole, which would not be as good without it. As Garcia says, "There exist in the teaching-learning universe many progressive cultures, each a rich complex, and worthy of knowing."

We must lead our students to understand that though cultures are different, no one culture is superior or inferior to another; that each not only is best for the people within that society, but that each culture benefits our society as a whole; that we all benefit from the ethnic and cultural diversity of American society. We must work toward the continuing development of a society which has a wholesome respect for the intrinsic worth of every individual. We must make allowances for difference. Let people be glad to be different.

Teachers are often not aware of the seriousness of the problems children have in being Indian in the non-Indian world of the school, problems rooted in the difference in cultures. When main-stream children enter school, the ways, ideals, and values they are taught reinforce and build on the teaching they have received since birth. The same ideas and behaviors are rewarded. However, entering school for the Native American can be a shocking experience. Many of the behaviors and expressed values are in direct opposition to what the child has been taught at home.

Before we can be really effective as teachers, we have to first be learners. We have to know the cultural values and experiential background of our students.

The Importance of Learning the Students' Backgrounds

Each cultural group has developed instructional techniques which are used throughout the children's growing years for teaching them in out-of-school situations. By the time children enter school, many of their values, skills, and ways of learning are firmly established. These have served the cultural group over a long period of time. There is no reason to feel that they will not serve well in the future.

Before a person teaches children within any social group, that person should think seriously about how the mores, the values, the learning methods of that group can be applied in the classroom. Imposing on children ways of thinking and acting that are foreign to their group may make these children less well adapted to living within their own culture. If the school uses methods appropriate to the children's background there is no reason that children of any minority group should make less progress educationally than those of the dominant society.

Even though you may be an expert teacher, failure to learn the local culture can doom you to failure in the Indian community. Orvando reported that only 10 percent of Eskimo children in his study felt that any large portion of their school instruction was of use in their native village life, and 72 percent felt that the curriculum should include more Eskimo cultural activities. These findings are also typical of studies of many American Indians.

Determining and describing the educational characteristics of American Indians is difficult because of the heterogeneity of the people. There are over 300 Indian tribes and each has its own customs and traditions. Some are common to most Native American groups. Others will vary with each tribe and each community. In talking about differences in cultures and making comparisons between them, as we will do in this chapter, there is always the danger that we will develop a stereotyped picture of a group of people and assume that all those within that group fit the pattern. We recognize that danger, and the problems that can arise from it. But we also know that we cannot develop an understanding of a group of people without discussing some generalities and providing teachers with some ideas of what to look for in adapting their instruction to the students they teach.

You must be observant and learn about your own community. No two Indian cultural groups are alike, just as no two Indians are alike, any more than you are like your neighbor. Yet, like you and your friends, they do share some beliefs and some ideals.

A culture does not consist of physical surroundings, places, or objects used. A culture is a way of life of a group of people, developed around a set of customs, beliefs, values, assumptions, attitudes, expectations, and behaviors. All of us accept changes in technology, yet our old values persist. These are taught consciously and unconsciously from infancy. Following them brings harmony and acceptance within the group.

Don't make the mistake of thinking that the old tribal ways and values no longer have meaning for your students, or conversely, of expecting that most of your students are well grounded in their own tribal heritage. Every Native child is somewhere between the two cultures. He may be doing everything the way of the dominant culture and appear to have lost all the Native culture; still he may deep down feel the way he is doing things is wrong. His inner feelings may still be Indian.

We can easily get some idea of the background of our students in general, and some idea of the experience of each student, but what is more essential is that we learn the cultural values around which our students build their lives. These influence their learning, attitudes, and behaviors even more than their experiences, but they are much harder to discover. They lie deep within the children's subconscious minds. They influence their behavior without them being aware of it, and they cannot be expressed clearly. The outward experiences of the Native child may not be much different from those of children from the dominant society, but the majority of Native children still retain many of the old values of their people. What are those values? Some are common to most Native groups. Others will vary with each cultural group and each community.

As stated by Jeanne Bearcrane (1990),

"It is important for teachers to become familiar with the cultural and linguistic patterns of American Indian students. Teachers must realize that there are many differences between American Indian tribes, and a wide range of differences between American Indian students and the white majority. The greatest stumbling block to full interpersonal acceptance is ignorance of a way of life which has ideals, habits, history and even language different from what seems standard. It is clear that the successful completion of school by American Indian students may well depend on the teacher's ability to understand the culture."

Three Paths to Mutual Understanding

1. Actively Promote Positive Values

> *"Schools that respect and support a student's language and culture*
> *are significantly more successful in educating those students."*
> —Indian Nations at Risk Task Force

Like people, cultures have good and bad points. As you learn the culture of your community, you are sure to find some things that are so good that you will want to accept them for yourself. As Gelett Burgess said, "If in the last few years you haven't discarded a major opinion or acquired a new one, check your pulse. You may be dead."

You are just as sure to find other things of which you disapprove. However, most values and ways of the traditional culture have the potential to be either helpful or detrimental in our classrooms, depending upon our attitudes and our adaptation of our instructional methods. For example, the children's willingness to share and to help each other may cause real problems for some teachers, but it can be a great benefit in most classrooms, particularly if the teacher plans her instruction to make use of it.

It is vital that you emphasize the *positive* and de-emphasize (not deny) the negative aspects of the culture at all times; not only in class but in your conversations with students, with people in the community, and with other teachers. If there are things about the culture of which you disapprove, talking about them will help neither you nor your students. Cultural ideals develop because they are useful. When people are critical of cultural values, it is often because they do not yet know enough about them to understand them.

As an example, two customs of the old life were frequently criticized in the books I read as a child. They criticized the men for letting the women carry the loads and for walking in front, "making the woman follow." I learned the reasons for these customs dramatically when I was living with the Yanowamo Indians of South America shortly after their first contact with the "outside world." A group of us had been gathering food and wood in the rain-forest. When we were ready to return to the village, one of the women had a huge basket of wood on her back, her baby on her hip, and still had to carry bananas and another bundle of food. I thought I could be helpful so I picked up her stalk of bananas and another bundle of food. She became extremely angry. I soon learned that I had in effect told her, "You are not of any value. You are not worth protecting." I should have been concerned enough to have my bow and arrows in my hands ready to protect the women when we started down the trail. I was also expected to lead the way. Believe me, I was glad when, on other occasions, a young warrior went ahead and was the first to face the jaguar, the bushmaster snake, or the raider from another village, and let me take the "woman's position," several yards behind. . . . Now I understand these customs, and the importance of understanding the reasons for a custom before we judge it.

As teachers, we should endeavor to know Native American cultural traits, especially the local culture, well enough so we can not only keep from being in conflict with the culture, but be able to discuss it and frequently point out to the students some of the values, the good things about the culture. If we put the values into words frequently, in a way that students can understand, then students can discuss them, express them in their own words, and feel freer to make their own comparisons and choices. As students see that we value the strengths that they see in their own families—generosity, the helping systems that operate within the family, the respect for each other—they will feel more self-confident, more free to express and discuss their ideas, and more willing to use their strengths in their academic endeavors.

To help children eliminate prejudice, we can talk over with our students the stereotypes of Native Americans and other minorities portrayed on TV and in books. We can help them look at these from the viewpoint of the person being described. In many groups there are still traditional clothing, braids, and so forth, which some students wear to identify themselves with their cherished heritage. These help them in keeping their identity. Criticism of them can be very detrimental to our relationships with the students.

As we explore the different cultures throughout the world and their value systems we help rid our students of prejudice against any group of people who are different. Whether we intend to or not, we will teach what we value. Our students learn from our actions.

2. Become a Part of Your Community

> *"Teachers should try to grow while they are on Indian reservations. .*
> *. . The children deserve teachers who are willing to keep learning."*
>
> —Dick Little Bear, Cheyenne,

We have talked about the need for knowing the culture and background of our students. But how do we go about getting that knowledge? The next step should be to study information available about Native American cultures in general, including that contained in this and the following chapters, but give special attention to any information you can locate which focuses on the local culture and the local community.

Some of the teachers who have been in the community for some time will have valuable information to share. The ones who are responsive to the community can provide you with valuable ideas about the culture, the things that work with the children, and even the political forces in the community. But remember that there are also many teachers, even with reservation experience, who still hold biases and prejudices.

Visit with the people in the community at every opportunity. Stop and talk when you see people in their yard. Let them see that you respect them and their culture, that you will be honest with them, that you are an open person easy to talk to, interested in other things in the community besides the school. Ask questions—not intrusive personal questions, but questions about any upcoming community activity, anything of interest in the area, about their opinions, or questions like, "How did you do this in the old days?"

Naturally, the most important people to visit with are the parents and grandparents. No other thing you can do will provide as much information about both the culture and the child as a visit to a home. Don't wait to talk to them until there is a problem to talk about. First impressions are long lasting. Don't make them negative, and don't wait for parents to come to visit you. It doesn't happen that way. No matter what you do to encourage them, some parents will never get to the school. The only way you will learn about their child is to visit their home. Even with parents and guardians who willingly come to the school, you will learn much more by a home visit.

In every school in which I have taught, I have visited the homes of most of the students. I have been told when arriving in a community, "Not here—you can't visit homes here—a lot of the parents are ashamed to have the teacher see their homes." But there has always been a welcome, even more in the poor homes than in the well-to-do ones. But then, I happen to believe there is as much love in a poor home as a rich one—not as much love of money perhaps, but sometimes more love of children!

Many parents have told me, "You are the first teacher that was interested enough to come to see us." Of course a positive attitude is essential. I have known critical teachers who even I would not have welcomed to my home!

Make ever contact an opportunity to learn, Let the community members see *by your actions* that you recognize your deficiencies, that you want to learn, to understand the culture and the ways of the community. Too many teachers, when they do venture into the community, hide behind a veneer of academic aloofness. Hesitating to make themselves vulnerable, they refuse to admit that they do not know; that they need to learn. They believe their educational facade will gain them respect. Not in an indigenous community.

The best way to gain respect is to show respect for others. And there is no more effective way to show your respect for people than to let them know that you want to learn from them, that there is much they can teach you.

Involve the parents and other community members in the school whenever and in whatever ways you can. Let them help you by working with projects and field trips, teaching crafts, and telling children about their work. And make every contact an opportunity to learn as much as the children do. For example, in the Kickapoo community, "the school identified and secured the participatory interest of more than 40 community members. They are providing enrichment support to the teaching staff in the areas of business, computers, science, nursing, government, industrial arts, language study, clothing, foods, and arts and crafts. These community members are called upon regularly to visit the school and participate with the regular teacher in enriching the cultural attention to the learning environment" Dupuis (1988).

3. Teach Through Culturally Relevant Activities

> *"If the dream of equal educational opportunity for Native Americans is to be realized, then education must be studied as a cultural process and this process must be made compatible with the Indian way of life. The Indian student dances to a different drummer. He/she hears Indian drums, not white man's drums."*
>
> —Dale Little Soldier (1981)

The historical and practical knowledge base of the community served must be valued and must serve as a starting point for the education of the children. We must involve the family and other Indian people of the community in the educational process. Whenever possible, basic skills should be taught using culturally relevant materials and experiences.

Dupuis and Walker (1988) have listed the following examples of activities through which the Kickapoo culture has been woven into the total fabric of the curriculum of their school. Such activities should be a part of all classes in all schools.

1. Oral presentations concerning the students' own culture.
2. Readings on contemporary Indian literature.
3. Stories on tribal history.
4. Studies on structure of tribal government.
5. Affective experiences through original art, music and dance projects.
6. Contributions to Indian community projects.
7. Recognition and awareness of current Indian issues that have potential impact on individual students.
8. Sharing of cultural enrichment activities with elementary students.
9. Performing and/or demonstrating skills in art and music.
10. Participating, with community resource people in the classroom learning environment.

Summary

Before we can effectively teach any group of students, we must know something of their background and culture. We must understand their values and motivations.

Since each Native American group has somewhat different customs, it is important that we not only have a knowledge of Indian culture in general, but that we also learn everything we can of the ways and beliefs of the local community.

There are many ways that the Indian values can be applied to make our teaching more effective, and there are many cultural activities that we can incorporate into our instruction. If we look for the possible values and actively promote them in the classroom, we will greatly improve our relationships with the students and their attitudes toward learning.

Then if we also go out and actively participate in community organizations and tribal activities, we will build the respect of the parents and their desire to back the school and encourage their children to do their best.

References for Further Reading

Bearcrane, Jeanne, John M. Dodd, J. Ron Nelson, and Steven W. Ostwald. "Educational Characteristics of Native Americans." *Rural Education,* Vol. 11–3. Spr. 1990. pp. 1–5.

Dupuis, Victor L., and Marjorie W. Walker. "The Circle of Learning at Kickapoo." *Journal of American Indian Education,* Vol. 27. Oct. 1988. pp. 27–33.

Indian Nations at Risk Task Force. "Part III: Task Force Priorities, a Strategic Framework, and Recommendations." *Indian Nations at Risk: An Educational Strategy for Action.* U.S. Department of Education. Oct. 1991.

Lewis, R. "Patterns of Strengths of American Indian Families." In F. Hoffman (Ed.) *The American Family, Strengths and Stresses.*

American Indian Social Research and Development Associates, Isletta, N.M. 1981.

Lin, Ruey-Lin. "Perception of Family Background and Personal Characteristics Among Indian College Students." *Journal of American Indian Education,* Vol. 29. May 1990. pp. 19–27.

Little Bear, Dick. "Teachers and Parents: Working Together." In Jon Reyhner, (Ed.) *Teaching the Indian Child: A Bilingual Multicultural Approach.* Eastern Montana College, 1986. pp. 222–231.

Little Soldier, Dale, and Leona M. Forester. "Applying Anthropology to Educational Problems." *Journal of American Indian Education,* Vol. 20–3. May 1981. pp. 1–6.

Chapter 4
Emphasizing the Positive Aspects of the Culture

"The [educational] system must respect and value the cultures of the communities served and the contributions of the people."
—Indian Nations at Risk Task Force

The customs and cultures of each of the many Native American groups vary somewhat from each other. It is therefore very important that we, as teachers, learn and adapt our instruction to the ways of the particular Indian nation, tribe, band, or community from which our students come. Yet, although each local culture is distinct, there are also many ways in which they are similar. In this chapter we will identify some of the values, customs, and characteristics which are common to many Native American groups. However, you must keep in mind that not all of these will apply to any one group. This listing is intended only as a guide to help you study and observe your own community. You must determine which items apply to the Native American children with whom you work.

Also, remember that each Native child will be living somewhere between the traditional Native American way and the traditional middle class Anglo way. Often a Native student acts more like the white child, but feels more akin to the Indian way. Remember also that all of these concepts are continually changing, both in the Indian and non-Indian societies.

It is very important that the aspects of the culture that you emphasize, not only in class, but in your discussions with students, with people in the community, and with other teachers, are those toward which you have a positive feeling, aspects that you can find ways of using to promote improved self-concept and academic achievement.

Possible Features to Consider

1. A People-Centered, Group-Centered Culture

In general, American Indian life and thought are centered around people, not things: the group, not the individual. People are more likely to be judged by their contribution to the group than by their individual achievements. The family and the community expect that an education should make the students more able to contribute to the group, to move them toward a self-determining society, rather than just get them a job or raise their individual standing.

Since the purpose of getting an education is to contribute to the welfare of the students' people, this should be recognized as a better motivating force than competition. If ways can be found for students, through their studies, to be helpful to the community now, they will more clearly see the need to apply themselves.

We must recognize that the relationship between the individual student and the group is more important to Native Americans than the relationship between the individual and the school. Any action that separates individuals from their friends will be detrimental to their desire to cooperate.

Being complimented or having their individual work discussed before the class may be upsetting to Indian children. Even being addressed individually by the teacher from across the room may be an embarrassment to the child as it calls attention to him or her as an individual.

Most Native American children will perform best when involved in group work. This is so important that we have devoted all of Chapter 5 to cooperative learning.

2. Respect for People, Especially the Elderly

Respect for people and their feelings is much more important in Native American society than it is in the general population. Light and Martin (1986) report that ''. . . it appears that helping systems that function within families and personal relationships are based on mutual respect. The overwhelming majority of Indian women reported that their family members respected each other, and that they in turn received great satisfaction from helping family members. These positive relationships appear to serve as a foundation of strength for Indian people.''

Indian people are generally very careful not to do anything that will show disrespect toward any individual, especially members of their family and the elderly. We hope that you can build your class into a unified group, with a ''family'' feeling. You cannot do this unless you are careful to show respect for every individual and their feelings at all times, and teach the children to do likewise.

Elders are particularly to be respected. One of the earliest lessons to be taught to a Cheyenne child is self-restraint and self-control in the presence of elders. If elders are talking, then the child is to cease talking, be quiet, and listen. The way to retain the values is to listen to and respect the elders.

Modern Americans often value youth and wish they were younger. Books and magazines are filled with advice on how to look young, feel young, and act young. Both Eskimos and Indians respect the elderly for their knowledge, which comes from many years of experience. In the old life, when people could no longer do hard physical work, they were given a place of social prominence and were searched out for guidance and advice. Even today, young educated Indians are often ignored and given few opportunities in their own communities because they have not yet reached the age for respect. However, some of the traditional Indians who twenty years ago looked forward to the time when they would be sought out as they reached the wisdom of age now find that today's youth have accepted the White culture's emphasis upon youth.

Elders, both male and female, although they may be somewhat shy about coming to the schools, are a good source of cultural information and wisdom, and they have many interesting experiences to tell students. Your inviting them also shows your respect for their wisdom and for the values of the people.

Grandparents, because of their experience and wisdom, have always been the chief instructors of the children in Indian societies. They may also be your best help in learning and teaching the local culture.

3. Courtesy, Privacy, and Autonomy

Indian children are taught not to interfere in other people's affairs or their rights as individuals. They should have respect for the individual's privacy, autonomy, and personal dignity. A person seldom gives advice unless it is asked for. You may find that Indian people will resent freely given advice, especially if it does not pertain directly to the instruction given in class. They may resist advice on personal matters of future planning. No one should presume to make a decision for another person or for the group, but cooperation with the group and consensus on group decisions is important. To the Navajo, good behavior means fulfilling their duties to the extended family, being generous, keeping their self-control, and minding their own business.

Indian children may not willingly share information about their families, especially their problems. In counseling sessions, Indian students are less likely than others to reveal either family or school problems. Counseling will require much patience because it usually takes a long time for the student to get down to the real problem. Non-Indians often think Indians seem aloof and reserved, while to Indians, European-Americans may appear to be superficial and hence untrustworthy. However, Sharon BearComesOut, an Indian counselor, tells me that her students are "becoming much more open and trusting when it comes to sharing family concerns and exploring ways to help themselves."

4. The Extended Family

"One of the greatest strengths of American Indian cultures is the extended family. It is not uncommon to find grandparents, aunts, uncles, cousins, or even friends of the family rearing the Indian child."

—Jeanne Bearcrane

Teachers should not assume that because a child is living with an aunt or other relative this means there is a problem in his or her immediate family. Most Indian children are welcome to move in with an aunt or uncle because these are their "other parents." In the Indian community, kinship is identified with even the remotest family tie. All clan members are considered relatives. Crow and Navajo mothers consider their sisters' children as close as their own. In Cheyenne and many other Native languages there are no words for aunt or uncle because they, in addition to the actual parents, are called mother and father. Cousins are called brother and sister. This extended family system gives extra support to all members of the family.

The Indian extended family includes more people, who we may consider "distant relatives," than the European extended family. It may even include nonrelatives if, as with the Sioux, a second set of "parents" is selected for each newborn child. This larger group of close relatives gives the children a sense of security and protection which they do not find in the world outside their homes. Among their relatives they can feel accepted and safe. Because of this extended family, there is less chance of jealousy, sibling rivalry, or emotional upset when a baby is expected.

The child whose parents have moved to a new location to obtain better opportunities for employment may have lost the benefits of the extended family. This may be a great loss especially if the child is a member of a broken home. If, however, the family remains in the community with the extended family, a broken home may not be nearly as serious for the Indian child as for the more mobile middle class. Deaths and family breakups seldom result in homeless children.

Teachers should not be surprised if aunts or grandparents show up for conferences in place of the parents, or if they show as much concern about the child as the parents. They may also be the ones who send permission for the child to participate in a school activity. Nor should they consider the child living with another relative an indication of problems at home. These are normal relationships. Appreciate the fact that the child has numerous people to go to for help or emotional support.

Indian children may have trouble relating to the basic reader stories in which each family stays within a separate house except upon very special occasions, where a family consists only of two parents and two or three children, and where life is child centered and adults frequently participate in children's activities. To them, the family consists of many relatives. Life is adult centered, and although children and adults do many things together, the children are participating in adult activities.

Understand that when adults other than the immediate family discipline a child, it does not mean the parents are neglecting their duties. It may be the responsibility of the uncles or other extended family members to do the disciplining and thus protect the close relationship of the parents and their children. When Crow children do what is not socially approved, it is the responsibility of their cousins to tease them about it and thus bring them into line.

Most Indian parents are affectionate people. Touching and closeness are part of the relationship between parents and children. If members of the Native community normally stand close to each other when they talk, don't keep backing away (your natural reaction) every time the person you are talking with steps closer. This gives the feeling that "teachers are cold." Pulling back when children touch you may make them think you dislike them.

If there is a death in the "family," understand why the children are out of school. It is essential that they be there and show their respect, for the elder, even the far-removed clan member.

Because in many families the older children need to help their families after school, they may not be able to participate in extra-curricular activities. Teachers should find out about their students' home situation before criticizing those who do not take advantage of extra-curricular opportunities.

The support and encouragement of the extended family are probably largely responsible for the fact that the self-concept of most Indian children is higher than that of the general population *when they start school.*

5. Nonverbal Communication and Eye Contact

Nonverbal communication is important in all societies, but more so in those cultures which tend to be less verbal than the typical urban American. This silent or invisible language applies especially to those behaviors that function to control the back-and-forth flow of conversation. These regulatory cues include headnods, gesticulations, gaze, proximity, voice pitch and loudness, utterance length, and turn taking pause duration, among others (Greenbaum).

Unlike verbal communication, two people who are trying to communicate (in the school, the teacher and child, or teacher and parent) can be using two different nonverbal systems without either being aware of the fact. Because of this, misunderstandings occur which are very difficult to identify and/or correct. Over time, these may become major obstacles to communication and develop into mutual antagonism.

Three nonverbal communication factors which frequently cause misunderstanding between the teacher and Indian people are the clues to turn taking in conversation, voice control, and gaze or eye contact.

A good example of misunderstandings and conflict that come from not knowing some detail of the culture is the attitude toward eye contact. Staring at each other while conversing is considered by a majority of Indians as impolite or even aggressive. Navajos stare at another person only when they are angry. The downcast eye is courteous. Persistently looking at a person is intrusive so being stared at is very disturbing. Unless they are quite acculturated, Indians in conversation are more likely to look off in the same direction than at each other. The more a person is respected, the less he or she will be looked at. Eye contact is limited to fleeting glances. Yet many teachers insist that when they talk to students there must be direct eye contact, considering this a sign of trust and respect, and looking around a sign of uninterest or dishonesty. A child who continues to look down is often considered stubborn.

What happens when you insist that a student look you in the eye? You make it even more impossible for him to do so!

At the high school level, it is important to teach students that when applying for a job or while working on the job, as a clerk in a store for example, they must learn to look the non-Indian boss or customer in the eye, and they should practice conversing this way. But this advice should be given only after discussing differences in customs and the importance of learning and adapting to the customs of the people with whom you deal, while retaining and valuing your own.

6. Voice Tone

Voice volume is used to indicate both meaning and emotion. Changing loudness or intensity is the chief way Americans of European background indicate that they are relinquishing their turn during conversation and giving an opportunity for speaker switching. Because many Native Americans habitually make their turns short and have longer pauses between speakers, they use less obvious clues as to when they are through. The children then don't understand, in talking to Anglos, when it is appropriate to talk. They may frequently interrupt the teacher at inappropriate times. The teacher should not interpret this as rudeness, but as a need for instruction and understanding. (And maybe of talking too long?)

Tone of voice indicates feeling. Most Indians speak in very soft tones. This upsets some teachers who think it indicates shyness, being unsure of what they are saying, obstinacy, or secretiveness. The teachers then raise their voices, being accustomed to people who will match their voice to that of the speaker with whom they are conversing. But this may only frighten the Indian students, who interpret it as anger, and they will probably speak in an even lower tone.

The Cree word for white man is "moniyaw"—"loud mouth," a term also used to indicate aggressive behavior. Athapascan parents interpret the loud speech of teachers as indicating rudeness or dislike for the students.

Teachers try to convey enthusiasm for what they are teaching or excitement over the story they are reading through higher and louder tones, hoping to increase the interest. Both Indian and Chicano children of the Southwest frequently interpret these tones as anger. They become intimidated and withdraw into themselves. Teachers then describe their students as sullen or evasive while the students say their teachers are mean, bossy, or always angry. This lack of understanding is obviously a serious obstacle to classroom participation and learning.

7. Time for Thought

"A man without patience is a lamp without oil."

—Andres Segovia

Native American people usually not only talk less than their Anglo counterparts, but the duration of the pause between speakers is longer. Even Native American teachers allow for longer pauses and less talk than non-Indian teachers.

During a discussion, Indian etiquette often requires a lapse of time before a response. A person should take time to think about a question. Grover Wolf Voice, a Northern Cheyenne elder, told me, ''Even if I had a quick answer to your question, I would never answer immediately. That would be saying that your question was not worth thinking about.'' Throughout a conversation, taking time and deliberating imply that what the other person says is worthy of consideration.

Appreciate the patience of your students. Don't expect immediate answers that come without thought. Appreciate, rather than becoming impatient with their slow, deliberate, unhurried discussions.

Nationwide, approximately 25 percent of Indian students are not fluent in English when they start school, so also keep in mind that Indian children may need a longer time to formulate an answer because, especially with a difficult question, they may have to translate the question into their own language, think it over, and then translate back into English.

In the classroom which contains both Indian and non-Indian students, the Indian student may never have a chance to speak. This may cause the non-Indian students and teachers to think the Indians are shy, withdrawn, disinterested, obstinate, unsociable, or that they are sulking or trying to ignore the teacher. When asking questions, few teachers allow enough time even for highly verbal urban children. What about the Indian children who are taught to wait, to think before answering? Many teachers never discover that some of their brightest students have answers because the verbal children with quick answers are the only ones who ever have an opportunity to answer. To motive Indian children to take part in class discussions, we must give them time to think out their answers—time to be right.

8. Lack of Pressure from Time

"Do not be anxious about tomorrow. Tomorrow will be anxious for itself. Let today's own trouble be sufficient for today."

—Matthew 6-34

The Native American characteristic which is probably most misunderstood is their concept of time. To European-Americans, time is very important. It must be used to the fullest. Hurry is the by-word. Get things done. Prepare for the future. They feel guilty if they are idle. They say, ''Time flies.'' To the Mexican, ''time walks.'' However, the Indian tells me, ''time is with us.'' Life should be easygoing, with little pressure. There is no need to watch clocks. In fact, many Indian languages have no word for time. Things should be done when they need to be done. Exactness of time is of little importance. When an activity should be done is better determined by when the thing that precedes it is completed or when circumstances are right than by what the clock says.

The fact that Indians habitually give less thought to time passing than non-Indians was evidenced by an experiment which indicated that Indian adolescents' estimates of the time required to do a job were less than half as accurate as the estimates of their non-Indian counterparts (Anderson, 1980).

Non-Indians often mistakenly interpret an Indian's relaxed attitude toward time as being a sign of indifference or irresponsibility, while some Indians think non-Indians are so dissatisfied with the present and so concerned about the future that they never really live in the present or enjoy it to the fullest.

Time to the traditional Indian and non-Indian may be a very different concept. European-Americans accept time as a straight line from past to present to future. Our language emphasizes this concept and helps us think in this way. We use the past tense most of the time in our descriptions and also put a great emphasis on the future. Many Indian people describe time as a circle, and many Indian languages are based almost entirely on the present. In some there are no future tense verbs. The future has to be indicated by the rest of the content, and the past tense is seldom used.

I arrived at a meeting and asked a traditional Indian what time he thought it would start. He appeared puzzled about why I asked. After a moment he said, "What difference could it possibly make? You're not going to miss it. You are already here!" Ask an Eskimo what time an event is to take place, and his typical answer is, "It will happen when we get there." He does not look at the clock; he looks at the weather. That is what decides his actions.

Patience and the ability to wait quietly are valued characteristics among Indian people. They may not understand the non-Indian's compulsion for continuous action and getting things done. Look carefully at the beadwork, quillwork, weaving, and other art works of the Indian people. Watch them at work. Understand the patience that is necessary to do these things.

When the typical non-Indian has criticism to make, he is often quite blunt. He gets to the point and expresses his feelings quickly. He may offend the Indian who is accustomed to much talk about the good things first. A teacher seldom has the patience to listen long enough to hear the Indian's concerns.

Pepper (1985, p. 182) suggests that Indian students have a unit of study on time, which would include use of time in the old cultures as well as in modern life. We have to teach the students that if they are to work successfully in the economic system of the dominant society, they must recognize the importance that others put on time and learn to work according to schedules; they have to think ahead to the effect of their present actions on the future. But we do not have to teach them that time is more important than people and human relationships.

Keep your scheduling flexible so that there is not a feeling of pressure to finish, or to stop in the middle of a task. However, also teach the students that they can't put off starting a project but need to learn to schedule their work so they can complete it by the assigned date.

9. Valuing Leisure

In the old life, and in the present life of the rural Navajo and others, there is no distinct line between work and play. They will both bring happiness if they are in harmony with nature.

Traditionally Indian people depended on nature to satisfy their needs. They used what was available. They grew what crops were necessary. They hunted only as much game as was needed. To take more was wasteful of both Nature, time, and energy. They were not concerned with producing beyond their needs, acquiring materials, or saving what they would not soon use. People did not work just to be working or to look busy. They worked when there was work to be done and enjoyed relaxation when there was not. The puritan work ethic had no place in their culture.

Indian students and their parents may well be frustrated when children are assigned work for the sake of work. Homework assigned just because you think they should have homework goes against their principles and will probably discourage them from being serious about assignments that are really important.

10. Sense of Humor

Many early explorers reported that "No other people laugh as much as the Eskimos." Since I knew the Yanowamo Indians of Venezuela before they had any contact with the outside world, I am more inclined to think that no one laughs as frequently as a Yanowamo. Native Americans have always had a deep sense of humor related to life, to inner feelings. It is one of the things that make difficult situations bearable. But humor is different in each society. Some teachers actually think that their Indian friends have no sense of humor. But that is not surprising since it is often claimed that the humor of a culture is usually the last part of the culture to be really understood. Modern Indians have accepted our light jokes, our open obvious humor, but much of their real humor is hard for the person new to the culture to detect. Jokes do not translate well, especially those that include idioms or puns.

Many Indians are especially good at condensing a statement into a few words, saying much with a verbal picture and a bit of humor. Often Indians will listen to a long discourse from a white man, then repeat it to their friends in two or three sentences which convey the overall idea, plus their own sense of humor.

Listen to the humor of your students and their parents. Learn to enjoy it. If you can put humor into your classroom, if you can let the students see you laugh at your own mistakes and problems, and if you can encourage them to laugh at theirs, you will have moved a long way toward understanding Indian humor, building mutual understanding with your students, and having a smooth running, enjoyable classroom.

11. Harmony with Nature and the Environment

In the old culture great effort was made to live in balance with nature. People were part of nature, so health and well being were possible only if they lived in harmony with nature. Early Indians did not understand people who wanted to own the land, to control it, to change it, to use it, and to be masters of it. Air, water, and land could not be owned. They were part of nature and people were to live with them, not control or change them.

Marie Reyhner told me that the Navajo regard nature as the best teacher. Nature is the basic source of knowledge of the natural order of things. It teaches us through the stars, seasons, wind, and animals to observe, respect, and learn from nature without disturbing the natural order.

European-American society since the Industrial Revolution has been more concerned with controlling nature. But we are moving rapidly toward the old Indian point of view. We should give the Indian people credit for their emphasis on the ecology. We should discuss this, and the importance of returning to the old point of view.

In science classes we should give the Native people credit for their knowledge of nature, of animal ways, and of the uses of plants. Nature, and the observation of nature, should be an integral part of our study. What better way could we begin the study of science than by honoring and using the Native people's knowledge of nature?

12. Spirituality and Health

Since all of the Indian's old way of life was surrounded by nature, and nature was spiritual, spiritual considerations were important in everything that was done.

Lewis (1981) lists three strengths of the Indian Family: (1) the helping systems that operate within the family; (2) the respect for each other and personal relationships; and (3) the courage and optimism obtained from spiritual life and religion.

The Indian Nations at Risk Task Force listed as one of the barriers Native children must overcome if schools are to succeed "a shift away from spiritual values that are critical to the well-being of individuals and society as a whole."

Although for many, modern life, as the Task Force notes, is causing a shift away from the spiritual values, they are still a powerful influence on many of our students. For the traditional Indian, religion and spirituality still have a place in every act and every decision, every day. Don't underestimate the importance of the spiritual in the lives of even some of the most modern of Indians. For many of them, it is much more important than for the majority of the general population. Lack of spiritual concerns and failure to cooperate with nature are considered better explanations for poor health, misfortune, or poor hunting than are scientific explanations. We should not try to avoid the spiritual aspect of life in the students' discussions, or downgrade it in any way. Accept the spiritual explanations for things, along with the scientific. They can provide two acceptable viewpoints that often go hand in hand.

And try hard to know enough about the beliefs of your local group so that you do not come in conflict with them. Dick Little Bear (1986) gives a good example related to his own tribe, the Northern Cheyenne:

"What is acceptable in one tribe may be taboo in another. For instance, in all Plains Indian cultures, eagle feathers are sacred. Yet among the Cheyennes, eagle feathers must not be touched by Cheyenne females. So something that seems logical for a teacher to do, like awarding an eagle feather, or a likeness of one, to a Cheyenne female for an athletic or academic accomplishment, is violating Cheyenne beliefs. Yet, doing so in a classroom with students from another Indian tribe might be perfectly acceptable."

Harmony with nature and spirituality are necessary to good health. The main purpose of many Navajo healing ceremonials is to restore harmony between people and nature. Poor health results from disharmony with Nature. It affects a person physically, spiritually, and psychologically. Indian 'medicine men' treated not just the affected part of the body, but the whole person. They believed that the mind and body were so closely linked that it would be foolish to treat one without the other. They were the early psychosomatic physicians.

Modern medicine is just beginning to recognize the importance of this. In 1984, St. Mary's Hospital and Health Center in Tucson hired Indian medicine man Edgar Monetathchi to teach their staff traditional Indian techniques of treating the sick with holistic medicine, relying on improvement of mental state along with treatment of physical ills. Since then medicine personnel have come from as far away as Mexico and Europe to study their methods, and other medicine men are training people in California and other places. Paul Ortega, Mescalero Apache medicine man, says that ancient healing methods, healing the mind as well as the body, speed the recovery of patients after their treatment with modern medical techniques.

If teachers as well as medical personnel recognize the validity of Indian medicine, it will be possible for individuals to have the advantages of both the old and the new, rather than having to make either/or choices.

13. Respect for Ceremonies

Most Indian groups still carry on many traditional ceremonies and other activities. These are a very important part of the life of the community and the teaching of the children.

Marie Reyhner, a Navajo mother, told me:

"Traditionally, the teachings of the Navajo were handed down orally. Knowledge was regarded as sacred, and the teaching was not left to just anyone, who may not respect the teachings. Navajo children are taught by the mother, father, uncles, aunts, and grandparents. The grandparents usually teach about the ceremonials, getting help from other elders if needed. Some of the ceremonials the Navajo grandparents would emphasize are a ritual for all at three months of age, a special ceremony for the baby's first laugh, the puberty ceremony for girls, healing ceremonies, welcome home ceremonies, thanksgiving ceremonies, and ceremonies of birth, marriage, death, protection, and others. They also teach about every area of family life: manners, personal relations, kinships, behavior, dress, not to be rude or immodest, to be gracious of relatives, considerate, and never stingy. Religion is very important—daily prayers of thanksgiving for food, clothing, family, relatives, for healing or wholeness, and for celebration.

"Many of these knowledges are important to the Navajo that may not be important to others. If one has determination to be good or to be accepted as one with knowledge, he learns what is essential for a Navajo to know, always stressing the good, suppressing the bad; encouraging sharing, giving, and compassion for your fellow men."

In most Plains Indian groups, the sun dance and the vision quest are the most spiritual of the ceremonials. There are many other ceremonies, pow-wows, and other traditional activities which range from the highly spiritual to largely recreational and social. These are all important parts of the lives of our students.

It hardly seems necessary to say that teachers should always show respect for the ceremonies or that comments or actions that can be interpreted as disrespectful could permanently damage a teacher's standing and effectiveness in the community. Rather, why not ask an elder to come and teach your class about the ceremonies? He could help the students to see that it is much more important to understand the values than the actions or costumes.

Learn which ceremonies and activities are open to the public. Plains Indian pow-wows are traditionally open to everyone. You will find few ceremonies that are not. There is no better way for a teacher to show an interest in the students and the culture than to be present and participate in the pow-wow.

14. Honesty

In most Native cultures of the past, honesty—telling the truth and keeping one's word—was one of the most important of all human characteristics. This was especially true of most North American Indian tribes. In other societies, such as the Yanowamo Indian tribe of South America, a people are supposed to tell the truth only to those of their own village and to personal friends. Lying to others is a respected practice so it is important to know if the person speaking considers you a personal friend, someone worthy of hearing the truth.

To the Indian child, trust must go both ways. The person who does not trust others is considered untrustworthy. To be trusted, a person must trust and respect others. Watching closely to see that a person does the right thing is disrespectful and destroys self-esteem.

15. Emotional Control

In most Native American groups, it is considered inappropriate for a person to express strong feeling openly in public. Actions that would evoke loud expressions of anger in most non-Natives are more likely to bring a shaking of the head and an expression of sorrow. Adults do not normally cry in the presence of others except in mourning.

Summary

Teachers should endeavor to learn as much as possible about the cultures of the communities in which they live. The chart below summarizes some of the common values and preferences of many Native American people, contrasted with those of the dominant society. Just as it is obvious that all the items in the first column do not apply to any one non-Indian, the items in the second column should not be construed as all applying to any one Indian, and only to an extent to any group of Indians. These are generalities—and there are no "general" Indians. The cultural patterns of each tribe are different, and Native Americans are individuals with their own ways and their own personalities. Instead of assuming that any particular statements apply to your students, use the list as a guide to aid you in knowing what to look for as you study your own community.

European American Values	Native American Values

The individual is all important.
  Promote your own welfare.
	The group is all important.
	  Take a back seat.

Support and get support from immediate family.	Support and get support from large extended family.
Emphasis on youth.	Respect for wisdom of the elderly.
Assertive, confident, doer. Dominate.	Passive, modest. Let others dominate.
Demonstrative.	Reserved.
Regimented lifestyle.	Independent lifestyle.
Expect direction.	Expect independent action.

Acquire, save. Possessions bring status.
  Wealth and security sought after.
	Share. Honor in giving. Suspicious of those
	  with too much.

Individual learning.	Group learning.
Compete. Excel. Be the best. Personal space required.	Cooperate. Help each other. Work together. Touching, closeness, affection.

Always look a person in the eye. Looking away
  means uninterest or dishonesty.
	Looking in the eye means aggression or anger.
	        Looking down is a sign of respect.

Reliance on verbal communication.	More reliance on nonverbal communication.
Vocal. Must talk. Embarrassed by silence.	Quiet. Say what is necessary. Enjoy silent companionship.
Be noticed.	Stay in the background.
Speak up, show enthusiasm.	Speak in a soft voice. Loud speech indicates aggression, anger.
Give instant answers to questions.	Allow time for thought.
Continuous conversation. Impatient.	Long pauses in conversation. Patient.
Criticism is immediate, blunt, to the point.	Talk about good things before criticism.
Time is extremely important. Get things done. Watch the clock, schedules, priorities.	Time is here. Be patient. Enjoy life.
Prepare. Live for the future.	Enjoy today; it is all we have. Live now.

Keep busy. Idleness is undesirable.
  Produce to acquire and build reserves.
	Enjoy leisure. Depend on nature and use what is
	  available.

Things of nature are here for man, to be used.	Respect nature. Do not disturb balance.
Health; concern for germs, cleanliness.	Health results from harmony with nature.
Traditions of varying importance.	Great respect for ceremonials and traditions.
Honor for the sports figure and individual achievement.	Respect for bravery, especially if for group benefit.
Accept public show of emotions: anger, sorrow, affection.	Little evidence of emotion in public.
Work is a virtue.	Work for survival.
Light humor. Jokes.	Deep sense of humor. See humor in life.
Few strong ties beyond the single family unit.	Close ties to entire extended family including many relatives.
Analyze and control nature.	Live in harmony with nature.
Science. Reason	Spirituality. Mythology.
Act according to logic.	Act according to what feels right.

Visitors, associates, teachers must be welcomed
  inside the home.
	Yard is appropriate place to visit teacher until well
	  acquainted and accepted.

Monolingual. English is the best and only
  important language.
	Bilingual. Values of culture are best expressed in the
	  language of that culture.

References for Further Reading

Anderson, Brooks, Larry Burd, John Dodd, and Katharin Kelker. "A Comparative Study in Estimating Time." *Journal of American Indian Education.* Vol. 19, 3. May 1990.

Bearcrane, Jeanne, John M. Dodd, J. Ron Nelson, and Steven W. Ostwald. "Educational Characteristics of Native Americans." *Rural Education.* Vol. 11, 3. pp. 1–5.

Beers, David. *It Happens When We Get There: Conversations with Teachers in Alaskan Villages.* Alaska Department of Education. 1978.

Fiordo, R. "The Soft Spoken Way vs. the Outspoken Way: A Bicultural Approach to Teaching Communication to Native People in Alberta." *Journal of American Indian Education.* Vol. 24. July 1985. pp. 35–48.

Florey, Janice E. *Identification of Gifted Children among the American Indian Population: An Inservice Model.* EDRS. 19486. 41 pp.

Galloway, Charles. *Silent Language in the Classroom. Phi Delta Kappa Educational Foundation.* 1976. 33 pp.

Gilliland, Hap, and Harriet Mauritsen. "Humor in the Classroom." *The Reading Teacher.* Vol. 24, 1. May 1971. pp. 753–756+.

Greenbaum, Paul E., and Susan D. Greenbaum. "Cultural Differences, Nonverbal Regulation, and Classroom Interaction: Sociolinguistic Interference in American Indian Education." *Peabody Journal of Education.*

Grudin, Robert. *Time and the Art of Living.* Harper and Row. 1982. 225 pp.

Indian Nations at Risk Task Force. "Part I: Why the Native Peoples Are at Risk." *Indian Nations at Risk: An Educational Strategy for Action. U.S. Dept. of Education.* Oct. 1991. pp. 1–12.

Lewis, R. "Patterns of Strengths of American Indian Families." In F. Hoffman (Ed.) *The American Indian Family: Strengths and Stresses.* American Indian Social Research and Development Associates. 1981.

Malony, Ray. "Ten Ways to Turn Out Terrific Kids." *Vibrant Life.* Jan/Feb. 1985.

Pell, Sarah J. "A Communication Skill Project for Disadvantaged Aleut, Eskimo, and Indian Ninth and Tenth Graders." Journal of Reading. Vol. 22, 5. Feb. 1979. pp. 404–407.

Blackfeet teachers plan together for a unit of study.

Phyllis Edwards, Blackfeet Indian teacher, plans a project with four of her Blackfeet students.

Chapter 5
Cooperative Learning: It's the Indian Way

> *"What's wrong with this world? There ain't but one word will tell
> you what's wrong, and that's selfishness."*
>
> —Will Rogers

In that one sentence, Will Rogers, a Cherokee, expressed the Indian viewpoint that you must be aware of if you are to understand the Indian way of life.

If you are a teacher who has never lived among Native American people and who is not familiar with the Native way of thought, you may not realize, at first, the importance of cooperation and sharing. You may expect to motivate children through competition, and you probably assume that any person would work to become better off than the neighbors. In the Native American community, you may become acquainted with a whole new orientation to life.

Consider the familiar middle-class urban children. They live in a world of things. People are supposed to work hard to acquire possessions and their value is measured by how many they manage to acquire. A person should save for the future. "A penny saved is a penny earned." A person must "put something away for a rainy day."

In contrast, the typical Native American child lives in a world of people. To him, people are all-important. Possessions are of value mainly because they can be shared. Family members may be suspicious of the person who collects many personal possessions. Rather, they believe "You can't get rich if you look after your relatives right." Having more than your neighbors may be undesirable. There is no respect for the person who puts possessions above relationships with friends and relatives.

I am not implying that owning the necessities is not important to the American Indian or that the dominant society disregards people. It is the emphasis that is different. This difference in priorities is noticeable and important. Since these attitudes affect the whole community, the children's relationships with the teacher and with their peers, and their motivation for school achievement, it is very important for us as teachers to understand the way of thinking the Native children learn in their homes. To which of these ways of thinking should we gear our instruction?

Why Not Compete?

"Man's unique agony as a species consists in his perpetual conflict
between the desire to stand out and the need to blend in."

—Sidney J. Harris, *Field Newspaper Syndicate*

Whenever we talk about eliminating competition and encouraging students to help each other, someone asks, "Shouldn't the students learn to compete so they can compete in the adult world? They will all have to compete as adults." Will they?

In a recent survey, several thousand employers across the U.S. listed the reasons the last three employees were fired. 80 percent of the employees lost their jobs because they couldn't work well enough with others, they couldn't get along with their fellow employees, they couldn't work as a team. They had not learned enough about how to work cooperatively. Less than 10 percent could not do the work or did not work hard enough.

People who develop as their main objective outdoing their fellow workers—proving that they are doing more—will never learn to get the willing cooperation of others. Nor will they get the help they need for doing a job well. Yet this is the attitude that is developed in the competitive classroom.

This attitude of competition, rather than cooperation, is detrimental to every student, but goes against the whole way of thinking of the Indian student.

Cultural Emphasis on Sharing and Cooperation

"It is well to give when asked, but it is better to give unasked,
through understanding."

—Kahlil Gibran, *The Prophet* (Knopf)

A look at the past will help us understand the Indian way of sharing. When the Plains Indian killed a buffalo, he shared the meat, not only with his relatives, but with all who needed it. He could do this with confidence, knowing that they would also share with him. One Indian, in describing his ancestors, said, "They were all fat or they were all thin." How better could you describe a society in which anyone who had food made sure that no one went hungry?

Some say the sharing way no longer works because there are now too many "red apples" who will take, without sharing in return. A group of us were discussing this on the Northern Cheyenne Reservation when Don Little, a Sioux, told us that although it may be true that sharing will not always result in others sharing with you at a later date, it does result in happiness, in health, in spiritual well being. It improves your mental health while it teaches your children your values and gives them good feelings and strength of character.

Along with sharing goes living cooperatively. In most Native American groups, cooperation, equalitarianism, and informality are more important than individual achievement, self-expression, or competition. Students do not feel any urge to out-do their neighbors, so competition does not produce motivation. Individuals who show that they can do better than their peers are teased and criticized, even ostracized. They feel ashamed. If the teacher points out their superior work to the class, they find it necessary to quit doing good work in order to regain their place in the group. However, if they do the same quality of work *as a member of a group,* they are then doing it for the benefit of others, helping others to learn. Their efforts are appreciated, and others are encouraged to also do their best.

Brewer, an Ogalala Sioux, says, "There is a constant fear of 'standing out' in a group that has deep roots in our culture."

The Importance of Cooperative Education

"Light is the task where many share the toil."
—Homer

As was emphasized before, if we try to teach any group of students using methods that are counter to their innermost values, we are doomed to failure. That's why cooperative learning is so important in Native American education. It is the *best* way of teaching *all* children, but it is especially important for Indian students and is effective with all Indian cultures and with students of all ages.

Slavin (1986), in reviewing a number of studies, says that although cooperative education improves the academic achievement of all students, the effects of cooperative learning have been even more dramatic for minority students than for white students.

Another good thing about cooperative education: Instead of the students feeling that they have to do a difficult task alone, they have the support, encouragement, and help of the group. It makes a great difference in the students' whole feeling about school.

As teachers, we can eliminate much frustration for both ourselves and our students if we do not expect them to be quick to respond individually. By having them work cooperatively, in groups, helping each other, we can stress the Native strengths: the enjoyment of self-created activities, reduced pressure to keep up with the Joneses, and freedom from the tensions of competition.

Thirteen Ways of Applying Cooperative Learning

Many educators have written about cooperative learning, describing one particular method or technique as if that one system was what constituted cooperative learning. Cooperative learning is not a single method, or several methods. It is an attitude toward students, a concept of learning, a whole way of life within the classroom and, hopefully, throughout the school.

It is not just something you use at particular times, or for a particular subject. In the Indian school, the cooperative way of thinking should permeate every hour and every part of the school day.

But you can't jump in and change everything at once. Following are suggestions of things you can do to get cooperative learning started in the classroom. You don't have to wait to make this a big project or learn all the techniques. Start small, but *start now!*

1. Develop an Attitude of Sharing and Cooperation

People are at their best when they are helping each other and working together. Regardless of race or cultural group, two heads are better than one. Working together is fun; it stimulates thinking; it helps develop children's thinking skills; it motivates the students because each feels a responsibility to the group; and it makes the individual feel that others care. Since cooperative learning requires communication, it also improves language and self-expression. This practice in communication skills is needed by many Native students.

In their own families and neighborhoods, when children see a brother, a sister, a friend or a neighbor having trouble, whether it is with another person or with a task, they know that they should try to help. Yet when the children are in class and a friend is squirming because he or she does not know an answer, they are told that helping is not allowed. Why? Couldn't we, the teachers, show the students that we appreciate their willingness to help? Couldn't the children learn from each other?

Then let's encourage students to help each other whenever possible. Let's talk about the importance of sharing and cooperation in the Indian community, past and present.

Tell your students, "In this class every student helps everyone else at every opportunity." Say it to the students often; then say it to yourself more often, until you convince both them *and yourself* that this is the right way of life.

I tell my students, "If anyone does poorly on this project, you are all to blame. You didn't give each other enough help."

Don't be the teacher who said, "Quit helping each other. This isn't our cooperative learning time." Encourage them to help each other all the time, in every subject.

Eliminate the word "cheat" from your vocabulary. It is impossible for anyone to cheat if he or she is *supposed to be* helping. Just make sure they understand thoroughly what helping is: that just giving someone an answer in math, for example, is not being helpful but harmful, because they are preventing learning. They are only helping if they make sure the student also knows how to get that answer.

2. Sit in Groups or Circles

The old style seating arrangement was purposefully organized to lessen students' contact with each other. Students who are working together in groups will need to sit together. For many activities, groups of four desks facing each other are most practical. This puts the students close enough together so they can see everyone in their group and talk together in low tones, promoting quiet cooperation. Of course, group size will vary for different purposes.

When students are not working specifically in groups, I like all the desks in one large circle, with my desk as part of the circle. Each student can see everyone else and no one is in front. This arrangement helps in getting the spirit of cooperation started.

3. Work in Pairs

The easiest way to begin cooperative learning is by having students work in pairs on their assignments. If you use workbooks, pairs of students can work with them, filling out only one form and discussing it together. They can each do a math assignment but keep checking with each other and discuss any disagreements, thus correcting any errors.

4. Try Peer Tutoring

> *"If you would thoroughly know anything, teach it to others."*
> —Tryon Edwards

Allowing older or more academically able students to help those who need extra help promotes the learning of both. The use of peer tutoring makes the students responsible for each other's learning. Both the tutor and the one being tutored feel responsible for doing as well as they can. Neither wants to disappoint the other. Helping each other becomes motivation for achievement, rather than a reason for holding back to keep from being resented by their friends.

Students boost their self-concepts by teaching each other. Nothing gives students more confidence in their ability to do a task than to know they have taught someone else to do it too, or that the teacher has confidence enough in them to ask them to help.

The best students are often not the best people to use as tutors, especially if the class consists of a racially and culturally mixed group. Often the gifted student cannot relate to the problems of the students who have real difficulty and they may also grow impatient or make remarks about their ignorance. The child who has had difficulty with a certain concept but has finally come to understand it is often the one who is able to understand and to help clarify the problems that another child is having with the concept. In addition, the tutors clarify the concepts in their own minds by putting them into words and explaining them.

Some parents, and a few teachers, think that peer tutors should not be used because they fear that this will be wasting the time of the students who are doing the tutoring and that the ones being taught are being deprived of the expert help of the teacher. This is the opposite from the truth. Teachers who think about it must realize that when they teach a skill for the first time, they learn even more than the pupils do. McWhorter and Leve (1971) found that when students tutored other students in reading, the tutors raised their own reading levels by an average of 2.4 years in four months, while those being tutored gained 1.1 years in the same period.

Older children tutoring younger or less skilled children can have double benefits if the older children themselves need practice. Sixth graders reading at first grade level may be indignant if asked to use primer type material for practice in reading. However, if they are reading it in preparation for helping a first or second grade child who is having trouble, reading this same material takes on status and responsibility. They build self-concept and self-confidence as they build reading skills.

One high school teacher lets some of the poor readers in her classes practice reading books they have chosen for younger children. They then are excused from her English class to go to the lower elementary classrooms to read to the students. Everyone benefits.

Students should also be encouraged to get together to help each other outside of class.

5. Form Bonded Partnerships

In one school, children were paired in partnerships that formed strong bonds between the students. The students learned to accept responsibility for each other's actions, for their academic success, and even for their attendance. The children agreed to call or visit their partners at least once a week, to help them or just keep in touch. This also got the parents more involved in the education of both their own children and their partners. It also produced cooperation between the two sets of parents.

Many of these partnerships developed into firm, lasting friendships, which some of the students lacked before.

The partners were kept together when assigned to larger groups, but were exchanged in the middle of the year, which, for most, added a new friend and partner. The change was also important in the few cases in which the original partners were not as compatible as they might wish.

6. Use Group Problem Solving

"By first doing a job together, each helper learns to do the job alone."

—Unknown

In a group-oriented, cooperative society the most effective assignments are problem solving assignments in which the students work on group solutions. Let two to six students work together on an assignment. Even in subjects like mathematics, many of the assignments can be given as group assignments that the pupils are to solve together. In science and social studies, assignments can be set up as group problems with small groups working together to find solutions.

Instead of individual oral reports, a group can have a panel discussion in front of the class. When students give a report for a group, shouldn't the entire group stand together with the student who is giving the report? The one giving the report will find it much easier to talk in front of the class and the whole group will feel a part of the achievement.

When it is necessary that each student work on a different topic, after each student has chosen a topic, the topics and who is working on them can be discussed with the whole class, and they can all be asked to watch for information on the other topics and to help each other find information. It is then the responsibility of the whole group to see that everyone is successful. The group is responsible for helping anyone who is having trouble. I tell my students that if anyone does poorly, they are all responsible. They didn't provide enough help! Individual praise, given quietly, should express appreciation for the help given to another more often than emphasizing individual achievement.

We must be very sure that before the students begin to work, their plans are very specific and are understood by each student, but that they are group-oriented rather than task-oriented. The plans are more likely to be understood and carried out if they are developed cooperatively by the teacher and the students.

7. Develop Student-Led Group Projects

After students become accustomed to, and adept at working in groups, there are many times, especially in the social studies area, where students can take the leadership role and develop their own student-led group projects. The teacher then becomes more a facilitator than a lecturer and students gradually become more adept at taking responsibility for their own and the group's learning. They learn to set up their own objectives and work toward collectively reaching group-established goals.

As stated by Forester and Little Soldier (1974),

> "The teacher remains the institutional leader, the manager of the setting for learning, but there is a shift in responsibility for student actions from the shoulders of the teacher to those of the student. The teacher is a resource and guide. They are there to help the students solve their own problems and to encourage them to explore alternative courses of action."

8. Try Team Games

We have emphasized the Native students' lack of desire to compete, yet on nearly every reservation and in every Alaskan village, basketball is the most popular activity and there is fierce competition between teams. The difference, of course, is that in team sports the individual is competing *for* his own group, while in individual competition, he would be competing against them.

In discussing this contrast, Dumont and Wax (1969, p. 85) say:

> "It has frequently been observed that Indian children hesitate to engage in an individual performance before the public gaze, especially where they sense competitive assessment against their peers and equally do not wish to demonstrate by their individual superiority the inferiority of their

peers. On the other hand, where performance is socially defined as benefiting the peer society, Indians become excellent competitors.''

Slavin (1988) has been a prominent promotor of what he calls ''TGT'' or Team Games Tournaments. Students are placed on learning teams, organized much like athletic teams. They know that their classmates are counting on them to do their best for the team, and support their academic efforts.

Students are assigned to four- or five-member heterogeneous learning teams each of which should include, as nearly as possible, all the levels of ability and cultural groups in the classroom. This is very important so that all teams are as equal as possible and competition will be fair. The teams remain together for five or six weeks, or for the duration of a unit of study. Each week the class is taught new information or skills. Each team then studies the material as a group, then competes with the other teams, either in solving a problem or a group of problems requiring this knowledge, or in a test over the material in which each individual score is totaled for a team score. This eliminates the stigma of some students standing out by excelling, and therefore being separated from their classmates. They are, instead, helping them by raising the group score.

This is an excellent system for *some* of the time, but it should not be considered the whole of cooperative learning. It is one of many techniques. If overdone with a class of Native American students, it could backfire because, even though the students are competing for their team, they still are competing against others of their friends. We don't want to base our motivation strictly on competition.

There are several articles and books by Slavin from which teachers can learn more about TGT techniques.

9. Apply Cooperative Effort to Learn Writing Skills

Another good opportunity for students to help each other is through the use of peer evaluation during the teaching of writing skills. When students are doing any type of creative writing, give each student an opportunity to write something; then let the students divide into groups and read and evaluate the writing of each student in their group, helping them with suggestions on how they can improve their work. Thus the students are the final authority. The teacher does not criticize the writing. The students have a real audience and a reason to write well. What they write becomes important.

Thorough planning is essential and must include an explanation of the importance of *helping* each other by pointing out the *good* things in the writing, rather than down-grading it, of helping writers to correct their errors, rather than criticizing them. The group must accept responsibility for seeing that each student ends up with a paper to be proud of.

10. Solve Math Problems Cooperatively

Since much of our mathematics class time should be practice in using mathematical thought processes to solve problems, it is the ideal place to apply group problem solving and team learning. If students are given tasks that require reasoning and the application of processes learned in solving life-like problems, then time together in small groups to discuss and solve the problems cooperatively will greatly increase understanding. Also, the type of problems groups of students are given can be much more difficult and require greater understanding than is reasonable when each student must solve problems independently.

When children use manipulatives, they need to verbalize what they are doing. It helps them relate what they are doing to words and symbols and encourages understanding. Students working in twos and threes are given an opportunity to talk about what they are doing and help each other clarify their ideas.

11. Develop Group Pride in Achievement

There are some teachers who are able to develop in their students a feeling of pride in belonging to a group of hard-working students. They build in their students a loyalty to one another. In effect, this loyalty to the group includes the teacher. When someone does good work, the whole group takes pride in it instead of envying or criticizing as they do in other classrooms. This group feeling seldom comes about through the influence of a good leader among the students. It more often develops through the attitudes shown by the teacher, the comments made to the students in and out of class.

12. Lessen Competition for Grades

In any group in which peer approval and peer relationships are important, some good students will intentionally make poor grades on tests or will refuse to turn in homework to prevent getting a better grade than their friends. Grades based on final tests of knowledge are unfair measures in any case. The tests are largely a measure of previous knowledge rather than of how much was learned in this class or how much effort was put into the learning. The child who has no knowledge of a subject to begin with has no chance of competing with the one who already knew more than other students will when they finish. Slow learners know that no matter how hard they work, they cannot compete with the gifted students who can make good grades almost without ever opening a book.

Emphasis upon learning, on the fun of learning, on helping each other, and on making use of the knowledge in some immediate way, is important. I taught for seven years in a school that gave no grades, so I understand the increased motivation when children are taught by the attitude of the whole school that the object is to learn as much as possible, not to get grades. Most of us are forced to give grades, even if we teach in a cooperative, noncompetitive society, but we can put the emphasis on the students' improvement in their own work, on interesting ideas, and on the fun of learning.

13. Replace Competition with Others with Self-Competition

> "There is nothing noble in being superior to some other man. True nobility is being superior to your former self."
>
> —Hindu proverb

While students should never be required to compete with their friends, they should be competing with themselves, trying to surpass their own records. If tests are used for evaluation, they should be tests of individual *improvement,* and the results should be discussed in that light.

In my elementary classes, at the beginning of any new study in social studies or science, I give a test over the entire unit of work. This is not only a basis for evaluating improvement, but a guide for study. When the students come to anything that was in the pre-test, they remember having seen it and know this is important. It is something to remember. Sometimes when I am talking to the class, someone will say, "Oh! You gave that away!"

At the end of the unit I give the same test again. I do not put a grade on the test. I mark the *correct* answers on both the pre- and post-test and return them to the student together. The only comparisons made are those the students make between their own final test and their beginning test. A common reaction from children of all ability levels as they compare the two tests is, "You mean I *didn't even know that!?*" Both the lowest and the highest ability students can see that they have learned, and this encourages them to work hard on the next unit.

It is only through this kind of comparison with their previous work that children realize how much they really do learn. Without this evidence they are unconscious of their increase in knowledge because no one can remember not knowing a thing. (Try naming some of the things about Indian education that you do not yet know!)

If you look for them, there are ways that you can let the community see that the Native American way of sharing and cooperation is important in your school.

On graduation day 1987, at the Lame Deer School on the Northern Cheyenne reservation, graduation was combined with a pow-wow and give away. The school picnic was held in the morning with most of the fun being non-competitive (no winner or loser) Indian games. In the afternoon was the assembly at which students were honored for scholarship, athletic achievement, and so forth. This was followed by the graduation ceremony. Next came a traditional Cheyenne feast. Following this was a traditional pow-wow with the entire community taking part. After two or three traditional Indian dances with everyone taking part, the singer/drummers

Honoring procession at Lame Deer School graduation ceremony.

would begin an honoring song and one of the graduates and his family would lead the dance around the floor with all those who wanted to honor that student joining in behind. At the end of the dance that family would bring out all kinds of gifts—star quilts, home-made beadwork, and others—that they had been gathering or making for the last year, and these were given to all those who the family wanted to honor for having been in some way helpful to the student, and to other people as well. This is the Cheyenne way—the person being honored honoring others and giving the gifts instead of receiving them.

Each community has its own activities which honor the sharing, cooperative way of life. Could these be incorporated in some way into the school program?

Summary

The Native American way of life is based upon sharing and cooperation, not upon acquiring and competing. Teachers who practice cooperative learning have found that in addition to raising achievement, it builds better attitudes toward school, it raises the self-esteem of the students, and it increases their concern for others.

Some of the ways in which cooperative methods can be applied in the classroom are encouraging students to help each other, group problem solving, observing and applying local family instructional techniques, peer tutoring, using group effort in improving creative writing, lessening competition for grades, having students compete only with their own past records, and developing school wide activities which emphasize generosity, sharing, or cooperation.

References for Further Reading

ASCD. *Cooperative Learning*. Series of 5 videotapes. Association for Supervision and Curriculum Development. 1992.

Brewer, A. "On Indian Education." *Integrated Education*. Vol. 15. 1977. pp. 21–23.

Dumont, R. V., and M. L. Wax. "Cherokee School Society and the Intercultural Classroom." *Human Organization*. Vol 28. 1969. pp. 217–226.

Forester, L. M., and D. Little Soldier. "Open Education and Native American Values." *Educational Leadership*. Vol. 32-1. 1974. p. 14.

Gilliland, Hap. *Wolf River*. Council for Indian Education. Ms.

McWhorter, Kathleen, and Jean Leve. "The Influence of a Tutorial Program on the Tutors." *Journal of Reading*. Vol. 14. Jan. 1971. pp. 221–24.

Slavin, R. E. *Student Team Learning: An Overview and Practical Guide*. (2nd edition.) National Education Association. 1988.

Swisher, Karen. "Cooperative Learning and the Education of American Indian/Alaska Native Students: A Review of the Literature and Suggestions for Implementation." *Journal of American Indian Education*. Vol. 29. Jan. 1980. pp. 36–43.

Chapter 6
Growth Through Native American Learning Styles

"Teachers who have viewed cultural differences as strengths have been able to create the type of atmosphere which motivates learning."
—Karen Swisher (1989)

The way in which people most easily learn and remember new or difficult information is their learning style. Research has shown that students taught through their preferred learning style achieved more academically, were most interested in the subject studied, liked the way the subject was taught, and wanted to learn other school subjects in the same way. It is our responsibility to learn as much as possible about the learning styles of each student in our classrooms and to adapt our instruction to those learning styles.

Cultures Affect Learning Styles

Let us re-emphasize here that nothing we can say applies equally to all tribal groups or to the individuals within any one group. It is generally agreed that preferred learning styles are the result of both inherited abilities and methods of instruction through which the child learned during his early years. Since the inherent abilities of the children within any Native group are as varied as they would be in a school of non-Native students, there will be a great variation in their learning styles. Also, there is not only a great deal of difference between the traditional cultures of the different tribal groups, but also in the extent to which the different groups still follow the traditional style of child rearing. For example, the learning styles of eastern Chippewa students are more like those of urban Caucasians than are the learning styles of the Northern Cheyenne or the Navajo. This would be expected since the Chippewa grandparents, the traditional exponents of the culture, were more exposed in their youth to a European-American educational system.

It can be expected, then, that there will be in every cultural group a great variety of learning styles. However, since there are similarities in Indian culture, there are also some learning styles that are more prevalent among Native Americans than among the general population.

It is not our purpose to review all of the research. It would require several chapters just to list and summarize the studies. The books and articles listed at the end of this chapter include some of the best reviews of the research. They summarize over 100 other studies which you can study if you so desire. Our concern is to suggest some methods through which teachers can try to help those students whose learning styles do not match the teaching style of the typical teacher.

Tests can give us clues to the learning styles of children, but mostly, we have to rely on observation of the children at work and on discussion with them. Many children, when asked questions about specific ways of learning, can tell us which is easiest for them. The important thing is to discover the learning styles of the students in our classes and teach them *through their strengths.*

Whereas a large proportion of European-Americans learn easily through lecture, sequence, and the building of a concept from details, a greater percentage of Native Americans learn most easily when watching, imaging, and reflecting are emphasized. Many Native Americans learn more comfortably when we begin with a holistic view of a subject and are more concerned with feelings than with cold evidence.

Ten Ways of Adapting to Native Learning Preferences

Although Native American preferences are not consistent enough to claim a "Native American learning style," they do vary from non-Native trends often enough to warrant careful consideration and adaptation to individual needs. Below are ten suggestions for recognizing the learning styles and tapping the strengths of our students:

1. Recognize, Encourage, and Use Alternate Ways of Learning

Although there are great individual differences, common patterns of thinking styles, learning styles, and interests characterize students who share a common cultural background. The effective teacher is one who can appreciate the ways of learning of the students and show humanistic concern for their problems while maintaining high expectations for their achievement. Unfortunately, some instructors have ignored learning style, thinking that recognizing differences in an individual or a culture is downgrading it. It should, instead, be considered an opportunity to build on the strengths of the students.

Ron and Suzy Scallon (1981) described four characteristic ways of thinking of many Athapascan people: a high respect for individual self-reliance, non-intervention in other people's affairs, the integration of useful knowledge into a holistic and internally consistent world view, and disdain for complex organizational structures.

When children reared with this type of mental set arrive at a school that values only the knowledge which comes from books and must be learned by reading and hearing rather than watching and doing, and when they are expected to show their knowledge through writing, speaking, and taking tests instead of action and demonstration, they have stepped into a strange and foreign world.

We should not expect them to check their cultural ways at the door and adapt immediately to a strange world where their ways of thinking and reacting do not fit. Rather, we need, through our actions, our discussions, and our ways of teaching, to show our respect for indigenous knowledge. By indigenous knowledge, we mean sources of knowledge and skills that are not derived from books, knowledge that is integrated into everyday life, knowledge gained from living, acquired through direct experience and participation in real-life experiences.

Can you help your students appreciate and build upon this background? Can you take the skills that are important in their daily lives outside of school and use them in the classroom? Can you help students to teach these skills to other students and to you through demonstration—through participation in meaningful activities that are beneficial to the school and the students?

We must help students of all ages, from first grade through high school, and even college, to explore the connection between what they learn in school and what they need to know to experience satisfying and productive lives.

The teachers who can challenge Native American students to achieve academically at their full potential are those who integrate into their teaching the historical and contemporary perspectives of the students. As Barnhardt (1991) says,

> "The most effective faculty members . . . have been those who have been able to engage themselves and their students in a process of sense-making and skill-building through active participation in the world around them. They use books and pencil and paper as a means to add breadth and depth to the students' understanding, but not as the sole source of knowledge. They measure their students' achievement through the students' ability to effectively perform meaningful and contextually appropriate tasks."

Crow Indian children at a pow-wow.

2. Learn About the Children's Early Training

> "An area of potential conflict in teaching Native children is the clash
> between the learning styles they have been exposed to at home and
> those used in the classroom."
>
> —Rachel Schaffer (1986)

Since lifetime learning patterns are learned early, it will pay us to learn as much as possible about the instructional methods used in the homes of the community in which we teach.

In the majority of Indian families, the children are highly valued from the time of conception on. Especially in non-urban settings, the parents, and more especially the grandparents, spend much time indoctrinating the children with the values of the culture. The first six years are very important and the children are with the parents most of the time. During that time the beliefs, ideals, norms, and values of the family have shaped the children's mental structure, their ways of learning and thinking, and their behavior.

The children have done most of their learning through direct experience and participation in real world activities. As the children grow, experiences in the community reinforce these learning patterns. We, as teachers, must recognize that these habitual ways of learning are not the same as those of the dominant society.

Education in most Native American homes is much more casual, informal, and unstructured than in homes of the dominant society; therefore the majority of Native American children work more effectively in an informal atmosphere. Rigid formal arrangements of the classroom may be inappropriate. This does not mean that your lessons should not be structured or well-planned, but after assignments are understood, letting the students sit on the floor to read or write, if they prefer, may promote better thinking. Try grouping around a table or putting desks in groups and allowing freedom of movement when students are studying.

Kleinfeld (1972) found that the teachers who were most successful with Native students were those who were personally warm and supportive, as opposed to those who concentrate solely on academic tasks or have a detached demeanor. It is possible to expect concentrated effort and high quality work and still be warm, accepting, informal, and democratic.

Talk to the mothers of your community. Learn about their children's early training. See what can apply to your classroom.

3. Use Family Instructional Techniques: Demonstration and Imitation

> "There are only three ways to teach a child. The first is by example.
> The second is by example. The third is by example."
>
> —Albert Schweitzer

In many Native American homes, the mother guides the learning by modeling household duties expected of the children. Children learn through observing over a long period of time, then begin to practice the skill as they feel secure in doing so. The system of instruction could be described as "watch me; then you try it when you feel comfortable with it." Verbal interchange and explanation are not a major part of this process. The process takes longer than the method of most classrooms, which is to listen and then learn though trial and error, but the children retain feelings of confidence and security throughout.

Studies of home learning styles of Navajo, Yaqui, Mayan, Athapascan, and Ogalala Sioux have all verified this home learning style. They all observe, then review, the performance mentally until they are sure they can perform the task well before they attempt it in public. As Brewer (1977, p. 32) says, *"Learning through public mistakes was not and is not a method of learning which Indians value."*

Indian children taught in this way are usually reluctant to exhibit before others clumsiness or inability to do a task. Only when they have observed until they feel competent do they feel that it is appropriate to take over and do the task.

It can be expected, then, that children accustomed to learning through imitation may appear hesitant when expected to do a task after only being told how to do it. And it is not surprising that teachers unfamiliar with instructional techniques of the Native American family mistakenly interpret the children's reaction as shyness or sullenness. One of the reasons some teachers think their Indian students never have an answer is that they do not give them the necessary time to think through their response first to be sure of the correctness of their answer before they speak.

Is there any reason why these family instructional techniques cannot be used in the classroom? Many tasks can be taught through demonstration, letting the children learn through their superior skills in observation. This can be followed by practice in small groups, letting those students who have learned the skill and feel more secure perform the task first and then help the others.

4. Let Children Learn from Children

Nearly all Native American children are a part of an extended family. Therefore, children are accustomed to spending much time with a small group of children who play and work together, and who learn with and from each other. They are thoroughly accustomed to a type of "peer tutoring."

In some more traditional groups, small children spend the major portion of their time under the charge of older children, and by the time they are four or five, they are full-fledged members of the group. The group provides a great deal of the child care and is charged with much of the daily work of the household. Parents relate to the group of siblings and their companions as a group, rather than dealing with each child individually. When an adult is pleased or displeased by what a child has done, the whole group may be rewarded or blamed. Children develop confidence in their own competence and their ability to act independently. This independence is an essential ingredient of their self-concept.

New information and skills are usually learned from siblings and companions. The children learn through both observation and participation. They develop competence gradually, as a part of a group, and their effort is accepted as a part of the group's achievement. By the time they start school, they are thoroughly familiar with a type of peer tutoring.

In many Native American communities that once relied on this kind of home training, the situation is changing rapidly, partly because of modern work schedules, but mostly because of television viewing occupying a major portion of the children's time. In some homes, however, the old peer group teaching is still in effect.

Since the Native Hawaiian system of child care is very similar to this American Indian system, the Kamehameha school puts this kind of learning into the classroom. The classroom is divided into several groups and the teacher works with each group for 15 to 20 minutes teaching a skill. She concentrates her efforts on this group, with little interruption from the other students, all of whom are sitting in groups, working. Children do not stay with the group with which they received instruction, but with a group which includes some children who are more skilled and some who are less skilled in the group activity. The children are practicing a skill in which they have received some instruction, but which they have not yet mastered. As they need help, they can usually get it from the other children in the learning center. The children understand that their behavior must not disrupt other groups and that they are to give each other help or feedback as it is needed. No child is forced to work alone. This primary school program has proved very successful, not only in their school, but in a number of other schools with ethnically Native Hawaiian children. They have raised the average reading scores of the children from below the 30th percentile to above the 50th, and achievement in other subjects comparably. Similar methods have been found applicable to other Polynesian and to some American Indian children.

The system works better with children who live in community situations and are with other children much of the time than with Navajo students, many of whom live apart and learn to work and play alone.

Philips (1972) says that on the Warm Springs reservation, when teachers used small groups, student directed, the Indian students worked effectively and were more cooperative than non-Indian students. What is important is that you look around, see how children are learning skills and responsibilities in your own community, then determine how you could apply some of the home instructional techniques of your own community to make your own classroom more effective for your students.

5. Utilize Visual Learning Skills

"Sometimes you have to be quiet to be heard."

—Swiss Proverb

The majority of middle-class Caucasian children begin school as auditory learners. They have been bombarded with verbal information since early childhood. Their parents talk to them a great deal. They are encouraged to talk, to learn new words, to express their ideas. Their parents have taught them many things through verbal explanations.

As shown in the examples given earlier, many Native American students have learned to do things by observing, by imitating. The majority have become visual learners.

Most Native Americans are expert observers. They learn easily from demonstration and note every detail. They also are good at reading non-verbal messages from actions, gestures, and facial expressions. They learn much about a subject or a person through observation. They usually do better than their non-Native peers on observation and visual learning tasks, visual discrimination, and spacial configuration. Why not teach through the skills in which they excel? If they do better after seeing a thing done than hearing a description, couldn't we use modeling to encourage learning? Instead of describing what we want done, we could do the task and have the children watch. Show them the right way. Ask the children to imitate what we have done. All children pay more attention to what we do than what we say.

In turn, when the children are reluctant to answer questions, they may respond better if we let them respond with action or demonstration rather than with verbal description.

Reading instruction can emphasize modeling, through oral impress instruction and tape recorded story books. We can use concrete objects, pictures, graphs, role playing, socio-drama, and creative dramatics. Have the children handle objects while talking about them. Teach vocabulary using word games.

With the new advances in educational TV, video, and films, we have the benefit of one more way of allowing learning through demonstration and observation. After the observation, most students enjoy discussing how they interpreted the content. If repeated observation can be followed by doing, and the students' understanding can be checked by their demonstrating that they can use the knowledge or skill in a meaningful situation, then we have turned the new technology into a culturally appropriate instructional tool.

Students who have good visual learning skills and good visual memory usually are good at recalling and creating clear mental visual images. This can be a real boost in developing reading comprehension and in understanding concepts in science and math. Students can be led to use this strength to visualize the action in a story or in a science experiment. They can then use visual imagery to recall the information at a later time.

All of this does not mean that the teacher can make assumptions as to the learning style of the individual. Although the majority of Native Americans are good visual learners, there will be a great variety in every classroom, and some students will be auditory learners. However, it does mean that the over-emphasis on verbal learning in most classrooms is not appropriate for most classes of Native Americans. The more verbal teacher must be careful to fully utilize the observational and imaging skills of the students.

6. Lower the Stress of Over-Verbalization

> "Nothing is often a good thing to do, and always a clever thing to say."

The very verbal teacher who presents most of the material through lectures may not meet the needs of many Native American students. Not only do many of them learn more easily through visual or multisensory modes, but since many of them may not be really fluent in the style of English used in textbooks and in teacher presentations, much of the meaning may be lost. If comprehension becomes too difficult, the student may just give up and quit listening.

Most Indian children are taught very early in life not to interrupt when adults are talking and not to interfere when adults are busy. Even toddlers do not become noisy and attempt to keep the attention of their parents.

Most Indian people value the ability to sit still quietly. They are comfortable with silence. Talking for the sake of talking is discouraged. When they talk the tone should be soft, never harsh or loud. And they should not appear to know more than the others in the group. The soft voices sometimes upset teachers who equate soft speech with secrecy. And the loud voice of the teacher upsets the students who interpret it as anger, aggressiveness, or bossiness.

Most Indians value the ability to express an idea in a few words. In a conversation between Indian adults, the length of each person's speech averages half the length of the turn taken by the average Caucasian. I have been amazed at how effectively many of my Indian college students can summarize a half-hour speech or discussion in a very few minutes. It is a skill that most of us over-verbal teachers would do well to practice and emulate.

At an informal party among strangers, a majority of non-Indians try to make talk with whoever will listen. They feel compelled to act, to make contact, to cover their uneasiness with talk, with action. Traditional Indians, on the other hand, will stand or sit quietly, saying nothing, watching, learning, trying to discover what is expected of them, and speaking only when they are sure of themselves. White people find their place by active experimentation, Indians by quiet alertness. One Indian said about a white acquaintance, "He'd rather be wrong than silent." Little Wolf described the need clearly: "Less mouth thunder; more hand lightning."

When I conducted a survey in which I had local Indian people interview 100 Indian parents on each of six reservations, one of the questions asked was, "What are the things your children dislike about their teachers?" The answer given more than four times as often as any other was, "He or she talks too much"!

7. Advance Holistic Intuitive Learning

Perhaps one reason many Indians can condense a great deal of information into a few sentences is their habit of looking first at the larger idea, then seeing the details that relate to it, rather than the longer process of building the generalities from the details as is done in most textbooks and curriculum guides.

The majority of urban Caucasian students learn easily when learning is done step by step, beginning with the parts and building toward the whole. They process information in a logical, sequential, linear fashion.

Many studies have indicated, however, that the majority of Native Americans are global learners who learn much more easily if they can see the overall picture before they concern themselves with the details. They are good at seeing the unity and harmony in the larger situation. Breaking up learning into a series of minute hurdles can be very discouraging to Indian students if you don't let them first see where the whole thing is leading.

Even though they may not like writing, most Indian students much prefer essay-type exams, which relate to an overall concept and its application, rather than multiple choice tests, which necessarily focus on details.

In social studies, forget about building concepts step by step from small details. Look first at whole emerging patterns; then let the children learn through stories, parables, pictures, imitation, music, and poetry. Begin with the larger concept, and from that develop the parts, rather than the other way round. For example, in studying the community, it is better to start with the characteristics of the community as a whole; then later, if helpful, discuss separately the social, political, and economic aspects. All children need to learn all the different reading skills, but when the emphasis is on phonetic instruction, linguistic materials, rhyming words, word families, and building words from word parts, and when you use formal organized instruction with few choices, much direction, frequent checking of work with specific time limits, and motivation by adults, remember that these are not the learning modes of most Indian students. Instead, in reading, whole word approaches, paragraph meaning, choral reading, and oral impress should precede breaking words into phonetic parts and comprehension into specific skills.

When I teach study skills to college students, I teach all of them, but particularly the Indian students, to *always* turn to the end of the chapter and read the summary, or the last two paragraphs if there is no summary, *before* they start to read the chapter.

8. Emphasize Application of the Information in Student's Daily Lives

If you want to motivate your students, you have to help them see how each thing they are taught can be immediately related to their own lives. If you can show them the applicability to their people, then complex concepts and theories can be associated with concrete memories, making them more comprehensible and more easily remembered.

Don't require rote memorization until the information to be remembered has been integrated into the overall picture and its application made clear. You can also expect students to find reading new information more meaningful if it is accompanied by discussion of how the information relates to them.

Encourage small group discussions where students can share their feelings and their personal interpretations. Let them talk about how the information relates to previously learned ideas. Specific facts seem irrelevant until they can relate them to a larger situation and their own experiences.

Walker, et al. (1989), suggest the following sequence:

"(1) Introduce topic with a short informational presentation, (2) Have students read a short passage with the important information, (3) Have small groups develop personal interpretations, (4) Review information and personal interpretations, (5) Expand on topic, and (6) Assess, using essay exams that ask for information and interpretation. Group discussion as an exam is also extremely effective."

9. Employ Active Learning Strategies

"Statistics show that we remember 10 percent of what we read, 20 percent of what we see, 50 percent of what we see and hear, and 90 percent of what we do."

—John Barth

Most Native American children learn much more readily when instruction is multisensory, relevant, and active, so they have several opportunities and alternate means to absorb the information, and they have the memory of concrete experience to which they can tie the principle.

For persons with tactile and kinesthetic learning abilities, we can use tracing of words written in crayon, writing in sand, demonstrating comprehension through action, and group activities. Give them freedom of choice, freedom in organization, and few time limits.

My Indian high school students enjoyed drama and role playing. Some of them almost never spoke in class previously, and when they did it was in such low tones they could hardly be heard. But when we began role playing, they were not their quiet selves; they were taking the part of someone else. They spoke out audibly and expressed themselves clearly. Chapter 20 of this manual includes excellent suggestions for relating drama to music instruction.

Throughout your teaching, use a wide variety of three dimensional objects and change these frequently. Provide freedom to move while learning, and use input from the children in planning so that they have a sense of control. More emphasis should be on teaching students how to think than on what to think, and they can learn it best through materials which they can feel, touch, and manipulate. Remember the Chinese proverb: "I hear and I forget. I see and I remember. I do and I understand."

10. Teach Through Stories and Legends

"Stories are one kind of truth and reality. They are maps of knowledge in memory."

—Sandra Rietz (1986)

The oral literature of the Native American people is much more than something to entertain the children and occupy the grandparents. It is an organized way of passing on the knowledge and behaviors necessary to the society.

Stories also slant the way a person sees the world, and in that way, change the world in which the child lives. The view of the world embodied in the stories of the culture becomes for the child the "natural" view. This is what is real. We experience the world not with impartial senses, but through our habitual ways of thinking, our memory, imagination, emotions, and will. The truths and the structure of the universe, as each person knows it, are partly the result of his or her own oral tradition. It has been said that "myths supply security in an uncertain world."

Traditionally, the teaching of proper behavior and moral values was indirect and informal. Much of this was through the telling of stories and legends. Most of the stories emphasized, but not obviously, one particular value, such as generosity, courage, or cooperation.

Just as children in the traditional Native home learned the values early through stories and legends, modern Indian children can begin from their first day of school learning proper behavior and values at the same time they are being interested and entertained through stories. There are many good Indian stories and legends in the books available that teach particular values. *Tonweya and the Eagles,* for example, teaches the importance of helping each other rather than competing; *Coyote's Pow-wow,* the need for sharing; *Red Horse and the Buffalo Robe Man,* being kind to animals; and *Northern Cheyenne Fire Fighters* builds the self-concept of the Indian while teaching the importance of bravery and being dependable in the modern world. The evil of outdoing friends or carrying competition too far is taught by the Crow legend *Blue Thunder,* in which two boys forget their friendship in competing with each other and end by destroying not only themselves but their families as well.

In most of the Indian legends, the moral behind them is not obvious to the learner. It was assumed that after hearing the story told many times, the children would have much time to think alone and glean the hidden meanings, that the values would become part of their subconscious minds and influence their way of thought. The hurried life of the modern student allows less time for individual contemplative thought, so discussion of what *the students* think is the value emphasized may be important. Some of the old fables from other cultures are also good to use with Indian children.

The oral literature of the community and story telling within your class can be the basis for your beginning instruction in reading and writing, as well as inspiration for much creative writing of older children. Written versions of stories the children have heard—in their homes and in class—can build the bridge between oral and written communication and make beginning students feel "at home" with the idea of reading, even if they have had no exposure to a reading environment before starting school. Stories from the local culture can also provide the basis for the development of other skills—speaking, writing, creative dramatics, listening, even mathematics.

In addition to the myths and folk stories of our community, another important source of stories we should tap is the real lives of Indian heroes, past and present. These should include the lives of tribal leaders and local elders. Telling the stories of the lives of real people and discussing what made them great can help shape the character of our students.

Traditional stories when told in the native language convey much more meaning and feeling than any translation can convey. The telling of stories can then be a very important part of the responsibility of the bilingual teacher or teacher aide. It can also be an important reason for bringing parents and grandparents into the classroom. Even if most of the students do not speak the Indian language, they will get a surprising amount from listening to stories told by elders in their own language. One school which I visited had children from several different cultures. Parents from each of these cultures came to the school and told stories and taught songs in their own language. While building in the children pride in their own heritage, it unified the class with a pride in their group as a whole and in their ability to cooperate and help everyone in the group.

Stories help people know their place in society. They give them a sense of perspective, a feeling of what is right and good. They help them understand relationships between people, and therefore, between themselves and others. Because these are so important, many of the traditional Native American stories are sacred to the tribe that tells them. Therefore however useful storytelling can be in our curriculum, we must preserve the traditions connected with it. If there are stories which are to be told only at certain times or places, these constraints must not be ignored.

Summary

All students have their own learning styles through which they can learn most easily. Although all learning styles are found in all groups of people, the majority of children learn most easily through the learning styles traditionally practiced by their own cultural group. Below are listed learning styles more common among Native American students, contrasted with those of non-Natives.

Suburban-Caucasian Learning Styles	Native American Learning Styles
Well-defined, organized.	Informal atmosphere.
Auditory learner. Prefers verbal instructions, explanations.	Visual learner, prefers demonstrations, illustrations.
Listens to explanations, then learns by trial and error. Wants teacher as consultant.	Observes carefully, then tries when secure in doing so. Wants teacher as model.
Prefers direct instruction. Likes to try new things.	Prefers to be shown. Likes learning through stories, pictures, activities.
Starts with parts, specific facts, and builds toward the whole.	Starts with general principles, holistic, overall view.
Insists on reason, logic, facts, causes.	Accepts intuition, coincidence, feelings, emotion, hunches.
Competes for recognition.	Cooperates and assists.
Task oriented.	Socially-oriented.
Impersonal, formal, structured.	Personal, informal, spontaneous.
Likes discovery approach.	Likes guided approach.
Relies on language for thinking and remembering.	Relies on images for thinking and remembering.
Likes talking and writing.	Likes drawing and manipulation.

References for Further Reading

Browne, Dauna Bell. "Scoring Patterns among Native Americans of the Northern Plains." *White Cloud Journal.* Vol. 3, 2. 1984. pp. 3–16.

Diessner, Rhett, and Jacqueline L. Walker. "A Cognitive Pattern of the Yakima Indian Students." *Journal of American Indian Education.* Vol. 25. Jan. 1986. pp. 39–43.

Macias, Cathaleene J. "American Indian Academic Success: The Role of Indigenous Learning Strategies." *Journal of American Indian Education.* Vol. 28. Aug. 1989. pp. 43–51.

Moore, Arthur J. "Native Indian Learning Styles: A Review for Researchers and Teachers." *Journal of American Indian Education.* Vol. 28. Aug. 1989. pp. 15–27.

Nelson, Annabelle, and Bisi Lalemi. "The Role of Imagery Training on Tohono O'odham Children's Creativity Scores." *Journal of American Indian Education.* Vol. 30. May 1991, pp. 24–31.

New, Douglas A. "Teaching in the Fourth World." *Phi Delta Kappan.* Jan. 1992, pp. 396–398.

Philips, S. U. "Participant Structures and Communicative Competence: Warm Springs Children in Community and Classroom." In S. B.

Cazden, *V.* John, and D. Hymes (Eds.) *Functions of Language in the Classroom.* New York, Teachers College Press, 1972. pp. 370–394.

Philips, S. U. *The Invisible Culture: Communication in Classroom and Community on the Warm Springs Reservation.* Longmars. 1983. 157 pp.

Rhodes, Robert W. "Measurements of Navajo and Hopi Brain Dominance and Learning Styles." *Journal of American Indian Education.* Vol. 29. May 1990. pp. 29–40.

Rietz, Sandra A. "Preserving Indian Culture Through Oral Literature." In Jon Reyhner, (Ed.) *Teaching the Indian Child: Bilingual/Multicultural Approach.* Eastern Montana College. 1986. pp. 255–280.

Ross, Allen Chuck. "Brain Hemispheric Functions and the Native American." *Journal of American Indian Education.* Vol. 28. Aug. 1989. pp. 72–75.

Swisher, Karen, and Donna Deyhle. "The Styles of Learning Are Different but the Teaching Is Just the Same: Suggestions for Teachers of American Indian Youth." *Journal of American Indian Education.* Vol. 28. Aug. 1989. pp. 1–13.

Tafoya, Terry. "Coyote's Eyes: Native Cognition Styles." *Journal of American Indian Education.* Vol. 28. Aug. 1989. pp. 29–41.

Tharp, Roland G. "The Effective Instruction of Comprehension: Results and Description of the Kamehameha Early Education Program." *Reading Research Quarterly.* 17–4. 1982. pp. 503–527.

Walker, Barbara J., John Dodd, and Rose Bigelow. "Learning Preferences of Capable American Indians of Two Tribes." *Journal of American Indian Education.* Vol. 28. Aug. 1989. pp. 63–69.

Wauters, Joan K., Janet Merrill Bruce, David R. Black, and Phillip N. Hocker. "Learning Styles: A Study of Alaska Native and Non-Native Students." *Journal of American Indian Education.* Vol. 28. Aug. 1989. pp. 53–61.

Wax, Rosalie H., and Robert K. Thomas. "American Indians and White People." *Phylon.* 22–4. Winter 1961. pp. 305–317.

Chapter 7
Discipline Through Motivation, Decision Making, and Self-Control

Classroom management, the control of the students, is the greatest concern of the majority of teachers throughout the United States and Canada. Every year from 1969 to 1985, lack of discipline was number one on the list of problems of public schools, according to the annual Gallup Poll of Public Attitudes Toward Education (Carter, 1987).

Although schools everywhere are having discipline problems, those with a majority of Native American students are less likely to have problems of serious violence, but fighting, picking on each other, ridicule, and poor attitude are common.

Suggestions for Culturally Acceptable Classroom Management
Some teachers fear teaching Native American children because they consider them undisciplined. Others prefer them because they find them so cooperative. Which behavior the students exhibit depends largely upon the teacher's ability to use culturally acceptable means of control and motivation. Eight means are recommended for maintaining a smooth running classroom.

1. Build Interest, a Love of Learning, and a Desire to Achieve
"Nothing great was ever achieved without enthusiasm."
—Ralph Waldo Emerson

A study of 500 well-disciplined U.S. and Canadian schools found that these schools focused on positive attitudes and prevention, not punishment; problems, not symptoms; faith in their students and their teachers; and they emphasized that their schools were places to do valuable, successful, productive work (Wayson, 1985.)

In the traditional Indian home, expectations were often quite definite, perhaps exact, but love combined with gentle discipline was the system of control rather than force. In fact, the Cheyenne, among others, said that the child must always be convinced, not forced. Developing interest, motivating children to want to learn, is always much more effective than telling them that they have to do a job. There is a saying: "Education makes people easy to lead but difficult to drive, easy to govern but impossible to enslave.'' Some teachers lead; others attempt to enslave.

Classroom control is about ninety-five percent motivation and interest and only five percent ''discipline.'' Motivation depends upon our learning the students' needs and interests. If we meet their needs, students will work willingly. If we provide for their interests, they will be enthusiastic. When there are discipline problems, it is well to look at our means of motivation. Have we given the children a reason to want to achieve? (Will they agree with what *we* give as reasons?)

The Sioux way is to not be concerned with eliminating bad behavior, but developing positive good behavior. This comes through shared responsibility. You and your students must work as a team to develop a pleasant atmosphere through mutual understanding. The cause of a great many discipline problems is depersonalization. Let the children know that ''You belong here. We want you. You are important as an individual.'' Show them through your actions that you mean this. They will not believe what you say unless they see it in your actions.

Both positive approval of good behavior and punishment of bad behavior give children attention. Both reward the behavior. If the only time children get any individual attention is when they misbehave, then it is this attention which gives them the sense of importance that they need. Naturally, they continue the behavior. The effective means of discipline then, is to recognize and compliment only good behavior. Except in extreme cases, ignore the bad. This also follows the system of control most often used in the homes of Indian children.

The secret is to support and reinforce the kind of behavior of which we approve. There are many ways of doing this: a touch, a smile, a wink, a pat, a helpful comment, giving the children more opportunity to go ahead their own way, laughing with them, or helping them to make their own choices. These are the kinds of rewards that are meaningful in the long run.

Show all the students that you believe in them. Challenge them. Let them know that you consider their misbehavior, like their other mistakes, as opportunity for them to learn and to grow. Show them by your actions that you see them as good, worthwhile persons. If you expect them to misbehave, why shouldn't they? It won't make you think any worse of them than you already do. But if you *know* they will do their best, they will.

The problem-free classroom is the one with a teacher who enjoys teaching and lets the children feel this enjoyment. Are you compassionate? Do you have an equal liking for children of all cultures? Is this evident from your *actions,* not just from what you say? Let them see that you still like them—even after they have ''screwed up.'' Don't be afraid to like your students and don't be afraid to let them feel it. Be sure they *all* feel it, not just the good students. As one teacher said, ''To love the world is no big chore. It's that miserable student in the corner who is the problem.'' The feeling that nobody loves them is the most common reason teenagers give for attempted suicide, drug abuse, and serious discipline problems in school.

Indian adults treat their children with the same respect that they expect the children to give them. That is what all teachers who want the cooperation of their students must learn to do.

If we can develop in our students a real curiosity about the things we teach so that the majority of the students are really interested and motivated, they will take care of discipline. They will work with us and will censure anyone who interferes with what they want to do most, which is learn.

2. Follow Cultural Patterns of Control

Most Native American parents, and more particularly the grandparents, discipline their children without the harsh words or physical punishment meted out by most European Americans.

Discipline is unstructured. Children are unfamiliar with the type of discipline in which they simply do as they are told without question. In the home, children are allowed to work together with very little supervision, giving them a feeling of autonomy, trustworthiness, and competence. They are given reasons, a knowledge of needs, then freedom of personal choice. They are responsible for their actions and the consequences. When survival depended on the right choices, this was all that was needed. It is no longer as easy for them to see the importance of doing what adults recommend. As Jeanne Bearcrane (1990) points out:

> It is common to see American Indian children, even the very young, running freely at traditional settings such as pow wows, hand games, feasts, certain ceremonies, and athletic events. . . . To those unaware of American Indian parental permissiveness, the children may appear unruly and their custodians apathetic. However, such permissiveness and the children's free-spirited behavior are not outside the norms for traditional American Indian settings.

Physical punishment usually had no place in the traditional society. The use of force to obtain discipline was almost unknown, and is rare in most Indian groups today. Most parents believe that both demeaning criticism and harsh or physical punishment, especially in public, are rude, disrespectful, and harmful to the child's self-concept. Frowning, ignoring, or shaming are more common means of showing disapproval. However, shaming in front of others can be devastating to the Indian child.

3. Use Peer Group Control

The power of peer pressure cannot be ignored or overestimated. Students often do things which are against their better judgment because they want the approval of their peer group, or because they want to avoid the criticism or ridicule of their peers. This peer pressure is blamed for a great deal of the present delinquency in our cities. It is an even greater force in the lives of American Indian students, who live in a group-oriented society based on cooperation and dependence on each other.

Peer groups are therefore an effective means of social control. Group approval is much more important than teacher approval. If an individual has to make a choice between cooperating with the group or the teacher, the group will win. To the autocratic teacher this means sure trouble. But for the teacher who can motivate the group, get them interested, and work with them, the peer group can greatly decrease the number of disciplinary problems.

Order, or disorder, can be created by the students as a group, depending upon their relationship to the teacher and their understanding of the value of the classroom activities. Let the students have a part in decisions, and in solving classroom problems. Talk with them, and *listen to their ideas*. If you don't listen to their ideas, you are saying that their ideas are not important and that therefore the students are unimportant. When you listen and expect them to have good ideas for solving the problems, you are giving them respect and building their self-concept.

Class decisions are better and receive better cooperation if consensus is reached, rather than being decided by a straight vote. Nearly all Indian tribes originally made decisions by consensus and some tribal councils still operate under that system. Instead of taking a vote and deciding a matter according to which side has a 51 percent vote, each person has an opportunity to voice his opinion. After each opinion is expressed, everyone tries to see how the plan can be changed somewhat to incorporate that person's ideas. In the end, everyone should feel that the plan is the nearest they can come to having complete agreement; all opinions have been considered, and everyone has yielded to reach consensus. "Tribal council" consensus-type meetings apply Native American values and are good training in democratic action because they require the involvement of all, with unselfish cooperation and mutual respect. The object of the individuals in the group is not victory, but a wise, workable plan, amicably decided upon. Roberts rules of order are more efficient in that they take much less time, but they are not nearly as democratic.

When rules and decisions on action are made by the group, rather than by totalitarian rule, the group will back the decision and control will be fostered rather than opposed by peer group pressure.

Most Native American parents never raise their voices to the shrill level. They use a voice that is soft, even in tone, non-judgmental and unemotional but firm. The children are not criticized as people. It is the act, not the child, that is disapproved of. When teachers hear Indian parents disciplining children in their Native language, they may not even be aware of what is happening unless they know the language, because the voice is low and calm, often lower than when just talking with the children. When parents hear teachers discipline in a loud, harsh tone, they think they have lost self-control. The teachers have lost the respect of both parents and children.

A few rules are necessary, but most discipline can be unstructured. Unstructured discipline is more flexible and is better understood by the Indian child. Indian children are often "thoughtless" but seldom intentionally disruptive. The reason they seem thoughtless is because school-type restrictions are so foreign to their way of life at home. It takes time and patience to develop an understanding of the importance of having a controlled atmosphere at school.

Problems that arise can best be handled through individual non-directive counseling. Once you and your students really know each other, individual discussion can eliminate most of your problems and make life happier for both you and the students.

In many tribes, discipline is the responsibility of the uncles, as this protects the close relationship between the children and their parents. The uncles usually use quiet admonition coupled with example. They also often use good natural humor and teasing as the best way of getting a point across, thus telling a child of their disapproval in a humorous way instead of with direct criticism. I have seen teachers who can use light teasing effectively for changing behavior in the Indian classroom, but this works only for those who can keep the atmosphere pleasant and do it without embarrassing the child.

In the Crow tribe, the mothers' sisters are also called mother, and their children are considered brothers and sisters, and their children are "teasing cousins." It is their responsibility when their cousins' behavior is not acceptable to tease them until they correct their ways. Teachers seeing the effectiveness of this method assume that the same method will work for them. However, in this situation the whole class may resent the teacher's teasing anyone because only a *relative* is supposed to tease the child!

In the community, most Indian people feel a great deal of responsibility for the actions of other members of their families. With proper nurture, they will develop the same feeling of responsibility for the behavior of other members of their class.

I once took 36 Indian high school students on a four-day tour of Montana. They had developed such a feeling of responsibility for each other that I never had to discuss behavior. At one location a boy and girl were walking with their arms around each other's waists. When we got back in the bus, I heard the other students telling those two, "We don't want to give anyone the impression we don't know what is proper. Don't do it again."

4. Let Students Know Your Expectations

"To err is human, to forgive divine—but to forget it altogether is humane."

—Gloria Pitzer's Secret Recipe Report

Whether on the athletic field or in the classroom, the students want to know the rules. But they have to know the reasons for them, and they have to be applied consistently. However, the fewer the rules, the better the game, and if the players can help set the rules, they will understand them and remember them better, and be more willing to follow them.

Whenever possible, the parents should have a part in developing school-wide rules. This way they will understand the reasons for them and feel that they are important. Otherwise, most Native parents consider discipline strictly the problem of the teacher. It has nothing to do with them.

Time spent establishing routines and giving students a sense of responsibility and mutual respect the first two or three days of school is worth more than many hours of correcting students and trying to enforce rules later.

Don't squelch discussion of the rules, and don't hesitate to revise them until all understand and agree with them. Don't assume that the students already know what is unacceptable behavior. You cannot have a rule that covers every specific situation. If the students internalize the principles, they should be effective even when they don't apply exactly. Indian children learn best by example. Find, discuss, and role-play some examples of situations to which the rules apply. If students agree that these rules are essential for cooperative living, they soon become effective and automatically obeyed. Whenever it is discovered that a rule is no longer needed, that it is ineffective, or that it causes more problems than it prevents, then eliminate it happily.

Rules must not only be understandable; they must be enforceable. Rules like "Be good," "Behave," and "Be polite" are neither. They are, therefore, useless. Be sure each rule is reasonable, and that the child is *able* to follow it. Once the rules are agreed upon and understood, insist upon their being carried out. You cannot love someone you let walk all over you. Nor can children love the person they walk over. A rule unenforced says: "Rules do not have to be followed."

High standards are essential, both in quality of work and behavior. When you do not have high expectations in class-work, students interpret your attitude as saying that what you are teaching them is not really important. When behavior standards are low, you are saying to the students, cooperation is not important, and I really don't care about my students.

A teacher should always expect respect from the students and not accept disrespectful behavior, but it has to go both ways. Indian students are very aware of the kind of respect you are giving them and cannot be expected to give respect if they are not also treated with respect.

Don't condone unacceptable behavior, but let your students know that rules are not to produce punishment, but to set clearly defined limits by which the group can live together more comfortably and effectively. The object is to have the rule followed, not to punish the one who doesn't follow it. Ignore irrelevant behavior. Pay no attention to the tantrum if the rule is followed. The goal has been achieved for this time, regardless of the attitude in achieving it.

If it is necessary to penalize a person for not following a rule, the penalty should be immediate. A penalty to take place later has little meaning to a student oriented to the present, and it makes for a long-range disgruntled attitude. In the old days, on the rare occasion when a person had to be punished for not following the rules, as soon as the punishment was over, so were all resentments. The person was treated as if nothing had happened. This is the way it should be in the classroom. If Indian children understand the reasons for restrictions, they will seldom hold any resentments. They will also assume that the incident is gone and forgotten on the teacher's part as well. Both of you can start the relationship fresh.

Once in a while you are bound to make a mistake in the punishment you mete out. Whether the cause is anger, or not having all the facts, or just not considering the child's viewpoint, if you see that it was a mistake or decide the punishment was unjust, don't ever hesitate to say you were wrong and apologize to the student. It will raise your standing as a person, identify you as a caring person, and make up for the act which the class has already recognized as unjust. No one should ever try to pose as a person who never makes mistakes.

Unfortunately, there are some school rules that must be followed which some students interpret as going against their way of life; there are also skills that students must learn to prepare them to be able to fit into both cultures. The children's attitude and cooperation in these cases depend largely upon the teacher's approach to them. Gloria Moore, a Navajo, described to me one such situation which occurred while she was teaching in a Navajo boarding school. One group of boys was intentionally not following any of the school's regulations for the lunchroom: putting napkins in their laps, eating with forks, etc. When Mrs. Moore reminded them of the rules, they retorted, "We heard you were Navajo. Now we know you're not. No matter what you look like, you're just another white teacher! We're proud of being Navajo."

Gloria's answer was, "I'm as proud of being Navajo as you are, but we all have to learn to live in different cultures if we're going to get along. When I'm in my mother's hogan, we sit on the ground cloth around the kettle. We all eat out of the same pot. That's the right way to do it, and I wouldn't want to do it any different. But when I'm here I eat the way they do here, so that when I visit other people I know what to do. This way isn't any better, but it's the right way when you are here, just like the other is the right way when you are home. You need to learn more than one way."

They all cooperated. If she had said, "This is the right way. The way you are doing it is wrong," she would have gotten nowhere.

A teacher who was not Indian might have said, "I am not saying this way is better, but it is something you will need to know when you go other places. I am trying to learn to do things your way, so I can do them correctly when I visit Indian homes. I will help you learn my way, and I hope you will all help me learn the Indian way."

5. Encourage Self-Discipline

> *"Democracy is the art of disciplining oneself so that one need not be disciplined by others."*

The whole system of discipline in the typical Indian home is based on self-discipline. If a person has self-esteem and if the reasons for behavior are made clear and discussed, then the individual will do the right thing. To do otherwise would decrease self-respect.

Children usually live up to the teacher's expectations. Threats indicate to them that instead of having confidence in them, you think they are not going to do the thing requested. If they can see that you expect them to cause trouble, why shouldn't they? It is not going to change your opinion of them. However, if all your actions indicate that you have confidence in their doing the right thing, they won't betray that confidence. They live up to your expectations.

Someone said that Cherokees treat their children as adults. A Cherokee answered, "No, we treat them as human beings. That is a status you only accord to adults, and usually only to adults of your own social status."

6. Help Students Develop Their Own Goals

"I have regretted all my life that I did not take a chance on the fifth grade. It would certainly come in handy right now, and I never go through a day that I am not sorry for the idea I had of how to go to school and not learn anything."

—Will Rogers

When people want something, they will work for it. The *want* precedes the achievement. Many Native American students define success in ways unrelated to school. Their only objective in school is to get through it—to endure it. If they are aware of goals in our classrooms, it is because we have set goals and told the students about them. They are not the students' goals.

During my first year of teaching, I told a seventh grader who refused to try to learn math, "In a few years you will be looking for a job, and you will have trouble getting one if you can't do any arithmetic." His reply was, "I can count my sheep. I want to be a sheep herder, and I can be a good one without any more math." His statement made me realize that here was a boy with a worthy goal and a belief in his ability to reach it, but it had nothing to do with anything I was trying to teach him. I had to find immediate uses for the math so he could see that it had value *now*.

Children develop confidence in their own abilities through their perceptions of how well they are fulfilling the personal standards that they have developed for themselves. They look at their abilities, their status, their roles, and they compare these with what they would like to become. Help them to develop goals that they can achieve and that meet their own needs. Try to find time to sit down individually with them and discuss their goals. Recognize that their understanding of success may be very different from yours, and allow for this. Give them an opportunity to discuss their problems, and set goals for eliminating them. Focus your own comments on the positive aspects of their behavior. Helping students to meet their own needs brings about a cooperative atmosphere.

7. Let Students Make Many Decisions for Themselves

"If the process of education is made gentle and easy and if the students are taught to think for themselves, we may call the man a good teacher."

—Confucius

Students need to make decisions and choices. They need to see themselves as responsible people. They cannot leave their decisions to others. They must learn to make them and live with them. Many Native American students have not learned to take this responsibility because they have not been given the opportunity. They need to be asked their opinions, to have their questions answered, and to see their ideas put to use so they can learn to see the consequences, good or bad. Only in this way can they become willing to make decisions and to base them upon reasoning and thinking.

It is only if you trust your students to make decisions for themselves that they will grow to be decision makers. Those who have had this opportunity will be in control of their adult lives. They will be the leaders of the community. As Peter Copen (1980) says, ''We believe that this is the key to successful adulthood: being self-directed, causing your experience and not merely feeling its effects, realizing that you have the power to choose and that there are clear options available to you.''

Most teachers ask questions. Some ask questions about the students' preferences. Only a few *listen*. Make sure your students know that you are listening—that their decisions are being carried out. The secret is constant recognition of their capabilities, their ability to make the right decisions, and letting them know that they have the right and the responsibility. Many Indian students don't believe they can make a difference, that they can decide for themselves and for their group. Help them to eliminate the words ''I can't'' from their vocabularies.

We must continually look for occasions when decisions can be made by the students instead of being handed down by the teacher, times when they can make a contribution, when their ideas can make a difference. I always start every social studies unit with an introduction to the subject to be studied, so the students have some background, then a pupil-teacher planning session, in which the students talk about what *they* want to learn about it. Then we *follow* their suggestions. We do this again throughout the unit, at every opportunity. Do we have discipline problems—students not wanting to cooperate? Not when the children are doing what they planned, when they are carrying out their own decisions.

8. Teach Decision-Making Skills and Character Education

> *''Rare is the teacher who can submit an idea for classroom discussion and then give up possession of it, who can lay a thought on the table for study and see it rejected and revised. . . . But if you can do this, you will be teaching your students how to become responsible citizens. . . . Your students will develop self-discipline and learn to consider the consequences of their actions.''*
>
> —Raymond Muesig

Before our Native students, or any other students, can build self-esteem by knowing they are trusted to make decisions for themselves, we have to do three things: (1) Teach them decision-making skills. (2) Give them a relaxed classroom atmosphere in which no students are afraid to express their ideas, so that there is free and open communication between us and our students. (3) Give them opportunities to make decisions, both individually and as a group, and have those decisions carried out.

Decision-making skills are taught through open discussion in which students not only make decisions for themselves, but discuss many hypothetical situations similar to ones they face daily. Then discuss openly and freely all the different possible consequences of the different decisions they might make.

It is much easier to start teaching decision-making skills if you have a planned program in ''decision making'' or ''character development'' with which to begin. Two examples of useful materials in this area are the decision-making kits, or ''tubs,'' available to all Alaskan schools from the Alaskan State Department of Education, and the *Character Education Curriculum* kits from the nonprofit American Institute for Character Education-AICE (1987).

The *Character Education Curriculum* contains some excellent material for discussions on making decisions. Among the many concepts covered are: 1. the difficulties created by trying to be one of the "in" group; 2. the influences which form a person's reputation; 3. the positive characteristics of a strong leader; 4. the effects of prejudice; 5. the benefits of generous, kind, and helpful behavior to ourselves and others; and 6. the need for trust in a working relationship.

The curriculum emphasizes the value of working cooperatively with others, an important part of the heritage of Native American students. It gives students experience in decision-making while endeavoring to shape positive attitudes toward life and school.

The purpose of this process is not to indoctrinate our students in an arbitrary set of values. It should provide an opportunity for them to examine their own choices, to help them develop their own moral conscience.

A good way to start these discussions is through a "story" that presents a difficult situation similar to one the students have faced; then let them discuss and decide what they might do and what the results would be. The discussion will be most successful in a relaxed, informal, open atmosphere in which every student is encouraged to speak, where every individual's beliefs and inner feelings are respected, and where no preference is shown for the response of one child over another. It may be necessary to teach the students to distinguish between constructive criticism and ridicule before they, too, can encourage everyone's participation. Our role is that of leader and observer. We can aid the discussion most with an occasional question: "How would this affect your family?" "Can you see why other people might feel differently?" "Are you saying this because you think that is what I want to hear?"

You should not hesitate to express your own values and feelings, but you *must* wait until the children have all had their say, then do it without being critical of their ideas. Explain why these values are important to you, being careful not to imply that all of them are right for everyone, or that the values of others are not as valid. The students should be encouraged to consider values from each of the cultures represented in their community, from their friends and family, and from their teachers. By choosing from all of these, they develop their own life style.

Discussions of values and decision making will become more meaningful if they are supplemented with role-playing of situations in which students must make decisions. To do this, set up a situation, get volunteers, give them time to plan the action, and prepare the class to listen and respond. You can follow with questions: "Was this true to life?" "Would you react the way Bill did?" "How was Wassie affected by this action?" "Are there other ways you could solve this problem?"

Pupil-teacher planning sessions in which the class as a whole makes decisions which will be carried out in the classroom provide practice in decision making and show students the importance of their own decisions. Students in a democratic classroom in which they have a voice in decision making not only have greater self-esteem, they also have more respect for the opinions of others and are more willing to cooperate. As Booker T. Washington said: "Few things help an individual more than to place responsibility upon him and to let him know that you trust him."

Summary

If students are interested in their studies, there will be few discipline problems. Effective classroom control develops when teachers know and apply the cultural patterns of control from the community, place responsibility on the students as a group, make their expectations clear, and encourage self-discipline. Students should have training in character development and decision making, then have a share in making their own decisions and setting their own goals.

If you continually watch for the good things, compliment them, and reward the good behavior, most of the problems will disappear. Build each child's self-respect, plan with the group and let them help you with control. Then a positive attitude will be easy to maintain, and you can be free to enjoy working with your Native American students.

References for Further Reading

Bearcrane, Jeanne, John M. Dodd, J. Ron Nelson, and Steven W. Ostwald. "Educational Characteristics of Native Americans." *Rural Education.* Vol. 11–3. Spring 1990. pp. 1–3.

Beare, Paul L. "Programming for Behaviorally Disoriented Native Americans." *Journal of American Indian Education.* Vol. 26–2. Jan. 1986. pp. 24–31.

Carter, Mildred. *A Model for Effective School Discipline.* The Phi Delta Kappa Educational Foundation. 1987.

Character Education Curriculum. American Institute for Character Education (AICE). 1987.

Copen, Peter. "Walkabout Lives!" *Phi Delta Kappan.* June 1980. pp. 703–705.

Garcia, Ricardo. L. "Classroom Management and Human Rights Strategies." Ch. 9, *Teaching in a Pluralistic Society.* Harper and Row. 1982. pp. 145–152.

Hyman, I. A., and J. D'Alessandro. "Good Old-Fashioned Discipline: The Politics of Punitiveness." *Phi Delta Kappan.* Sept. 1984. pp. 39–45.

Light, Harriet K., and Ruth E. Martin. "Guidance of American Indian Children: Their Heritage and Contemporary Views." *Journal of American Indian Education.* Vol. 25. Oct. 1985. pp. 42–46.

Malony, Ray. "Ten Ways to Turn Out Terrific Kids." *Vibrant Life.* Jan./Feb. 1985.

McGinnis, Alan Loy. *Bringing Out the Best in People.* Augsberg Publishing House. 1985.

Muesig, Raymond. *Aphorisms in Education.* Phi Delta Kappa Educational Foundation.

Parenting Education: Discipline Skills. National Indian Child Abuse and Neglect Resource Center. 1981. 18 pp.

Pepper, Floy C. "Effective Classroom Management Practices." *Effective Practices in Indian Education: A Teacher's Mongraph.* Northwest Regional Educational Laboratory. 1985. pp. 41–110.

Thornbush, Cheryl, and Sandra J. Fox. *Bridging the Challenging Years: Tips for Working with American Indian Teenagers.* ERIC Clearinghouse on Rural Education and Small Schools. 1988. 91 pp.

Wax, Rosalie H., and Robert K. Thomas. "American Indians and White People." *Phylon.* Vol. 22. No. 4. Winter 1961. pp. 305–317.

Wayson, W. "The Politics of Violence in School: Doublespeak and Disruptions in Public Confidence." *Phi Delta Kappan.* Oct. 1985. pp. 127–132.

Chapter 8
Working with the Parents
by Sandra Kay Streeter

The involvement of parents and grandparents in the education of the children is especially important with Native American people since there has often been a feeling among Native families that school has little relation to "real life" and parents may therefore have little interest in the school. Children learn more when their parents are involved in education (U.S. Dept. Ed., 1986; Lyons, 1983). A study of 250 California elementary schools found parent involvement related to student achievement (Herman & Yen, 1980). Umansky (1983) makes the point that when parents and teachers work together the child will identify both the school and the home as places to learn. Native American parents, historically, were systematically excluded from participation during the mission, boarding, and day school era (Little Bear, 1986).

In situations where the school and the child come from different cultures the child looks to the people at home to find out if it is "OK" to participate in this new environment. Little Bear points out that the past exclusion of the Indian parents from the education of their children has only served to make Indian parents suspicious of modern American education. This suspicion many times is demonstrated by a hesitancy to participate in the child's classroom. Consequently, the parents may send a message to the child that it is *not* "OK" to participate fully. The classroom teacher is then faced with the problem of encouraging family cooperation. Following are some techniques teachers can use to encourage parental involvement in the child's learning environment.

Preparing to Interact with the Parents
The success of the parent-teacher relationship is based upon mutual self-respect. When teachers move into a new school it is their obligation to familiarize themselves with the cultural background of their students. Little Bear (p. 227) points out "There is no such thing as a generic Indian for which a standard Indian history, culture, and language curriculum can be designed." It may be helpful for teachers to think of themselves as students of the new culture. The parents and extended family of the students can be excellent resources for this educational process. The following suggestions are guidelines to help teachers facilitate interaction with the parent population:

1. Familiarize Yourself with the New Environment

Read one or more books written and/or recommended by tribal members or a professional educator in the school system.

Visit with several older people about the local culture. In your search for information focus on traditions, values, and specific ideologies (Little Bear, 1986).

Look for tribal cultural events such as pow-wows or feast days, and ask a tribal member if you will be welcome to attend.

Become aware of tribally-specific differences. Little Bear points out that what is acceptable in one tribe may be taboo in another tribe.

Explore the land in order to create a visual and effective image of the students' environment and resources.

Limit your own vocalization and *listen*.

2. Talk to Local Head Start Personnel

In many Native American communities, Head Start has provided a beginning in parental involvement in the child's classroom. However, since this parental participation component involves pre-school education, many times the parents as well as the educators do not know how to effectively and appropriately transfer this model into the elementary school system. One help for the new teacher might be to talk to the local Head Start personnel to find out what parent activities worked well in that setting. If some of these activities could be transferred to the elementary classroom, this might be a comfortable activity to use for the first parent participation activity.

Implementing Parent Participation

Once a teacher has made the commitment to interact with parents the "how to" becomes important. What does parental involvement mean? What should the teacher be striving for? The first step in this process is to recognize that, in spite of cultural differences, the parent and teacher have a common goal. That common goal is to provide the best possible education for the child. Many new teachers get frustrated because they are unrealistic; they expect the same degree and kind of interaction with every parent. Parents are as individual as the students. If a teacher welcomes diversity in parental response, then the teacher's expectations are not as likely to exceed the participation level of most parents. McConkey (1985) suggests that a teacher can interact with the parent on five different levels.

1. Individually, on a one-to-one, face-to-face basis.
2. Individually, at a distance.
3. Group, face-to-face.
4. Group, at a distance.
5. Parent networking: Encourage parents to be involved with other parents.

1. Individually, on a One-to-One, Face-to-Face Basis

Many parents are comfortable interacting in the classroom or as sponsors for class trips. In communities where Head Start was active, parents already understand how important they are in the educational development of their children. They may have developed important interactional skills during their child's pre-school experiences that can be utilized in the elementary and secondary classroom.

One-on-one direct interaction between a parent and a teacher also takes place when the parent attends a parent-teacher conference. Parent-teacher, one-on-one interaction can take place outside of the school environment. Out of school contact with the parent may be especially important when the parent did not have a good experience in school as a child. A parent, even though now an adult, may see the teacher in the school setting as an authority figure and remember feeling powerless and helpless. A home visit by the teacher may indirectly address the feeling of powerlessness. The teacher when in the parent environment may seem less threatening.

Casual, unplanned visits with parents take place when the teacher is participating in community activities such as sporting events, shopping, church, and money-making suppers. In these casual settings the parent also has the opportunity to see the teacher as a person in society.

2. Individually, at a Distance

Working with individual parents at a distance might include the following activities:

A telephone conversation with the parent.
Writing a personal letter to the parent.
Sending home a picture of the child interacting in the school setting.
Sending home report cards.
Sending home "home work" assignments.

3. Group, Face-to-Face

Many Native American adults feel uncomfortable when they are in the "minority" in the school building. Consequently, arranging a time when several parents can come to the classroom together to learn about what their children are doing might increase participation. An important consideration when working with parents is to make the school room an emotionally and socially "safe" environment. During group gatherings, the children might serve refreshments and show the parents "their" classroom. Pictures and script depicting Native American roles in today's society can demonstrate that this classroom is dealing with the issue of the relationship of education to the loss or change in Indian identity. The classroom should also reflect the culture of the community and demonstrate in words, pictures, and displays the ways education impacts life.

4. Group, at a Distance

Some suggestions for this mode of parent-teacher interaction include:

A class newsletter edited by the children could provide the parent with information on class activities.
Bulletin boards and class displays in the window of the local store could provide a means of disseminating information to the parents and community.
Parent study groups might also work in select locations.

Perhaps local agencies could also be supportive of parental involvement in the classroom by providing a "get to know the teacher" social occasion. For example, the kindergarten teacher might be invited to participate in several of the spring Head Start activities so that the children and parents could become acquainted with the teacher on the parent and child's "turf." This might also be done by several church or social organizations in the early fall as a way to demonstrate community support for parental involvement in education.

5. Parent Networking

Encourage parents to maintain contacts with other parents and to participate in school board decisions. If success in school is important, then the community, tribe or family needs to address the issue of what can be done to help parents provide active support for their children. Watson et al. (1983) suggested the following guidelines:

1. Parents must have a community support network from which they can draw in carrying out their roles.
2. Parents must perceive their role as "educator" and their children's role as "learner" as important and vital to the functioning of the family.
3. Parents must act on their perceptions that learning is essential for healthy family living.
4. Parents must have an understanding and knowledge of young children.

Parental Attitude

Watson also indicated that many parents believe it is important for children to learn but never actively pursue education for their child. Maynard and Twiss (1970, p. 96) express a similar concern with Indian parents:

Of great importance in the lack of motivation to learn is the indifference or disinterest of Indian parents in the education of their children. Some parents feel that they are obliged to turn over their children to the schools which they regard as alien institutions, completely separate from their home life. What goes on in the school is out of their hands and of no concern to them. Consequently, these parents offer little encouragement to their children to do well in school and show no interest in what they are learning.

Attitudes such as these may need to be addressed by the teacher if, in fact, parents are going to participate in the school setting. Parents from a minority culture need to provide their children with active as opposed to passive support in the education setting. Active parental support might be facilitated by providing the parent with explicit information on teacher expectations for each parent-teacher contact. Once the parent is comfortable in the school setting, parental expectations and concerns can then be addressed.

References for Further Reading

Herman, J. L., and Yen, J. P. "Some Effects of Parent Involvement in Schools." Paper presented at the American Educational Research Association Meeting, Boston, April, 1980.

Indian Nations at Risk Task Force. "Recommendations for Parents." *Indian Nations at Risk: An Educational Strategy for Action*. U.S. Department of Education. 1991. p. 23.

Light, Harriett K. *American Indian Families*. Journal of American Indian Education. Vol. 26, 1. Oct. 1986. pp. 1–5.

Little Bear, D. "Teachers and Parents: Working Together." In J. Reyhner (Ed.), *Teaching the Indian Child: A Bilingual/Multicultural Approach*. Billings, MT: Eastern Montana College, 1986.

Lyons, P., A. Robbins, and A. Smith. *Involving Parents in Schools: A Handbook for Participation.* Ypsilanti, MI: High/Scope. 1983.

Maynard, E., and G. Twiss. *That These People May Live.* DHEW Publication No. HSM 72–508, 1970.

McConkey, R. *Working with Parents: A Practical Guide for Teachers and Therapists.* Cambridge, MA: Brookline, 1985.

Umansky, W. "On Families and the Re-valuing of Children." *Childhood Education.* 59, March/April 1983, pp. 260–266.

U.S. Department of Education. *What Works: Research about Teaching and Learning.* Washington, D.C.: U.S. Department of Education, 1986.

Watson, T., M. Brown, and K. J. Swick. "The Relationship of Parents' Support to Children's School Achievement." *Child Welfare,* 62–2, 1983, p. 175–180.

A Yupic Eskimo girl builds a relief map of Alaska.

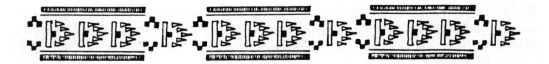

Chapter 9
Social Studies and Native Americans
by Adrian Heidenreich, Jon Reyhner and Hap Gilliland

"Respect for diversity is the hallmark of democracy."
Asa G. Hilliard III (1992)

Regardless of the culture from which our students come, they need to get a true picture of Native Americans and all other racial and ethnic groups in their Social Studies lessons. Teachers need to learn more about Native Americans both in the past and present so that they can adequately teach their students. Information about the Social Sciences given in this chapter can be used in all classrooms with Native American and non-Native American students because we all need to learn more about each other.

What Are the Social Sciences?
In Social Studies lessons, the individual and group behavior of people is studied along with how people relate to the environment in which they live. Modern Social Studies and behavioral sciences include the disciplines of anthropology, economics, geography, history, linguistics, political science, psychology, and sociology. Social Studies refers to the combined use of methods and data from the several social and behavioral sciences to understand and predict our own behavior and the behavior of others.

The overall goal of the study of the social sciences is to understand the social forces and institutions which affect us. They help us understand human and institutional behavior and to establish facts and theories which will provide a basis for more rational management of human affairs in both our personal and group life. This understanding helps to fulfill a major goal of education: to prepare students to be participating citizens in a democratic society.

In teaching the Native student, there ought to be an emphasis on development of practical knowledge and effective democratic political skills which can be of benefit to the individual and the community. Much of this focuses on becoming freed from institutional and other forms of racism, poverty, economic exploitation, political powerlessness and alienation, and low self-esteem. Key concepts for the Native American that relate to these issues include *culture, tradition,* and *ethnocentrism.*

Culture is the complex totality which is the way of life of a group of people. Each culture is patterned and includes social structure, knowledge, belief, art, environmental adaptation, and other customs learned by people as members of a society. Phrasing this more generally, Vine Deloria, Jr., writes:

> Culture, as Indian people understood it, was basically a lifestyle by which a people acted. It was self-expression, but not a conscious self-expression. Rather, it was an expression of the essence of a people. (1969, p. 185)

All cultures are characterized by both persistence and change. They adjust and adapt to changing environmental conditions as well as to the creative thinking of the people who make up the culture. The Laguna Pueblo poet Carol Lee Sanchez writes of Indian identity as creation:

> Each tribe adapted various
> forms of European beads and
> ruffles and braids that
> became traditional
> ceremonial dress by
> the late 1700s—
> but—they are Indian!
> because: We wear them!
> because We put them together
> in a certain way. (Hobson, 1981, p. 241)

Culture is characteristic of the unique quality of humanity as defined by N. Scott Momaday (1975), Pulitzer Prize-winning Kiowa Indian and author of *The Way to Rainy Mountain:* the ability—as individuals and as groups—to imagine ourselves into existence.

Tradition is the link with the past which influences our behavior through time-tested and honored ways of living. Sometimes it keeps us from repeating old mistakes, and other times it keeps us from progressing. Whether students accept or reject traditional beliefs, they need to learn about their traditions and respect them.

One of the characteristics of all traditional cultures is ethnocentrism, the feeling by each culture, each group, that they are the chosen ones, the most important people in the world. This idea that the group one is born into is better, and that other groups and cultures are inferior, must be overcome if different cultures are to live together in harmony.

The major goal of multicultural education is to give students an appreciation of other cultures. Ideally children must learn to adapt and be able to live in several cultures, not just their own (which itself changes). It is important for students to learn about their own culture, those of other tribes and groups, and the "mainstream" or national cultures with which they will have to interact as adults. However, a month-long unit, or several month-long units on Indian culture, can only give an introduction to what normally takes a lifetime to learn.

Eight Suggestions for Improving Social Studies for Native Americans

1. Teach from a Multicultural Viewpoint

Help all students to see multiple points of view. Social Studies is an opportunity for students to learn about both their own culture and others. Studying other cultures and emphasizing the viewpoints of people from other cultures can help overcome ethnocentric attitudes.

Many states and the National Council for Accreditation Teacher Education (NCATE) have multicultural and/or Indian studies requirements.

2. Allow Time for Native American History and Culture

It is important that Native American history and culture be included in the Social Studies curriculum. Both historical and contemporary social, economic, and political issues that affect Indian people should be included. Ignoring Indian history and culture, or distorting it, is detrimental to all students. Indian students need to learn about the world they will live in and how it came to be the way it is, and non-Indian students need to be aware of Indian issues. For example non-Indians elect representatives to government that pass laws affecting Indian Reservations. Many non-Indians have mistaken ideas such as the myth that all Indians receive money from the government for being Indian. Education about the relationship between the federal government and tribes can correct such myths.

In a major study of Indian education, Estelle Fuchs and Robert Havighurst (1973, pp. 170 & 187) found that the most common suggestion by parents was that "schools should pay more attention to the Indian heritage" and that Indian community leaders were "overwhelmingly in favor of the school doing something to help Indian students learn about their tribal culture."

The curriculum of the schools in most communities allows for the teaching of a unit on American Indian life and culture only on about three grade levels in the elementary school. Little is said in most textbooks about Native Americans after the time of the Civil War and the "closing of the frontier." Perhaps once in the primary grades when studying the home, and again when studying state or provincial history, and again with national history, some mention of Native Americans is made. However, any school with an appreciable number of Native American students should include at least one unit on Indian life and culture every year. History textbooks need to be supplemented with additional information about Native Americans, especially for the period after the Civil War.

Learning is gradual, and one unit every two or three years does not necessarily lead to understanding the complexities of a particular culture or of social relations generally. There should be awareness of the levels of understanding of the information studied; for example a seventh grade class will not be able to comprehend sophisticated knowledge about concepts such as kinship and religion to the degree that a twelfth grade class could. It took Cheyenne priests years to learn the proper knowledge about the Sun Dance, both its performance and theology. A one or two hour interview or a week-long topical unit on the Sun Dance will not be the equivalent. But it will encourage the student and provide entry into the skills and knowledge of Social Studies.

One of the most difficult issues in discussing the findings of the Social Studies regarding Indians and Indian-White relations is the matter of the feelings and anger brought out, on the part of both Indians and non-Indians, for different reasons. This can become quite sensitive when the Indian students appreciate the information or focus and the non-Indians feel that they are being attacked or feel guilty and vulnerable. One of our students wrote in evaluating one of us that "he is so sympathetic to Indian culture that he hates other cultures," an impression that was certainly not intended.

Sensitive topics can be approached from a variety of ways. For example, an overview of Plains Indian history can emphasize the brutality of warfare and the massive number of deaths which occurred in smallpox epidemics. Or it can emphasize the constant heroism of individuals and ultimate survival of the group, and the creativity developed by the tribes in their continual adaptation to new conditions. Or, there can be a balance in presenting both of these issues as they relate to Indian culture and history.

3. Give Native Americans Their Rightful Place

A study of groups in world history should give Native Americans an equal place with other groups from Europe, Asia, Africa, and the Islands of the Pacific. Textbooks should not leave the impression that "American" history begins with European settlement. Along with other great leaders, great Indian leaders should be given equal prominence. Pontiac (Ottawa), Tecumseh (Shawnee), Pope (Tewa-San Juan Pueblo), Benito Juarez (Zapotec), Ely Parker (Seneca), and Plenty Coups (Crow) among others should be mentioned in textbooks and included in biographies.

Indians should not be studied just in terms of their relations to the European invaders. Relationships within the Indian society and between tribes should also be studied. When the Indian way of life is discussed, it should be described as the way of life of a particular group at a particular time. In the words of Dick Little Bear (1986), a Northern Cheyenne, "There is no generic Indian."

An eighth grade text on American history used on a Montana Reservation recently was examined for Native American content. In the 400 page textbook, there were three pages on Indian life and culture, beginning with the sentence: "There were savage Indian tribes that hunted the buffalo for food. They made clothes of the hides, and used skins to cover their tents. The Indians often attacked the covered-wagon trains." The Council on Interracial Books for Children (1841 Broadway, New York, N.Y. 10023) publishes guides for evaluating history books, *Stereotypes, Distortions and Omissions in U.S. History Textbooks,* and *Guidelines for Selecting Bias-Free Textbooks and Storybooks.*

Tribal governments need to be studied as well as state, county, and city governments. Teachers can collect their own materials, or for some of the larger tribes like the Navajo, published material is available. The Navajo Curriculum Center (Rough Rock Demonstration School, Rough Rock, Arizona 86503) publishes a whole series of books including *Our Community— Today and Yesterday* and *Navajo Police.* The Bilingual Materials Development Center (P.O. Box 219, Crow Agency, Montana 59022) published in 1986 a bilingual history of their tribe for the intermediate grades titled *Spsaalooke Bacheeitche.* Many more books like these need to be published. When they are written, it is often owing to the dedicated efforts of classroom teachers who recognize the need for such materials.

4. Assure Historical Accuracy

Materials in the classroom need to present a balanced, honest portrayal of Native American history and society. Battles and strange (usually unexplained) customs should not be emphasized. Theories and educated guesses based on incomplete evidence should not be stated as simple facts. Native American traditional views and oral history should have a place in the curriculum along with archeology, historical analysis, and other scientific/humanistic interpretations.

Particular cultural practices of the past should be considered in comparison with contemporary practices in other parts of the world rather than with current practices. For example, writers have made scalping a significant aspect of Indian life and used this as evidence of savagery. Usually they do not make clear that the Indians of the New England and Southwest areas were encouraged to take scalps by the French, English, and Spanish, who also took scalps and paid bounties to the Indians for scalps of their enemies. Similar "savage" customs in Europe are usually downplayed or ignored.

Native Americans also are portrayed as nomads who did not use the land when in fact many more Native Americans lived in villages growing corn and other crops that they had domesticated over the years than hunted buffalo on the plains.

5. Teach Native American Contributions

Social Studies is more than battles and political events. It should include the daily life, the ideas, and the values of each group of people studied, as well as their contributions to our thought and well-being. For example, the contributions of Native Americans to the field of medicine which are described in Virgil Vogel's *American Indian Medicine* (Norman: University of Oklahoma Press, 1970) should be studied. The contributions of the Mayans, Incas, and Aztecs to the fields of astronomy, genetics, mathematics, and architecture are largely ignored in most history books as well as the political contributions of groups like the Iroquois to our democratic institutions.

John Collier (1947, p. 154–55) believed that Indians had a "power to live . . . the ancient, lost reverence and passion for human personality, joined with the ancient, lost reverence and passion for the earth and its web of life" which they have tended as "a central, sacred fire" and from which modern America had much to learn.

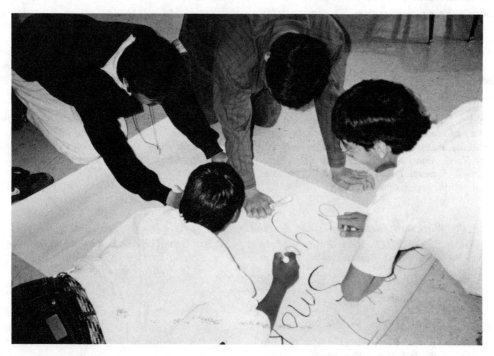

Blackfoot students work together on a poster on the dangers of smoking.

6. Teach Social Studies as On-Going and Dynamic

In addition to having tribal elders come to school and talk about the old ways, the current issues for tribes of self-determination, land and fishing rights, and economic development should be discussed in classes. Tribal councilmembers should be invited to talk to classes, and students should go on field trips to tribal offices and might interview tribal officials or other community leaders.

7. Integrate other Subjects into Your Social Studies Unit

A good Social Studies unit will add interest to all the other subjects in the curriculum, and will provide an opportunity for application of the knowledge learned to those subjects. During your unit on Indian life, your language arts time can be used for recording and revising information obtained in committee work and for writing down stories and information acquired from tribal elders, parents, or guest speakers. Music, physical education, science, art, and even a little of your mathematics program can be integral to parts of your Social Studies unit.

8. Learn More about Native Americans

This chapter provides only a starting place for teaching Social Studies to Native Americans. Teachers are encouraged to read more and take classes in Indian history and culture, such as those offered by tribal community colleges and Native American Studies Programs in regional colleges. Below are some suggested sources for more information about Native Americans:

A. General Works on Native American History and Culture

America's Fascinating Indian Heritage. (1978). Pleasantville, NY: Reader's Digest.

Debo, Angie (1970). *A History of the Indians of the United States.* Norman: University of Oklahoma.

Kehoe, Alice B. (1981). *North American Indians: A Comprehensive Account.* Englewood Cliffs, NJ: Prentice-Hall.

Schneider, Mary J. (1986). *North Dakota Indians: An Introduction.* Dubuque, IA: Kendall/Hunt.

Smithsonian Institution. (1978-ongoing). *Handbook of North American Indians.* William C. Sturtevant, General Editor. (Will be 20 volumes on various regions and topics)

Utley, R. M. (1984). *The Indian Frontier of the American West 1846-1890.* Albuquerque, University of New Mexico.

Vogel, Virgil. (1972). *This Country Was Ours: A Documentary History of the American Indian.* New York: Harper & Row. (Contains a list of famous Americans of Native American Descent).

Weatherford, Jack. 1988. *Indian Givers: How the Indians of the Americas Transformed the World.* New York: Fawcett Columbine.

Wissler, Clark. (1966). *Indians of the United States.* Garden City, NY: Anchor Books. (Revised American Museum of Natural History edition).

B. Specific Works on Particular Tribes Abound. Only a sample list is given here:

Ewers, John C. (1982) *Blackfeet: Raiders of the Northwestern Plains.* Norman: University of Oklahoma.

Underhill, Ruth. (1983). *The Navajos.* Norman: University of Oklahoma Press.

Weist, Tom. (1984). *A History of the Cheyenne People,* Revised Edition. Billings, MT: Council for Indian Education.

C. Reading Material (Stories) for Students

The Buffalo of the Flathead (1981) and other books in the *Indian Reading Series.* Portland,

OR: Northwest Regional Educational Laboratory.

The Council for Indian Education (Box 31215, Billings, MT 59107) has a number of booklets containing stories about Native Americans.

Gerrard Publishing Company (1607 North Market Street, Champagne, IL 61820) has a series of ten Indian biographies at the third grade level as well as two books on "Indian Patriots."

Grandfather Stories of the Navahos. (1968). Rough Rock, AZ: Navaho Curriculum Center.

Kleitsch, Christel, & Stephens, Paul (1985). *Dancing Feathers.* Toronto, Canada: Annick.

Linderman, Frank B. (1972). *Pretty Shield, Medicine Woman of the Crows.* Lincoln, University of Nebraska.

McDermott, Gerald (1977). *Arrow to the Sun: A Pueblo Indian Tale.* New York: Puffin.

Ryniker, Alice D. (1980). *Eagle Feather for a Crow.* Kansas City, MO: Lowell.

Sandoz, Mari. (1985). *These Were the Sioux.* Lincoln: University of Nebraska Press. (First published in 1961).

D. Directories, Catalogs, and Lists

Canyon Records (catalog). Major producer of Indian records, 4143 No. 16th St, Phoenix, AZ 85016; (602) 266–4823.

Native American Directory. (1982). San Carlos, AZ: National Native American Cooperative. (Includes tribes, museums, organizations events, stores and so forth.)

Newberry Library Center for the History of the American Indian. Bibliographic Series. Fran-

cis Jennings, General Editor. Chicago, IL (Includes tribes, regions and special topics.)

Weatherford, Elizabeth (1981). *Native Americans on Film and Video.* New York: Museum of the American Indian (Broadway at 155th Street, NY, NY 10032). A listing with descriptions of about 400 films and videotapes.

E. Teaching Guides

American Indian Education Handbook. (1982). Sacramento: California State Department of Education.

Oklahoma's Indian People: Images of Yesterday, Today, and Tomorrow. (1983). Oklahoma City: Oklahoma State Department of Education.

Summary

James Banks (1987) has declared that developing "the ability to make reflective decisions" should be the main goal of multiethnic education. Native American and non-Native American students need to be exposed to the truth about the history of the United States, including unpleasant truths about slavery and discrimination and more pleasant truths about the cultural strengths of the Native tribes and the various immigrant groups. Only when armed with the truth can students make realistic decisions, both personal and political. Teachers of Native Americans need to allow students to explore their past and present and facilitate that exploration by being knowledgeable about Native Americans in general and the specific groups near their schools in particular. Teachers must be advocates for their students by searching out culturally related materials and by encouraging their schools to procure books and other materials on native history and culture.

References for Further Reading

Antes, J. M., & B. J. Boseker. "Using an Indian Community in Social Studies Education." *Journal of American Indian Education,* 22, January 1983, pp. 28–32.

Banks, James A. *Teaching Strategies for Ethnic Studies: Fourth Edition.* Boston: Allyn & Bacon, 1987. (Chapter 5 is a good introduc-

tion to American Indians and Chapter 6 is a good introduction to Native Hawaiians).

Burnes, B. "Teaching about Native American Families." *Social Education,* 50, January 1986, pp. 28–30.

Collier, John. *The Indians of the Americas.* New York: Norton, 1947.

Deloria, Vine. *Custer Died for your Sins: An Indian Manifesto*. New York: Macmillan, 1969.

Fox, Sandra. *Indian Culture Unit; American Indians and their Foods*. Washington. 1411 K. Street, NW, Washington, D.C.: Indian Education Act Resource and Evaluation, Center one, n.d.

Fuchs, Estelle, & Robert Havighurst. *To Live on This Earth: American Indian Education*. Garden City, NY: Anchor, 1973. (Reprinted by the University of New Mexico, 1983).

Hilliard, Asa G III. "Why we must pluralize the Curriculum." *Educational Leadership*. Jan. 1992. pp. 12–16.

Hobson, G. (Ed.). *The Remembered Earth*. Albuquerque: University of New Mexico, 1976.

Hurlburt, Graham, Randy Kroeker, and Elden Gade. "Study Orientation, Persistence and Retention of Native Students: Implications for Confluent Education." *Journal of American Indian Education*. Vol. May 1991. pp. 16–23.

LeBrasseur, Margot, & Ellen Freark. "Touch a Child—They Are My People: Ways to Teach American Indian Children." *Journal of American Indian Education*, 21, May 1982, pp. 6–12.

Little Bear, Dick. "Teachers and Parents: Working Together." In Jon Reyhner (Ed.), *Teaching the Indian Child* (pp. 222–231). Billings, MT: Eastern Montana College, 1986.

Momaday, N. Scott. "The Man Made of Words." In A. Chapman (Ed.), *Literature of the American Indians* (pp. 96–110). New York: New American Library, 1975.

Noley, G. B. "Historical Research and American Indian Education." *Journal of American Indian Education,* 20, January 1981), pp. 13–18.

Turvey, J. S. "Investigate a Culture: Map, Research, Present, and Write." *English Journal, 75,* January 1986, pp. 82–83.

Winkler, J. K. "Bringing the American Indian into the Mainstream of Colonial History." *Chronicle of Higher Education.* Vol. 36–A3. June 20, 1990.

Chapter 10
Selecting and Producing Valid Material for Reading and Social Studies

Children learn about cultures and values, their own and others, through the things they read. Most of the culturally related reading in your classroom will be in Reading and Social Studies. It will require time and effort for you to find an adequate amount of materials and separate them from those which could be damaging to self-concepts and inter-group relationships. There are many ways in which you can also produce some locally relevant materials to meet the needs of your students, but you will have to be creative and alert to the possibilities. However, the difference in achievement and attitude that good materials make will be well worth the effort.

Selecting Multicultural Materials

If Native American students are to build self-esteem, a feeling of personal worth, and a sense of their place in history, their reading must include culturally and historically accurate material about their people.

If non-Native children are to develop an appreciation for the Native culture and its contributions and are to learn to accept their Indian neighbors as friends and equals, then the books they read must be culturally and historically accurate, and they must be realistic enough so that students can see the relationship to the Native people with whom they are acquainted.

It is not necessary that all reading be culturally related. To have a well-rounded and complete instructional program in Reading and Social Studies, the school will need to use other materials also, but it is necessary that enough cultural materials be included to give the students a feeling of their place in history, of the importance of their people in American culture, and to provide a reading program that is relevant to the lives of the students. As teachers, we must be aware of student backgrounds and interests and be on the alert to obtain as much relevant material as possible.

All students should be exposed to other cultures and new ideas. However, the way in which those cultures and values are presented is important. If they portray urban, middle class values, do they imply that the culture and values of other groups are wrong, or even that they are less worthwhile? If so, they may do great harm to the self-concept of the Indian or other minority students, in addition to causing them to develop a dislike for reading and the study of history. Therefore, you must have an understanding attitude toward all cultures to guide you in selecting materials and in guiding class discussions on any culture. Whenever possible, local community members and tribal cultural committees should aid teachers in producing, examining, and choosing cultural materials to be used in the school.

There is now so much good material that there is no longer any excuse for using inaccurate materials. However, we must select carefully. Keep in mind the ten criteria listed below. These criteria will apply whether your students are Indian or non-Indian, and whether the material is to be used as a part of a lesson in social studies, reading, literature, or for recreational reading. These same criteria should be considered by parents, librarians, editors, and anyone else who influences the selection of books for children's reading.

1. Is Adequate Material Provided?

We cannot rely on our history and social studies texts to supply adequate information on the American Indians or on their rightful place in history. Nor can we rely on our basic readers and anthologies of literature to provide adequate fiction either by or about Native Americans.

There is almost nothing in first grade basic or supplementary reading material to which reservation Indian children can relate, and this is the time when they are struggling to adjust to a new environment and a new way of life. It is the time when they most need to see that they, their people, and their way of life have a place, that they are important. It is the time when they are developing permanent attitudes toward school. And it is the time when they will begin developing reading skills and an interest in reading, if they are provided with material that is both interesting and comprehensible to them.

There are a few beginning reading materials written especially for Indian students available from the Council for Indian Education and from the Northwest Regional Laboratory, and there are a few trade books that are appropriate for reading to the children, but these are hardly adequate. Most primary teachers of Native American students will have to develop much of their own reading material.

As the reading level rises, the number of Native American stories and Native authors increases, until at 9th to 12th grade there is a fair representation in the anthologies. However, there is an overabundance of stories of the old days, which gives the impression that Indians lived only in the past and no longer exist. Many school children away from Indian populations actually believe this. Also, the majority of stories of the old days are about the Plains Indians. The few present-day stories are mostly about the Southwest. Although there is some material about Indians of the Northwest and Northeast, there is almost nothing about the Southeast, California, Alaska, or Canada, all of which have large Native American populations.

It is especially difficult for teachers of either Indian or Eskimo students in the Alaskan "bush" or in Northern Canada to find relevant material. Consider the Eskimo child who had never seen a car and is expected to answer test questions about a stop light, or the Aleut students to whom I was supposed to administer a comprehension test over a story about a boy mowing a lawn. When it was over, they all wanted to know what a lawn was, and what was a lawn mower!

It is obvious, then, that teachers of Native children are going to have to draw most of their material for reading, literature, and social studies from sources other than textbooks. It is also essential that school librarians locate and obtain as much *good* Indian literature as possible.

2. Is It Interesting?

High interest materials that promote a desire to read are particularly important to students who have not had a great deal of exposure to reading in their homes and have not built a habit of reading for recreation or a feeling for the importance of reading. Fiction should be fast starting, fast moving, and with enough action to maintain interest throughout. Even the top Indian students will often state that they are turned off by thick books and small print.

Topics should be of interest to the particular children in the class. While urban children may have developed an interest in science, geography, and technology, most Indian students center their interest on people. Most of the beginning reading and much of the reading at all levels should be about people and life to whom the children can relate, people whose lives are similar enough to the local way of life to seem real to the children. It is through much reading about their own people and their own interests that children gradually expand their interests to other people and other subjects. TV has broadened interests and backgrounds for reading to some extent, but students will still build reading skills, comprehension, and interest in reading best if most of the reading is something to which they personally can relate.

3. Is the Readability Level Appropriate?

Can the students for whom the material is intended read it easily enough to understand it and enjoy it?

The material which is used must be at a reading level appropriate to the individual student. Children will not develop an interest in reading and read enough to become good readers unless they enjoy what they read. The cannot enjoy reading if the vocabulary or comprehension level are such that they have to struggle to read or understand it. If the vocabulary level is too difficult, they may lose both self-confidence and interest in reading. They will also make little if any progress in reading skills, because, faced with too many unknown words, it will be difficult for them to remember any of them, and they will not read enough material to get adequate practice.

There are numerous readability formulas available that will give you an approximate reading level of books that you want to evaluate. Formulas such as Fry's, which are based on sentence length and number of syllables, give a quick estimate. However, for books written with a high interest and mature format, but easy vocabulary, intended for remedial readers, the estimate will be much too high. For these you need a formula based on word lists of common words, but analysis with these formulas takes longer. There are also computer programs available that will quickly give you readabilities from several different formulas.

Readability, however, is more than sentence length and difficulty of vocabulary. It is also how well the sentence construction, vocabulary, and means of expression match that of the reader, and how the content fits the students' backgrounds and their desire to read. For this reason, although formulas will give you some indication and help you eliminate some very inappropriate material, they will not accurately tell you how difficult the material will be for the Indian students in your class.

4. Is It Accurate?

There are inaccuracies regarding Indian life and culture in many historical materials. There are many more in "historical" fiction. Do the Indians portrayed live and act according to the Indian customs and habits of the particular area at the time the story takes place? Does the material over-emphasize one particular aspect of the culture to the point that it gives a false concept of a way of life?

In 1965, a committee from the American Indian Historical Society, an all-Indian organization, appeared before the California State Curriculum Commission choosing textbooks for use in California Schools. They wrote:

> We have studied many textbooks now in use, as well as those being submitted today. Our examination discloses that not one book is free from error as to the role of the Indian in state and national history. We Indians believe everyone has the right to his opinion. A person also has the right to be wrong. But a textbook has no right to be wrong, or to lie, hide the truth, or falsify history, or insult or malign a whole race of people. That is what these textbooks do. . . . A true picture of the American Indian is entirely lacking. (Costo, 1970, p.7)

What was true of textbooks was just as true of fiction. Most of the Indians portrayed were stereotyped. Battles between Indians and whites were emphasized, with Indians usually in the wrong and having no right to protect their land from invaders. Indians were either described as savage beasts, nomads, or drunks, or as noble savages living in an ideal world. Neither view made them appear as real people with faults and virtues, people with whom a child could relate.

Not only were many authors of the past misinformed, but editors chose the stories which perpetuated the stereotypes because "that's what the readers want." In 1955, I wrote a short story which included an Indian who I thought was very realistic. The editor's first comment was, "Your Indian character speaks English as well as your other characters. Indians don't talk like that. Make him talk like an Indian."

While less *distortion* of facts occurs in present-day writing, the *omission* of facts remains a serious fault of much of the literature. The treatment Indians received is usually omitted from children's literature, as are Indian contributions to agriculture, medicine, architecture, biological science, and other aspects of modern life.

Writers seem unaware of the Indian's philosophical thought, close family ties, emphasis on cooperation and sharing with others, respect for the land and all of nature, hospitality and generosity, and the relationship of all of these to the Indian's spiritual life.

Do your history books treat Indian people as the original Americans and study their civilization, then bring in the arrival and contributions of each group of people, including Asians? Or do they sound as if all history began in Europe and nothing important happened unless the European-Americans did it? The book from which I had to teach California history started with the statement, "The history of California begins with the Spanish settlement"!

There has been a great deal of effort made to improve the books published more recently. Editors are refusing to publish books that are blatantly prejudiced. The majority of authors of history texts and many writers of fiction are trying to present a more balanced and accurate picture of Native people, but too many are not well-informed. They cannot write what they do not know, and if they have prejudices they are unaware of, these will be obvious to the Indian reader. Most of the fiction writers learned about Indian life mainly from other fiction writers who perpetuated the biases of the writers who came before them.

After reviewing ten of the most complete studies of history textbooks and the American Indian, O'Neill (1987) says that although much of the biased language found in earlier textbooks has been eliminated, the Indian is still most often portrayed in extreme, simplistic, stereotypical roles. "The evidence, as based on published sources, is overwhelmingly conclusive. The status of the North American Indian in most history and social studies textbooks has not substantially improved in the last 20 years.''

5. Do the Illustrations Authentically Depict Indians of the Time and Location?

Books as well as motion pictures sometimes depict Indians of the Southwest wearing Plains Indian headdresses, New England Woodland Indians living in teepees, or Navajos living among Saguaro cactus. These errors do not necessarily reflect upon the knowledge of the writer, as the author does not always see the illustrations that the publisher will use, but it does indicate that all of the content needs to be checked for accuracy. The illustrations themselves can teach misinformation regarding the history and culture of the people depicted.

6. What Are the Author's Attitudes toward Native American People?

Authors may be very accurate in the historical facts they present, yet reveal attitudes toward the Indian of which they may not even be aware. Even though unintentional, if the author shows prejudicial feelings or attitudes of superiority, the material will be damaging to the child who reads it.

Authors' attitudes show through their writings in many ways. Books, both old and new, should be checked for stereotypes, prejudices, and loaded vocabulary. It is the little innuendoes which are often missed by the non-Indian reader that may do the most harm to the self-concept of the Indian child or develop lifelong prejudices in the non-Indian. Often the authors who intend to say something good are actually, because of their own feelings, downgrading the Indian. Consider this statement: ''He was an Indian, but he was a very smart man.''

It is the vocabulary used which often brings out the writer's attitudes. Battles won by soldiers are called ''victories'' while Indian victories are ''massacres'' even when they were the result of surprise attacks by whites. Settlers who protected their homes were ''patriots''; Indians who did the same were ''murderers.'' Indians who did not disclose their military plans to the white man were ''treacherous,'' but the word is not used for the generals who made treaties, then broke them, or who attacked the Indians who were abiding by these treaties. Modern workers who must move with their jobs are not termed ''nomads,'' but an Indian who only changes location from summer to winter is ''nomadic.'' All Indians are called ''primitive,'' even those who were creative artists, skilled architects, or builders of great irrigation systems!

7. Does It Portray Indian Values?

Are values interpreted in terms of an Indian or non-Indian point of view? How is success described? Are people respected only if they get ahead in the white society? To gain acceptance, do they have to get A's, excel in sports, and make money?

Many stories which accurately portray historical events and the physical environment of the Indian completely misinterpret Indian values. The concepts of sharing and cooperative living are missed, along with the differences in feelings about property, time, family relationships, the significance of nature, and the importance of spiritual life. Authors who have not lived among Indian people are prone to give their Indian characters the same motivations and values as their non-Indian friends. Watch for these fallacies. If you must use these books, discuss the misconceptions as you read with your students.

Compare the values by which Native American characters in your book live with those described in Chapters 3, 4, and 5. Unless the majority of them are similar, perhaps you should study the book carefully before you recommend it to your students.

8. Does It Portray Indian People in a Positive Way?

In the majority of basic readers, the only Indians are Indians of the past. Modern Native American children see no relationship between the feathered warriors of the plains and the people of their own neighborhood. If they look for it, they find only fighting warriors, not loving families with close relationships and concern for each other. Then they read about the ideal family of the basic reader, about happy children living in ideal homes and ideal neighborhoods where there is no poverty, and they are never told that loving families are better than expensive toys, or that helping others is better than driving fancy cars. Will the book you use help your Indian students identify with and be proud of their heritage? Will it foster a positive image of present-day Indian people? Will it encourage Indian students to want to achieve?

9. Are Indian Authors Represented?

Many of the problems of misinformation in stories and books about Indian life and culture can be eliminated by selecting material written by American Indians. It is important that as much as possible of the information on Native American thought, values, and philosophy should come directly from Native writers. This is especially true for high school students, whose reading should include social, political and philosophical essays by American Indian authors. These are scarce in the anthologies, but they are available if you search them out.

10. Is There Balance in Cultures Portrayed?

We must insist on books that give all cultural groups their rightful place in history. Many of our social studies books have endeavored to meet the demand for a multicultural curriculum by making trivial changes in their texts, that is, by adding a sprinkling of minority individuals, rather than incorporating information on the influence of all groups on human history. Basic readers have done it by adding a few stories of the buffalo days on the plains or a story about the Southwest. Then, of course, they add a story or two of modern city life in which there are Indian names and illustrations with black faces, but which show no real understanding of the way of life. Many schools are wisely throwing out all basic readers in favor of teaching all reading from a wide range of materials that can be selected with the particular students in the school in mind.

Clark (1990) provides a bibliography that shows the huge gap between what is known and what is taught about the place of people of African descent in world history. We need the same kind of listing for Native Americans, Hispanics, and Asians. As Hilliard (1992) says, we must "find the true stories of the roles of all groups in human history so that we could include them in the school curriculum. Nothing less than the full truth of the human experience is worthy of our schools and our children."

Developing Locally Relevant Material

Although there are many good books on Indian life and culture, many of these will be only slightly relevant to any one group of Indian students. Penobscot children of Maine or Abnaki children of Quebec may prefer stories of the Navajo and Apache in Arizona to stories of the dominant society since Indian children are usually interested in how other Indian children live, but to really build interest in reading and the self-concept that comes from knowing of the importance of your own group, children need reading material that is about them, their people, material that is "real." Many different groups have worked on developing their own materials, so some may be available, but there are almost never enough of these to adequately supplement the commercially available materials. Therefore, most teachers find it necessary to somehow supplement these with locally developed materials. Below are descriptions of seven ways that some of us have produced materials for our own classes. Perhaps you will find some of them applicable to your classroom and your school.

1. Record Children's Experiences

Recording of children's own experiences can begin very early in the first grade and continue at all levels. If the stories are typed, bound, and kept on file, they can provide much good reading material for other children as well as those who write or tell them.

These stories have the advantage of being about local people and typical local experiences. They emphasize that the children's own experiences are worth writing about and reading about. They have the further advantage of being in the local vernacular, the vocabulary and way of speaking of the children themselves. Be sure to keep them that way.

The writing of "language experience" stories is not just an activity for the beginning reader. It is equally appropriate for older students. In the Reading Clinic at Eastern Montana College, they have been an essential part of the reading instruction for remedial students of all ethnic groups and all ages from primary students to adults. They have been especially valuable for Indian adult beginning readers.

A more thorough discussion of language experience for Native American children is included in the chapters on teaching reading skills and the whole language approach.

2. Produce a School Newspaper

In Arctic Village, a small Athapascan village in Northern Alaska, the little two-teacher school published the Arctic Village News, about four dittoed pages, that came out every two weeks and was distributed to everyone in the village. The children all wrote news items, and parents also contributed news. The whole village was always anxious to read it, so it gave the children a real incentive to write, as well as providing reading material of importance to them.

The same idea could be adapted to many situations. In a larger school the paper could be distributed just to the students, or it could be for the members of one class and their parents.

As part of this, a teacher can take pictures of students and their activities, as well as other activities around the school and community. Young children can write captions for the pictures. Older ones can write news articles about them. The children are usually very enthusiastic when their pictures are included. Although it is not a recommended method of copying photos, copies made on the school's copy machine are usually adequate for school use.

3. Let Students Conduct Interviews

Students on the Pima reservation interviewed their parents, grandparents, and other elders, and collected stories. Some were old folk stories or legends. Others were the experiences of the people interviewed. The students then wrote the stories. When they had difficulty expressing

Pima ideas in English, they talked them over with each other or with a bilingual teacher aide and tried to agree on a translation. When the stories were completed, they were typed. Most were one or two pages long. "Reader's Digest type" blurbs to interest the reader were put at the top of each story. Any words that other children reading the story might not know were defined or used in a defining sentence in the wide right hand margin. Each story was then put into a bright-colored cover which included the title and illustration. A number of copies of each story were made and put into the school library so that any teacher could check out enough copies for a reading group or a whole class. They became an important supplement to the reading program, as well as preserving much information that could have soon been lost as the elders passed on.

In a similar project at Tuba City, Navajo and Hopi students and parents produced a book called *Desert Wind*. The school at Craig, Alaska, published *Kil-Kass-git*, a small magazine that included stories and photos about their Haida community. Similar projects have been found practical and have benefited many schools and communities since Elliot Wigginton and his Appalachian students set the example with their *Foxfire* magazines, which began in 1972. These magazines come from extensive interviews the students conduct with community elders. As Wigginton (1992) has pointed out, "The fact that students are *of* a culture does not automatically mean that they will know very much about that culture or have more than superficial notions about its history or its worth."

Wherever these projects have been tried out, they have produced not only improved reading and writing skills, but also a pride in the students' culture and increased interest in other literature. The gains are much greater than they would be by simply finding published reading material about the students' culture.

As the students learn, they are using and developing many academic skills, as well as their ability to relate to and work cooperatively with people of all ages, and most of all, an enthusiasm that lifts them out of the monotony of routine.

4. Develop Local Culturally Related Books

Northern Cheyenne teachers, tribal council leaders, parents, and other elders formed a committee under the chairmanship of John Woodenlegs, who was the tribal president, to produce a series of small books from which Northern Cheyenne children could learn to read using material relevant to their own lives. After several books were printed the group felt that their books should be shared with other tribes and others should share with them, so the non-profit Council for Indian Education was formed to continue and expand the project. They have now published over 100 of these small books about Indian people throughout the U.S. and Canada (Gilliland, 1970).

Others have developed similar materials. Crow teachers and teacher aides have developed a Crow Easy Reading series for their library. The Menominee have produced folk stories and even a science book. Consultants working with Winslow teachers and parents at Kayenta developed some small humorous books about local present day Navajo life. This kind of project is a good opportunity for teachers and parents to work together and get parents interested and involved in the school. If all such projects would share and make their materials available to the others, there would be more than adequate material to carry on a complete culturally related reading program.

5. Invite Local Storytellers

The interest and knowledge of any class can be enhanced by inviting local storytellers to come to the class to talk and tell stories. If they do this, ask the storytellers to allow you to turn on the tape recorder while they are there, and to write the stories out later. If they are telling the stories to the grade level for which you intend to use them, most of them will naturally, without being told, adjust the vocabulary and language structure to the maturity of the students. If they tell the stories to you, you will have much more adaptation to do.

If your guest storytellers speak the native language, record at least half of the material in their language so the children can use it for listening. Feelings cannot be expressed as well in English, and there is much description and humor that is lost in translation.

Guest storytellers can also be a good way of getting children interested in storytelling, and this can greatly improve the program in oral English. A relaxed storytelling time at least once a week could do more for students' oral English than many standard uninteresting drills.

6. Inspire the Writing of Creative Stories and Poems

Both the recording of stories from interviews and writing their own experiences can lead children into writing purely creative stories and poems. Many Indian children have great ideas for creative fiction and they love to write poetry if they can be inspired. I have watched Mick Fedullo as he works with Indian students writing poetry. He has every student writing with enthusiasm. Try out the ideas in his chapter in this book on teaching creative writing to Native students and you may end up with much good material that can supplement your reading program.

If you work with remedial reading for high school students or with adult basic education, your students may hesitate to write because they think they can't write well enough. Explain to them that you need material for your first and second grade students. Ask them to write about their own experiences when they were younger but that they should be sure to write using easy words that these children can read. It may work wonders for you. It did for me.

7. Rewrite Material at an Easier Level

Tribal information material, occupational, consumer information, adult education, and other materials written for adult use are often more appropriate for high school students than those provided for their use, as the students can see more relevance to their own use. Some teachers have provided material by rewriting these at the reading level of their students, with terms not familiar to the students paraphrased to aid understanding and vocabulary building.

Summary

If Native American children are to build reading skills and a good self-concept, if they are to be interested and gain an adequate understanding of the history of both their own people and society in general, they must have a wealth of culturally and historically accurate materials. As teachers we must select carefully the materials we will use to separate truth from untruth and the biased from the unbiased. Are the materials accurate, complete, and informative? Do they portray Native values positively? Are the characters and the illustrations true to the way of life of the particular group at the time depicted?

When adequate materials relevant to the local way of life are not available, they can be supplemented with materials developed in the classroom through children writing about their own experiences, their creative ideas, and material that has been told to them by local people. Parents and elders can help to produce additional relevant material.

References for Further Reading

Antell, Lee. *Indian Education: Guidelines for Evaluating Textbooks from an American Indian Perspective.* Education Commission of the States. 1981. 32pp.

Charles, James P. "The Need for Textbook Reform: An American Indian Example." *Journal of American Indian Education.* Vol. May 1989. pp.1–13.

Clark, John H. "African People in World History." In A. G. Hilliard III, L. Patyon-Stewart, and L. Obadele (Eds.). *The Infusion of African and African American Content in the School Curriculum.* Aaron Press. 1990.

Gilliland, Hap. *Indian Children's Books.* Council for Indian Education, 1980.

Gilliland, Hap, Editor. *Indian Culture Series.* Small books for Indian children, published by the council for Indian Education, Box 31215, Billings, MT. 1970 to present.

Gilliland, Hap. "The New View of Native Americans in Children's Books." *The Reading Teacher* 35, May 1982. pp. 799–803.

Hilliard, Asa G., III. "Why We Must Pluralize the Curriculum." *Educational Leadership.* Vol. 49–4. Jan., 1992. pp. 12–16.

Indian Reading Series, Small books of stories and legends of Northwest, Plateau, and Northern Plains Indians. Northwest Regional Educational Laboratory, Portland, Ore.

McEachern, William Ross. *Supporting Emergent Literacy Among Young American Indian Students.* Appalachia Educational Laboratory. 1990. 3 pp.

New, Douglas A. "Teaching in the Fourth World." *Phi Delta Kappan.* Jan. 1992. pp. 396–398.

O'Neill, G. Patrick. "The North American Indian in Contemporary History and Social Studies Textbooks." *Journal of American Education.* Vol. May 1987. pp. 22–27.

Reyhner, Jon. "Native Americans in Basal Reading Text Books: Are There Enough?" *Journal of American Indian Education,* 26–1, Oct. 1986, pp. 14–22.

Rietz, Sandra and Norma Livo. *Storytelling: Process and Procedures.* Libraries Unlimited, 1986.

Slapin, Beverly and Doris Seale. (Eds.). *Through Indian Eyes: Books Without Bias.* Revised Ed. 1989. 452 pages. [Excellent Resource]

Unlearning "Indian" Stereotypes: A Teaching Unit for Elementary Teachers and Children's Librarians. Council on Interracial Books for Children, 1977.

Vogel, Virgil J. "The Blackout of Native American Cultural Achievements." *American Indian Quarterly.* Winter 1987. pp. 11–31.

Wigginton, Elliot. "Culture Begins at Home." *Educational Leadership.* Vol. 49–4. Jan. 1992. pp. 60–64.

Chapter 11
A Whole Language Approach to the Communication Skills
by Sandra J. Fox

The instructional philosophy called the "whole language" approach is the natural way to teach language. It incorporates oral language practice, language experience activities, and the use of culturally relevant materials, the three most recommended strategies for improving the reading achievement of Indian students.

The majority of Indian students are "holistic" learners. They learn more easily if they see the whole picture first, then learn the details as a part of the whole. This holistic method is preferable for Indian students as it provides for the practice of language skills in a meaningful way as interrelated and useful tools. It allows students to explore life experiences, then to look at language in relation to those experiences rather than doing meaningless workbook pages, spelling and vocabulary lessons which are isolated parts of language and have no experiential basis. Whole language instruction includes reading, writing, speaking, and listening activities.

Principles of Whole Language
The principles of whole language instruction include:

- It is student-centered. Much of the content of instruction comes from the student's own language and experience.
- It is comprehension-centered. Aspects of language are learned as parts of a "whole" language rather than being learned as isolated parts. For example, words are learned in the context of meaningful language experiences. Sound/symbol correspondence (phonics) is learned from sounds within words which students know and use.
- Instruction is based upon active learning, hands-on strategies.
- Communication skills are not taught in isolation. Students learn to read from writing and vice-versa. Oral language and listening activities are important for improving reading and writing.
- Students are taught to enjoy and appreciate literature—the written works of others.

- Students are involved in planning activities based upon a selected theme for the whole language lessons.

Strategies for Teaching

Nine strategies for teaching language as an integrated whole to Indian students are recommended.

1. Begin with Language Experience and Continue at All Levels

A basic activity of the whole language approach is writing a language-experience story. Basal reader stories are usually far removed from any of the experiences of Native American children. Language experience is based on the children's own experiences. Therefore, the instruction relates to their backgrounds, interests, and culture.

You can begin language experience instruction by providing a group experience such as doing a project, seeing a movie, or going on a field trip. After the experience, the class discusses what they did and you ask the students to "summarize" the experience so they can write a story about it. As they summarize, you initially lead the students with questions such as "What did we do?", "What did we see?" Later on, the students will give summary information on their own. Write the story on the board while students give you the information. When writing the language-experience story, you are modeling writing for the students. The finished story is used for reading instruction. The students see their own words written down and practice reading words from their own experience. They have practiced speaking when discussing the experience and when providing the summary information for the story. Illustrating the stories encourages students' visualization and reinforcement of concepts. Thus, the language-experience story involves students in reading, writing, speaking and listening, all in the same lesson, and all related to the students' own experiences.

For students at higher grade levels, the language-experience story technique is usually adjusted so that students write their own individual stories from their own or group experiences. Language-experience stories, both group and individual, can be "published" as books the students have written. These books are then available for others to read.

The idea of the language-experience story can be extended to activities such as the writing of a daily class newspaper (including the date, weather and news items about the class, school, or activities in the community), the writing of real get-well cards or thank you notes, and the writing of plans for class activities. In this manner, children learn communications skills from language which is within the realm of their own experience and communication needs.

The procedure for writing language-experience stories (experience, discussion, summarizing and writing) can be used with older students to help them keep class notes in notebooks. This is an especially good technique for classes such as Indian culture classes in which there are no single textbooks for use, but the technique can also be useful in all academic areas. Students can refer to their notebooks for purposes of reviewing the material; they are simultaneously practicing language skills and the actual process of notetaking.

2. Bring Familiar Language to the Classroom

The language-experience story allows students to read and write their own language. In addition, students can bring jingles and words from their favorite television shows and commercials, words of rhymes they know, words of their favorite popular songs and words relating to sports or other activities in which they are especially involved. Students can also examine words which are the names of things within the classroom, within the school building, and in the community. They can examine their own slang, popular expressions or terms. These words, this familiar language which students bring to the classroom, then become word lists for you to use in reading and writing instructions.

Students can make word lists based upon the theme of the whole language lessons. For example, if the theme is "grandmothers" the students can give words they use to describe grandmothers. You, the teacher, can write the words on the board or flip chart. The meanings and spellings and grammatical usage of the words can be discussed. These words are from the students' oral vocabulary, words they know and use but may never have seen written down. These words can then be used by the students to write short stories and essays.

3. Incorporate Instruction in the Reading Strategies

The words in the language-experience story and in other language brought to the classroom by the students are the primary medium for teaching word attack skills—the skills involved in sounding out or pronouncing words. In addition, words encountered in literature being read and in experiences taking place are used for word attack instruction.

When stories or words are on the board or flip chart, you have an opportunity to point out words with sound/symbol correlations or examples of the phonetic analysis which you want to stress. You thus build upon certain things which the students already know about phonics and also use words which they already know as examples.

Students can write words from language-experience stories and other activities on word cards. These cards should then be kept in the students' bank of words (the collection of words they already know how to read). Each student should have a personal box or bank. Other students may prefer to write in word notebooks the new words which they encounter. The words from these word banks can be used by students in several ways:

1. The words can be put in alphabetic order.
2. The students can make new sentences with them.
3. Students can identify words with the same beginning sounds, etc.
4. Students can review the words as flashcards.
5. The words can be analyzed for spelling and word attack information.

It is important that you include all the important phonetic and structural analysis skills. Some teachers are very adept at pointing out aspects of phonics and structural analysis in words as they arise. Others choose to rely on some guide to be sure all skills are included.

It is also important that all the comprehension skills (word meaning, main ideas, retelling, searching for answers to questions, predicting happenings, etc.) are practiced both with student - written and published culturally relevant material. Concept mapping and semantic webbing are helpful for assisting Indian students in improving comprehension skills.

4. Read to Your Students Every Day

Students who become good readers usually have been read to when they were preschoolers. They got the idea of what reading is. They learned there were words on the pages and often memorized the book so they knew exactly which words were on a page. The reader dared not skip a word or a page. These students learned to enjoy a book. They also saw adults "model" reading behaviors. Reading to students is important at school for these same reasons and students never get too old for this activity. This is especially important for Native American students, as many of them have never been read to at home and some have never seen anyone read until they entered school. It is an important learning activity.

Students who are being read to are practicing comprehension and the important communication skill of listening, which is not stressed enough in our schools. Students learn how to listen for information and they hear new words which can increase their vocabularies. When reading to students, you can help them practice good reading habits. Help students relate happenings to their own experiences. Stop to examine meanings and spelling of words encountered and include comprehension questions and higher level critical thinking questions to promote analysis.

Often good Indian literature is left on school shelves or only a few students read it. Reading to students is the perfect way to include these culturally relevant Indian materials. The material read to students should be something in which the group of students is interested. For kindergarten and first grade, favorite books or poetry can be read over and over again.

Groups of all ages can be read to, or tutors or older students can read to individual students. Older students can listen individually to books or other materials which have been taped by tutors and they can follow along in the book while listening.

The idea of the importance of reading to students, especially in the primary grades, should be extended to the home. Parents should be urged to read to their children, and vice versa. If there is any one way Indian parents can help their children with reading it is by reading to them.

5. Have Students Do Much Independent Reading

Time should be spent having students read silently. Allow students some selection of their reading material.

A variety of reading materials at various reading levels should be made available. Although students may not choose books at their independent reading levels, they should be available for them. Remember though, that the more interested the student is in the subject matter, the easier it will be for him/her to handle more difficult material. Although reading of entire books should be encouraged, many Native students, even the best high school students, hesitate to attack a full sized book. Supply plenty of poetry, short stories, and materials such as *Reader's Digest Reading Skill Builders* so students can choose shorter selections which may help to build their confidence. Guide students to materials with their interests and reading levels in mind. Record students' special interests for this purpose. The available materials should include Indian culture materials and also books and magazines on subjects being studied in social studies and science, and materials on themes being used for other language activities. For older students who do not read well, high interest-low readability level materials should be made available. There are now many of this type on the market.

When students read silently, you should read silently as well. This can be sustained silent reading time. Some term it DEAR time: Drop Everything and Read. Students at Wingate Elementary School on the Navajo Reservation surpassed their goal of reading 1,250,000 minutes in the dormitories during the 1985–86 school year through the whole language program.

6. Encourage Students to Share the Literature They Enjoy

There should be time when students and the teacher or tutor share poetry, stories or books that they especially like. The sharing can simply be showing books and recommending them, giving short oral book "sales talks" which entice others to read the books, or actually reading aloud the poetry, short story, book or a portion of a book. When sharing literature, the sharer should stress the name of the author and illustrator so students begin to recognize their names and importance. Written book reports which are displayed can also be a form of sharing literature, but don't force students to quit reading by telling them they must write a report when they finish.

Older students who have difficulty with reading can read lower readability books to younger students, or make tapes for them. Younger students can listen to or read along with these tapes. The older students are practicing their reading and helping younger students with reading at the same time. This is a great self-image booster for all involved.

7. Have Students Write Every Day

Students should write every day. Writing should be made a very important activity. Students should have writing folders or large envelopes in which to keep their written work. Classroom rules should emphasize the importance of silence when people are writing. The cooperative effort and sharing which are essential parts of the Indian culture can be utilized by having students help each other with "editing." This helps to prevent the discouragement from writing that usually results from the correcting process. Thus, students also regularly get helpful suggestions from other students about their writing. Students should often work in pairs.

There are two kinds of writing to be done in school: controlled writing and independent writing. These lead to the two kinds of writing which are necessary for life's communication needs: exact writing and imaginative writing.

Controlled Writing Controlled writing is that in which you, the instructor, control the topic and the form of the writing. This is useful for beginning writers and for older students who need to improve their exact writing skills.

One form of controlled writing is to simply have students copy written works. In the early grades, students copy poetry, songs, language-experience stories, and other short works. The best materials to copy are things already familiar to the students, things that they have memorized or at least heard.

Dictate sentences for your students to write. The length and number of the sentences depend upon the level of the students. The sentences can include students' spelling or vocabulary words or can be from an experience which the class or student has had. After each sentence is written by the students, you can write it correctly on the chalkboard for the students to compare with theirs. This provides immediate feedback as to their success at writing, correct spelling, punctuation, and capitalization. Then, direct students to check to make sure they have capitalized, put a period, and so forth—one aspect at a time, stressing the things with which students are having difficulty. More advanced students can have short paragraphs dictated to them. No hints are given, such as "end of sentence"; only the words are dictated. Students then have to check to see if they have divided the materials into sentences correctly, whether they have properly indented the first line, and have correct spelling, capitalization, and punctuation. Remember, however, that there can sometimes be more than one correct form. Short papers can be dictated to see if students can divide ideas into paragraphs, as well as checking on other skills. Teaching these skills this way means that you will not need to emphasize them at the expense of more creative writing.

Another method of controlled writing is converting questions into statements. After you explain or review the difference between questions and statements, students can be directed to write a paragraph of statements in which they use sentences to answer questions such as:

> What is your name? What school do you attend? What grade are you in? What is your teacher's name? How many students are in your class? Is your school work easy or hard?

The length of the sentences and the paragraph will depend, of course, upon the level of the student or group.

Another type of practice is having students write sentences using their spelling or vocabulary words. A simple record of types of errors being made should be kept and the teacher should discuss the types of errors being made with each student. This technique worked very well with high school remedial students on a South Dakota reservation. Students saw, after writing the same number of sentences each week, that they were making fewer and fewer errors.

Controlled writing should be done as long as needed and the content of it should depend upon the types of errors being made by students.

Independent Writing   Students should be encouraged to put their thoughts and ideas on paper. It should be stressed that their ideas are important. Writing should be viewed as the ability to write one's own ideas and present them in a form for others to read. The ideas can provide real or imaginary information—fiction or non-fiction.

Independent writing should be stressed from the first day of school. Children want to write, as evidenced by their crayon marks and scribbles. They should be encouraged to write in kindergarten, because from the beginning, they must believe that they can write. So they are allowed to scribble, draw pictures, or even write alphabet letters if they know them. Ask what they have written and praise them for what they have done. Some whole language teachers write what the children want to say under the children's ''writing'' for the children to see and copy. Soon they begin seeing the children's writing evolve naturally.

Children can also begin expressing their ideas on paper in kindergarten through drawing or painting pictures. Artists can tell about their pictures, and you can extract two or three sentences that will describe each picture or tell the story. By the next day, attach a story strip to the bottom of the child's picture with the two or three sentences on it. The class can then share the pictures again and read the ''stories'' that go with them. Later on, students can write their own stories for their pictures.

First grade children often have limited spelling-usage vocabularies. If their flow of thought is interrupted by idea gaps and spelling problems, students may feel frustrated about writing—putting their own ideas down on paper. As a transition from controlled writing, a set of completion blanks is sometimes desirable in initial writing lessons to get students started writing, and so that they can see completed selections more quickly. Be sure to leave an open sentence or two at the end that allow students to write as much or little as they like.

I have a pet and its name is _____. It has _____ fur. It likes to _____ . It sleeps in the _____. One day it _____.

ME

My name is _____. I live in _____. I am _____ years old. My father's name is _____. My mother's name is _____. I have _____ sisters and _____ brothers. My tribe is _____. I like myself because_____ (or One day I _____ or, My friends and I _____).

After the students fill in the blanks, they should copy the entire paragraph to make it their writing. For older students who need this kind of motivation to get anything written, type a story but leave out the adjectives or the verbs so they can be creative by filling them in and making the story their own.

Sometimes you can provide the beginning of incomplete sentences or the ending of sentences in order to get students started.

Before the students begin writing, stress that they must work quietly so all can think. Music may be played if it is soft music with no words. Tell the students that if they come to a word that they want to use but can't spell, they can put the first sound down and leave a blank so they can ask you or their writing partner later. For the time being, they shouldn't disturb anyone.

Written works should be illustrated regularly. This reinforces the ideas which were used in the writing as well as the skills which were practiced. Students can also write captions for cartoons.

Modeling, rather than just telling, is important for Indian students, so demonstrate writing for them. After you choose a topic, or the class helps choose a topic, you can show the class how you gather your thoughts and organize your writing. You should actually write short papers on the chalkboard, making corrections and reorganizing ideas as you go along. As students' writing becomes more complex, there will be a need for outlining and other higher level writing skills which you should also model for students.

Making corrections in independent writing should be viewed as "editing." Editing should start out simply, with all students turned into editors after being writers. They can edit their own work or they can edit each other's work. At first, they should simply read the work to see if it makes sense. Later, they can check for capitalization, punctuation, correct writing of the title, spelling and paragraphing, etc. Older students might have a checklist of things to look for.

You can be available to help students edit. Some papers may be edited by you as examples of how to edit. Copies can be made of one paper for all to see as you point out the things to be changed, or sentences from many papers can be extracted for the teacher to use as examples. For this purpose, you should be careful to choose papers written by the students who are better writers so as not to squelch the creativity of those who are less confident about their writing.

Some materials should be "published." Sometimes students' works are displayed on bulletin boards or compiled and actually bound into books to be read by others. Students can write individual books also. The teacher is the "senior editor" in these cases and reviews "drafts" for final copies with students. They do not necessarily have to be perfect. It depends upon the level of the students and the teacher's expectations of students and their levels.

A project for older students is based on the Foxfire concept of gathering information about the local community. The students' writing is then made into a book. Students can also write articles on any topic for local and school newspapers, or their own class newspaper.

Poetry adds spice to the writing program. For early writers, rhyming words—after the first one—can be left out of poetry so that students can fill in the blanks. Later, students can write their own poetry. They get to feel and use a lot of language when they write poetry.

The class should have many opportunities for writing. Students can keep journals and write in them every day. In the early grades, the teacher can provide the topics. They can be as simple as: Tell how you feel today. Describe your shoe. Journal notes are not "corrected" or edited. You may, however, review them and make comments like "me too" or "I agree" or "nice," etc. Older students may not want their teachers to review their journals. Or journals can actually be written dialog back and forth between teacher and student, and they prove useful as a counseling technique. The classroom could have a message box where students can answer and send messages to the teacher.

8. Provide Oral Language Practice

Oral language practice is involved when students write language-experience stories, bring familiar language to the classroom and share literature. There should, however, be other opportunities for practicing oral language. Reciting of poetry, participating in skits or plays, giving short oral reports, speaking into tape recorders, sharing experiences and discussions—all these things should be included in the whole language program. Two-thirds of the students at Wingate Elementary School on the Navajo Reservation tried out for the all-school Christmas play after having gained confidence in themselves through the school's whole language program.

9. Organize Your Language Program Around a Theme

The ideas presented in this chapter are just a few of the ideas you could use in a whole language program. There are many others. There is no set way to organize them. To provide some structure to a whole language program we suggest a thematic approach. A language unit can be based on a topic being studied in social studies or science, a book or a special happening of interest to your students. If the topic is chosen with student interests in mind, the students will have many ideas for activities. Use them.

For example, suppose you choose the theme "pets" for students at about the third grade level.

1. *Oral language practice.* Students can tell about their pets or pets they know. They can tell the kind of pet, describe the pet and tell something funny the pet does.
2. *Reading to students.* Read the book *Dog Story* by Oren Lyons to the group. It is culturally relevant to some tribes and is by an Onondaga author.
3. *Reading Strategy.* Pick out words encountered in reading *Dog Story* for meaning analysis and word attack instruction. The students do a concept mapping of the story.
4. *Language-experience story.* The students can research various kinds of dogs and summarize their findings in a language-experience story format.
5. *Students reading to themselves.* At their independent reading levels, the students can read stories about pets.
6. *Sharing literature.* Some students can tell about stories or books about pets which they have read and especially enjoyed.

7. *Students bringing familiar language to the classroom.* Students can tell about dog foods or dog food commercials they know about. Write and discuss the words in dog food brands or words of commercials.

8. *Writing every day.* Students can write papers on "Why Pets Are Important." They can work together in groups to edit these. They may keep daily journals. They may have some controlled writing also.

Students will come up with other activities based on the theme. As the group plans activities, they may outline them in the form of a concept map or web so they see a picture of their plan. Students may be allowed to choose from proposed activities.

The various activities of the whole language approach don't have to be in any particular order. Concepts from other academic areas, such as math or science, should be included if they relate to the topic. Whole language promotes the idea of the teachable moment—teaching a concept or exploring an idea if it relates and if the students seem ready for it. Students learn to do research to learn more about topics they are interested in.

The whole language classroom should be full of stimuli for reading, writing, speaking, and listening. Some whole language classrooms have reading, writing, speaking, and listening centers.

The whole language approach is a much more exciting way to teach than just following textbooks. You will find many more ideas in the books listed at the end of this chapter.

The procedures of the whole language approach can also be used in content areas such as science and social studies. You and your students can plan your reading, writing, speaking, and listening activities on the topic being studied. The procedures of the whole language approach can also be used for bilingual programs using the native language.

In a culturally appropriate way, the whole language approach stresses the importance of individuals, their languages, their experiences, and their interests. One whole language teacher I know has a mirror in her classroom. Above the mirror are the words, " I AM SPECIAL."

References for Further Reading

Allen, Roach Van, and Claryce Allen. *Language Experience Activities.* Houghton Mifflin Co. 1982.

Fletcher, J. D. "What Problems Do American Indians Have with English?" *Journal of American Indian Education,* 23. Oct. 1983.

Goodman, Kenneth S., and others. *Language and Thinking in School: A Whole-Language Curriculum.* Third ed. Michael C. Owen Pub. 1987.

Graves, Donald H. *Writing Teachers and Children at Work.* Heinemann Educational Books, 1983.

Grobe, Edwin P. *300 Creative Writing Activities for Composition Classes.* J. Weston Walch, Portland, ME.

Indian Culture Series. Council for Indian Education, Box 31215, Billings, MT 59107. Many small books of Indian stories.

Indian Reading Series: Stories and Legends of the Northwest. Educational Systems, Inc., 2360 Southwest 170th Ave, Beverton, Oregon 97005. Contains good discussion of language-experience approach.

McCracken, Robert A. and Marlene J. *Stories, Songs, and Poetry to Teach Reading and Writing: Literacy Through Language.* American Library Association. 1986.

Pacific Northwest Reading and Language Development Program. Northwest Regional Educational Laboratory. Contains many oral language activities.

Rich, Sharon J. "Restoring Power to Teachers: The Impact of Whole Language." *Language Arts.* Nov. 1985.

Smith, Frank. *Joining the Literacy Club.* Heinemann Educational Books. 1988.

Watson, Dorothy. *Ideas and Insights: Language Arts in the Elementary School.* National Council of Teachers of English, Urbana, IL. 1987.

Weaver, Constance. *Reading Process and Practice: From Socio-Psycho-Linguistics to Whole Language.* Heinemann Educational Books. 1988.

Excerpts from this chapter have been printed in *Whole Language Approach to Improving Reading and Other Communication Skills.* IEA Resource and Evaluation Center One, NAR/ORBIS.

Chapter 12
Developing Reading Skills

Reading is the most essential of all academic skills because in our system of education it is necessary to the learning of all subjects. For the Native American, reading can be the road that leads from poverty and second class membership to full participation in American society.

There are four essentials that must be kept in mind in teaching reading to Native American students. First, reading is comprehension. Comprehension is more difficult for the child whose background of experience, vocabulary, and spoken language are different from those for whom the textbooks are written. Comprehension must be emphasized and checked in all reading throughout the school day. Second, reading is part of a whole language experience. It must be seen as a part of the whole experience of the child if the child is to put full effort into learning all of the skills. Reading skills must be taught, not just during reading period, but throughout the day, in relation to all subject areas. Third, the detailed parts of the reading process, such as phonics and sequence, are parts of a larger experience, and for the Native American student, even more than for some others, it is essential that instruction begin with the larger view so that the details have meaning. Fourth, extra effort must be taken to relate reading to oral language in the thinking of the students. Reading must be fun. This means that reading of good literature in the interest areas of the children must exceed the amount read from textbooks.

If the ability to read is going to be successfully developed in Native American children, then teachers must be willing to be flexible and innovative. Native American children can develop reading proficiency, but in order for this to happen, teachers must be willing to adapt their instruction to meet the needs of the children. This means that teachers must go beyond "canned" basal reading programs. Although some teachers may feel most secure when using a basal reading series, the majority of instruction and practice should be through broader reading from many materials. Children should read many times the amount included in the basic readers. You can't learn to play tennis by being taught how in a classroom, although the information may be helpful. Likewise, you don't become a good reader through instruction and skill practice alone. Most of the reading time must be spent *reading!*

How Should Reading Instruction Begin?

Teachers who have taught in middle class communities assume that their pupils will begin school with some knowledge of reading, that they have seen parents reading and have been read to, and that they already have a desire to learn how to read. This will be true for some Native American students but not for all. For instance, one teacher on a Montana reservation had 22 students beginning school, 21 of whom had never seen a book or newspaper, or held a pencil in their hands. These students needed a great deal of readiness before formal reading instruction could begin.

Development of fluency in speaking, along with an adequate listening and speaking vocabulary, is a must in preparing Native American children to read. In a study of the Crow and Northern Cheyenne first graders, Simpson (1975) found that these children used less than one fourth of the vocabulary of middle-class urban children in describing the same pictures and objects. As part of their beginning reading experiences, Indian children must be given opportunities to develop their language ability. This means that children must be exposed to language, encouraged to speak, and have their speech accepted without being corrected.

1. Read to children

Reading to children is probably the most important thing either a parent or teacher can do to prepare them for reading. While it teaches them what reading is, it also develops an interest in reading and learning to read.

Teachers should read a variety of stories to children. It is usually beneficial for as many stories as possible to be about the children's own people, their tribe, and the life they know. Such reading sessions should be made as comfortable as possible. One way this can be achieved is sitting on the floor with the children, and if possible letting them see the pictures as the story is read. During the reading, children should be encouraged to talk abut the stories, express their ideas, ask questions, and tell their own experiences. Such sessions serve to help develop print awareness, develop listening skills, and promote language development, all of which promote future success in reading.

If you have an opportunity to work with one or two children at a time, let them watch the book as you read, and follow the words in the book with your finger as you read. This not only orients the children to the whole process of reading from left to right, but many of them will watch the words as you read and begin learning the more common words. This fits well the Native American learning process discussed earlier of learning through careful observation.

2. Use Language Experience

Language experience is one of the most successful means of teaching beginning reading to Native American students. It should be a part of the instruction of every primary school student and every student of every age who is reading at a primary level.

Reading and print must become the "personal property" of every child. Make captions for pictures the children have drawn, labels for things they have made, and put picture books with just a few words where they are always available. Encourage those who can read them to read them to the others.

An excellent way to begin reading is to let children select key vocabulary words. A key word has special meaning for a child and is chosen by him or her. Once a child has chosen a word, the teacher prints it on a piece of tagboard and gives it to the child to take home, show to people, and bring back to school the next day. The next day, children normally return with "crumpled" words, words which will be remembered. Children's words can be kept and reviewed periodically (say twice a week). This review should be a "fun" activity. If a child does not remember a word "instantly," then that word is filed away without criticism and a new word takes its place. Known words can be used to construct sentences and stories. This approach, known as the "Key Word Approach," was first made famous by Sylvia Ashton-Warner (1963) with the Maori children in New Zealand and is an excellent technique for Native students. For a detailed description of key words see J. Veatch, et. al. (1979).

Most early language experience sessions will be group projects ending with a story which the teacher puts on a large chart which the class can read together. The session usually begins with a conversation between the teacher and a group of students about a topic in which they are interested. Students should be encouraged to change the subject of the discussion as much as they desire. Field trips, pow-pows, an incident at home, the weather, or a television show may provide ideas for discussion. When enthusiasm for a subject has developed, the teacher suggests that the children tell about the experience. The teacher records their story on the chart.

Stories should be kept short for beginning readers and lengthened as the children grow in confidence. The stories should always be recorded in the exact words of the children. This is what makes it *their* story. "Correcting" the language not only decreases motivation, but may make the children feel that they are being criticized, instead of having their self-confidence boosted, as writing a story should do.

Individual language experience can begin with the same type of group motivation; the children each think of a story they want to write, and draw a picture of that story. As they draw, the teacher moves from one to another and writes the story for each child. Having them draw first, then tell the story, allows all to start at the same time, and the dictations of stories can be spread through all of the drawing-writing period.

As soon as the children know some words and letter sounds, they can begin writing their stories, writing what words they know, sounding some out, and putting a beginning letter or just a blank for the other words. This helps them remember the story as they want it, and the teacher can help them complete it. Before long, the children will be writing their stories independently.

Both individual and group language experience stories can be used for oral reading practice, work on sight vocabulary, and practice on word analysis skills. The more important words can be analyzed and discussed to aid word recognition, but students must realize that they are not expected to recognize every word. The stories can be bound into individual scrapbooks or into class anthologies; they may also be used on bulletin boards made by the class members, or they may be combined into class newspapers. After students have read a story several times, they may wish to take it home to read to others.

When students feel confident enough in their writing abilities so that they want to, they can begin to take the responsibility for writing their own stories. If a child feels more comfortable recording stories on tape, this is possible too. One teacher created a recording booth from a refrigerator box and put a cassette tape recorder inside. Whenever children had a story to record, they would go into the recording booth, turn on the recorder, and tape their stories. A volunteer teacher's aide typed these stories and had them ready for the next day's reading. It is a good idea to keep many of the stories or copies of them in class anthologies, to be used as reading material for students later in the year and for future classes.

The language experience method is especially appropriate for Indian children because it uses the English spoken by the children, not textbook English, which may be very different from the language and vocabulary with which the children are familiar. Also, the subjects of the stories are familiar and understandable, which is an important aspect in promoting fluency, ease of reading, and comprehension. It is, however, important that children read each other's material as well as their own stories. Otherwise, they may not have the inspiration which comes from reading new material and learning through reading, or the practice in developing comprehension.

Too often, language experience activities are assumed to be appropriate only for the beginning reader. This is unfortunate since they can be used equally well with older students. Older students can benefit from studying a topic and constructing "stories" about that topic. These stories are shared with the other students in the class. Language experience activities are also an essential part of the reading instruction for remedial students of all ages.

How Will We Teach Word Recognition?

Word recognition is an important facet of reading. While recognizing and being able to "say" the words will not guarantee success in reading, the child with a large sight vocabulary has a better chance of being a successful reader.

1. Learn the Children's Strengths and Match Their Learning Styles

To be effective at recognizing words while reading, students must have a large number of words which are recognized at sight. They must also have a means of identifying words not seen in print frequently enough to be remembered. This requires the combined use of the meaning of the word in the sentence and the sounds represented by the letters. Most Indian children are better at holistic learning than analytic learning. That is, they learn more easily by looking at the whole picture, then analyzing the parts, studying the details, and putting them back together to make the whole picture. Therefore, more of them are better at sight word recognition that at phonics. Of course, it is essential that every child learn both to become a really effective reader, but we find it easier for most Native Americans to begin by learning some words through language experience, then use other clues for the words they don't recognize through recall and context.

As you work with groups reading charts made through language experience, you can point out letters and name them, then begin finding words that begin alike, that begin like their names, that end alike, or that have letters in the middle that they have learned as beginning sounds. Flash cards can be made from words in their experience stories and these can be used for comparison of beginning sounds.

Before students can use phonetic analysis, they need to recognize small differences in the sounds within words. This is difficult for many Native American students, who are either visual learners or have a Native language as their first language. Furthermore, native Americans who are more fluent in their native language may have difficulty distinguishing the sounds not in their first language. At age nine or ten, most people's "sound system" is set and they can learn to recognize or speak new phonemes only with great difficulty. How much difficulty this causes will depend upon which of the many Native languages they speak. I worked with Hawaiian students who had, until the age of ten, only spoken Hawaiian. These students had great difficulty because Hawaiian has 12 sounds or phonemes: five vowels and seven consonants. Of the 44 sounds of English, these were the 12 they heard and pronounced. In contrast, Kuchi, an Alaskan Indian language, has 95 phonemes: 75 consonants and 20 vowels.

Children who have difficulty with sight recognition can learn the letters or words that cause them particular trouble by practicing them kinesthetically. They can draw the letters in loose salt on a cookie sheet, or they can close their eyes and write large letters on the chalkboard using both hands together.

It is important that we teach all the skills through all possible mediums so that all children, regardless of their particular learning style, can learn them. If children have difficulty with a particular kind of learning and you spend additional time trying to teach them to read through that mode, you will probably condemn them to frustration and poor reading. It is much more advantageous to emphasize and reinforce strengths, and let children learn to read through them.

2. Try Oral Impress

Most Native American children are especially good at learning through demonstration. One of the best ways to improve word recognition, and one which makes use of this ability, is the oral impress method. It is particularly applicable to Indian students since it is a whole word approach, focuses the child's attention, and culturally-related material can be used. It is, however, an individual approach so it cannot be used in its pure format in a large class if there is no outside assistance. But it can be taught to parent volunteers or a teacher aide, and may very well be the best possible use of a volunteer's time.

When using oral impress, sit behind the student, close enough so that you are speaking almost into his or her ear. The child holds the book from which you are both reading. As you read point to the words with your right hand. Read aloud and the child reads aloud with you. Read at a slow-normal reading speed, not hesitating or waiting for the child. At first, if there are unfamiliar words, the child is likely to be half a word behind, but that is alright. The child's job is to try to stay with you, saying every word if possible. Be sure to move your finger, smoothly along, keeping it directly under the word being read; the child will follow your finger, and must be looking at each word as it is said. Read slowly and clearly with good emphasis and rhythm, since the oral reading of the student will be patterned after yours.

Each daily oral impress session should last from 5 to 10 minutes—never longer since it requires a child's concerted, unwavering attention. With most children, you can expect to see a change in their vocabulary, speed of recognition, phrasing, and fluency within the first two hours (three weeks) of instruction.

Another method, which includes the sharing that Native children enjoy, is pairing the children. Children are put with either an older child or a better reader, who reads aloud, pointing to the words, as the partner listens.

The cassette tapes of the stories that are available with some of the supplementary reading materials are useful if the children will make an effort to watch the words closely and read with the tape.

One reservation teacher reads a story every Monday morning from a supplemental basal reader. The children watch in their copies as she reads; then she tells them they may read the story as many times as they like, but they must all read it at least once that week.

Many Indian children enjoy poetry; they enjoy its rhythm, its rhyme, its vivid pictures, and they enjoy reading it together. Choral reading of poetry is an excellent way of practicing smooth, rhythmic reading and learning new vocabulary without being corrected when they make mistakes, and without anyone being aware of their errors.

How Should We Develop Comprehension?

The answer to this question is neither easy nor simple. Reading comprehension is an interaction between various factors, during which a reader constructs meaning. Some of the factors which affect comprehension by Native students include prior knowledge about a topic, motivation, language facility, and familiarity with how to read different kinds of print materials.

Reading means comprehension and reading comprehension involves more than successful decoding, fluent oral reading, or ability to recall information. While the ability to recall information is an important aspect of comprehension, developing the comprehension ability of Native students involves more than students answering questions over material they have read.

1. Adapt to the Children's Background

In comprehending a passage, a reader's mind does not just record the information in the passage and then give it back. Readers are not passive recipients of knowledge. Instead, they construct meaning by taking ideas from the page and relating them to ideas already in their minds. The text serves as a sort of "blueprint" that guides the reader in building a mental model of what is meant through supplying clues to what the author intended (or what the reader thinks the author intended). During this "building" a reader fills in points and makes inferences; after all, no text can explicitly give all of the information, underlying concepts, and relationships necessary to understand what the author is talking about. Consequently, comprehension requires a reader to play a very active role in constructing meaning.

Good comprehension, then, depends upon the reader having the necessary background information *and* being able to relate that background information to what is being read. It is fair to say that "reading is caught through books that fit." The subjects, topics, locale, and activities of characters must be such that the students can relate to them. Stories with exotic and difficult language, or about strange situations or far away places, are for good readers who have read enough to expand their backgrounds. The Native American student who is just trying to learn how to get some understanding from the material is not yet ready for strange and far away places, which may include urban or suburban locations.

Prior knowledge is very important to comprehension. The more a person knows about the subject of a passage, the easier that passage will be to read and understand. Whether the material read is fiction or a textbook, comprehension requires that the reader have enough prior knowledge to relate what is being read to what they already know.

Prereading activities prepare readers for the material to be read through introducing and building background knowledge. They are especially important when students are asked to read something outside of their normal experiences. Prereading preparation involves introducing a topic, students relating to that topic, and students forming a purpose for reading. It might sound strange, but readers are more likely to be successful if they talk about the subject before reading—rather than after reading.

Among the prereading activities which have proved successful with Native American children are brainstorming and mapping. In mapping, the teacher records the information on a board, so the students can see the results. This helps the students identify what they know and what they might not know about a reading selection.

2. Use Active Reading Strategies

Children need help in becoming active readers. An active reader interacts with the print and tries to make sense of what is being read. In order for students to become active readers, they need to be exposed to and have an opportunity to practice different strategies. These include previewing difficult material before reading, using cues within the text to make predictions about what is likely to occur next (and reading to confirm those predictions), and switching the rate of reading to fit the material.

Most teachers test comprehension; they don't teach it. Simply asking questions after the students read a passage, then telling them whether they are right or wrong and what the right answers are is testing. One way of doing this checking that also teaches is, when students do not know the answer to a question, have them go back and locate the place where the information was given, then reread to locate the answer, decide on the right answer, and use quotes from the material to prove the answer. Another method when studying textbooks is to have students always read the questions at the end of the chapter first, then read to find the answers, or work in a group, turning each heading into a question, reading the passage, then discussing and agreeing on the answer to the question.

An active reading technique which has proved very successful with Native American students is Stauffer's (1976) Directed Reading Thinking Activity. This activity involves predictive reading: the students guess or predict what will happen and read to confirm their predictions. The steps are simple and this procedure can be used with students of any age.

First, read the title and let students guess what the story or chapter will be about. Let them read a page to confirm. Then, let them guess what will happen next. Give them hints, not of the content, but how they should think: "What did the author mean by . . ." or "What do you already know that will give you an idea what will happen?" Be sure to make it a fun activity, help them laugh about the surprises they did not predict so that they will not feel embarrassed about making a wrong guess.

Two observations about this strategy. First, teachers must model the process. Show the students how you do it, then work together by having students tell you their predictions. Second, it takes use and repeated practice before children will use this technique for improving comprehension in independent silent reading.

Another active reading strategy is ReQuest (Manzo, 1969). ReQuest is a form of reciprocal questioning which helps students ask questions about what is being read. This strategy involves students and teachers taking turns asking each other questions about the material being read.

Introduce the lesson by telling the students that they are going to have an opportunity to be the teacher and ask you questions. Then, the students and the teacher read the first paragraph silently. The teacher closes the book and urges the class to ask any questions they want over what has been read. After the students' questions stop, the teacher switches roles and asks the students questions. The process is then repeated with the next paragraph.

Two points about ReQuest: First, if you, the teacher, don't know the answer, admit it. Second, most students ask only literal questions. Model higher level thinking by asking questions such as "What in the book makes you think that . . . "

How Do We Assure Adequate Practice?

This is done by making actual reading an important part of the instructional time every day. It is safe to say that if teachers want their students' reading to improve, then students should spend more time actually reading than in related exercises or listening to someone tell them how to read.

Where can teachers find the time for reading? One way is by cutting out the unnecessary. A prime example of the unnecessary is workbooks. Instead of having students practice unnecessary and frequently unproductive workbook lessons, have students become involved in more independent reading and writing. Remember, reading comes *first* and students learn to read by reading.

As a general rule of thumb, every reading lesson should include twenty or more minutes of reading. To this, teachers often say, "But there aren't enough reading materials available at the primary levels for this much reading." Yes, there are sufficient materials available. The trick is finding them. Be innovative; ask parents if those with children's books at home could send some to school to be shared with other students. If you are teaching in a Native community in which there are no materials in the home, then ask other teachers, officials, and people you meet if they can help you to find some books for your classroom. One teacher did this and was "adopted" by a church in a city. The members of this church sent books and the children wrote thank you letters. Another six grade teacher, on a Montana reservation, went to a paperback wholesaler and was given a pickup load of unsold books.

Reading is FUNdamental is a national program to aid parents and local groups in giving books to children so that all of the children can own books that they can read and enjoy. They give special help to Indian schools. For information, write to Reading is FUNdamental, 600 Maryland Avenue S.W., Room 500, Smithsonian Institution, Washington, D.C. 20560.

Materials are important. Reading is enhanced by materials which are available and varied. Every classroom should have culturally relevant materials, humorous materials and educational materials available at all reading levels, to fit every student. For information on developing your own materials see the chapter on "Selecting and Producing Valid Material for Reading and Social Studies."

Conclusion

Improving and developing the reading ability of Native American students is facilitated by teachers who are willing to teach to a child's strengths and enthusiastic enough to make reading an enjoyable experience. Reading can be fun, both because of the content and because of the environment. If reading is approached as a meaning-based function, students will be more likely to have a positive attitude and grow in ability when we let them read.

References for Further Reading

Ashton-Warner, Sylvia. *Teacher*. New York: Simon and Schuster, 1963.

Cooper, J. David. *Improving Reading Comprehension*. Houghton Mifflin Co., 1986.

Dubois, Diane M. "Getting Meaning from Print: Four Navajo Students." *The Reading Teacher*, 32, March 1979, pp. 691–695.

Feeley, Joan T. "A Workshop Tried and True; Language Experience for Bilinguals." *The Reading Teacher*, 33, 1979, pp. 25–27.

Gilliland, Hap. *A Practical Guide to Remedial Reading*, second edition. Charles E. Merrill, 1978.

Mallett, G. "Using Language Experience with Junior High Native Indian Students." *Journal of Reading,* 21, 1977, pp. 25–28.

Manzo, Anthony V. "The ReQuest Procedure." *Journal of Reading,* 11, 1969, pp. 123–126.

McCarty, T. L. "Language Use by Yavapai-Apache Students: With Recommendations for Curriculum Design", *Journal of American Indian Education, 20, October 1980, pp. 1–9.*

McNeil, John D. *Reading Comprehension: New Directions for Classroom Practice,* second ed. Scott, Foresman and Co., 1987.

Pearce, Daniel L. "Improving Reading Comprehension of Indian Students." In Jon Reyhner (Ed.) *Teaching the Indian Child: A Bilingual/Multicultural Approach,* pp. 70–82. Billings: Eastern Montana College, 1986.

Simpson, Audrey Koeler. *Oral English Usage of Six-year old Crow and Northern Cheyenne Indian Children.* Doctoral Dissertation, University of Maine, 1975.

Simpson-Tyson, Audrey K. "Are Native American First Graders Ready to Read?" *The Reading Teacher,* 31, April 1978, pp. 798–801.

Chapter 13
Teaching Creative Writing to Native Students
by Mick Fedullo

Regular and frequent creative writing in the classroom helps expand Native students' potential by offering them ways in which they can express their thoughts and feelings in words. When we encourage Indian children to write from their inner selves, from their own experiences as Indian people, language becomes a tool with which their young minds can begin exploring limitless possibilities. And when Indian children tap the source of their own creativity, the act of using language becomes pleasurable and truly meaningful, and the students become empowered.

Creative, or imaginative, writing should be viewed as consisting of skills separate from the skills of revising or editing. Its objectives include helping children learn their own value as individuals as well as developing their own natural talent for artistic expression. The creative writing ideas in this chapter should be seen as forming an essential element of what Sandra Fox calls *independent writing* in her chapter on "whole language." It is recommended that her model be used, and that the ideas herein become a basis for getting first-draft material from students. For revising and editing this material, see Fox's chapter.

Setting the Mood for Writing

Before having students write, it is crucial to set a fostering, creative mood in the classroom. The students, in order to exercise their creative imaginations, must be relaxed, confident, and eager to write. We want them, after all, to discover that writing can be pleasurable and not intimidating, to learn to give structure to their ideas and feelings, and to experience the success that comes with effective written communication.

When students are tense with the anticipation of failure, the chances are they will fail. This anticipation may express itself in any of a number of ways. Often, students who claim boredom with, or a dislike for, a classroom activity are actually expressing an underlying fear of failure. In establishing a class mood conducive to creativity, it is necessary that every student view the writing activity as relatively simple, personally relevant, pleasurable, and a break from regular academic studies.

It is helpful to tell the students that writing poems and stories is an artistic activity, and that they should think of each piece of writing they produce as a work of art. In creating this kind of art, the students, instead of using lines and color, are using words and sentences. Encourage them to visualize, to create clear images. When youngsters come to see creative writing as another art form, they find that it is indeed pleasurable.

I often tell students that the best way to conjure mental images is to daydream. I explain that daydreaming is an activity that may hinder the learning of academic skills, but that in order to be creative, daydreaming is quite useful. Students are sometimes startled when told that they may daydream in class, so I explain to them that daydreaming is one way we actively use our imaginations, and that it is from the imagination that all creative writing is born. It is important that the students realize that the most valuable aspect of creative writing is indeed their own imaginations working in relationship with their own personal experiences. Each individual is so filled with memories, perceptions, thoughts, and feelings that there are countless potential poems and stories in everyone. The students should be told repeatedly that they, as individual human beings, are worthy, priceless resources for their own writing.

One crucial way to take pressure off the students and establish a relaxed, creative environment is to stress the fact that *every* member of the class can achieve success. For Indian students, defusing the competitiveness of an activity goes a long way in assuring that each and every student will participate with maximum effort. Let the students know that every one of them can achieve success if they simply use their imaginations. Although they will write their poems and stories individually, success of the group as a whole should be emphasized over success of the individual. It has often been noted that Indian students at times do not strive for success because they are afraid of "standing out" from their peers. Being perceived as apart from the group, whether positively or negatively, runs against the Indian value of cooperativeness over competitiveness. When success of the entire group is underscored, the students will not want to "stand out" negatively.

Another important way to keep enthusiasm for creative writing alive is to offer positive criticism on every piece of writing a student completes. These individual creative efforts should never be criticized negatively. Suggestions may be offered to improve the efforts, but emphasis should always be placed on what was successfully accomplished. It is not hard to find something positive to say about what a student has created. The one cardinal rule is: Never praise falsely. If positive comments from the teacher cannot be backed up by specific, concrete examples in the poems and stories, the students will lose confidence in the teacher's judgment, or assume that the teacher always says something positive whether or not it is true. The list of things to praise is endless. A few that teachers can look for are: clear, detailed images; well-made similes or metaphors; adept personifications; exciting verbs; accurate adjectives; interesting overall vocabulary; notably rhythmic lines; inherent or developed drama; effective sequencing; evocative mysteries; intriguing character portrayals; thoughtful meditations; non-sentimental emotions; clever repetitions of words or phrases; crisp, pointed endings; striking syntactical variations; culturally relevant ideas or concerns; complex logic; biting ironies; imaginative free-verse forms.

Although it may be valuable to have the students read their work aloud, it is recommended that the teacher read the poems and stories first, making positive comments. If students lack confidence in what they have written (and we are all our own worst critics), then hearing it in their own voices does no good. They will not read their work with the authoritative voice it deserves. This may further reinforce negative feelings. But when the student hears the poem or story recited by an adult voice, there is often the realization that the work is much better than originally assumed.

Providing students with model writings can often mean the difference between success and failure. When teaching similes or alliteration or any other writing technique, and while suggesting various topics and forms, teachers should show the students sample writings, especially ones that are culturally relevant—that is, writings by American Indian authors. At the end of this chapter are listed major anthologies of American Indian poetry and short fiction. Teachers are urged to acquire at least two or three of these, especially *Harper's Anthology of 20th Century Native American Poetry* and *Talking Leaves: Contemporary Native American Short Stories*. Models for the following writing ideas, and for many others, can be found in most of these anthologies.

Writing Techniques

1. Parallelisms

A simple form of parallelism that also makes a convenient poetic structure is the repetition of the initial words of each line of a poem. There are infinite possibilities—"I see," "I dreamed of," "I like," "I wish I was," "We heard," "We believe," "She imagines," "He goes to,"—just to name a few.

The students first select the opening words of each line, then compose their poems. I tell the students to "stretch" their lines by providing details, especially of description, action, and location. By doing so, they create something more than a list—they exercise their ability to construct images. Instead of:

I see a horse.
I see a tree.
I see a mountain.

the students might come up with:

I see a white horse galloping through the wheatfields.
I see the tall pine trees swaying in the wind.
I see a snowy mountain rising into the clouds.

Variations can include starting each line with a *different* item of the same kind, such as animals, plants, or natural geographical features. Again, the variations are endless.

Rather than use the technical term "parallelism" with younger students, I tell them that this form is a kind of "puzzle poem." Usually I ask the students to write the opening of each line a certain number of times down the left side of their papers. Then they go back and, like a puzzle, fill out each line with details.

2. Personas

One of the most common strategies of childhood play is the imaginative assumption of being someone or something else. From the four-year-old Crow grandson of a friend, who, when introduced to me, announced that he was a "transformer" (a robot toy), to a young Navajo girl who, playing with dolls, informed me that she was their mother and proceeded to explain her tribe's clan system from that point of view, the game is the same: the child is no longer him- or herself.

Writing persona poems, in which the author takes on the identity of someone or something else, is, therefore, natural and enjoyable for children. Again, there is such an incalculable number of possible choices that this strategy can be used over and over.

Have the students select identities from whose point of view their poems will be written. I often suggest that they choose an animal, an old person, or an object. Stress that whenever they use the pronoun "I," it must refer to their choice; they must *be* that other animal, person, or object. The students can include in the poems anything they want, including the following suggestions: what they physically look like; a description of where they live; what they do; what they think about; what memories they have; what secrets they have; what desires they have; what they think of others around them; what they hope for.

3. Personification

To personify something is to give human qualities or characteristics to something that is not human. Writing poems or stories in which the students use personification is fun for them.

After giving the students examples, and perhaps having them verbally invent some (the branches sang all night; the trees are bothered by the wind; the sleeping desert; the mountain stream laughed), ask the students to write a poem or story in which they personify two or three items from nature. You may want to have the students write their own list of five or more personifications from which they may then draw for use in their poems or stories.

4. Addressals

Most children are familiar with writing notes or letters to one another. "How are you? Me, I'm fine," is a typical opening. Letter writing represents for children a pleasurable activity and offers a basic structure in which they can express themselves through writing.

The assumption behind letter writing is that one person holds a private conversation with another person. In so doing, the person for whom the letter is intended is addressed by the use of the pronoun "you," just as in verbal conversation.

One strategy that works well with students is to have them write letters or poems to other things besides individual people. They may hold a "private conversation" with anything they choose. A poem may be written to, or addressed to, a specific group, such as one's tribal people (My Apaches, you are proud and brave"), or to all people—the general "you" that addresses the reader ("You walk upon the earth; you are part of the earth").

There are many variations, so the addressal can be used many times. The students can address objects, ideas, emotions, or things from the animal or plant kingdoms.

5. Questions

"Why is the sky blue?" "Why does the grass grow?" "Why do people have two eyes?" Every parent (and teacher) has been both delighted and plagued by the infinite curiosity of youngsters. And children, as they grow and continue asking questions, learn that not all questions are answerable and that some are answerable in different realms of understanding: cultural, spiritual, scientific, to name a few. Into adulthood we continue to ask, to wonder, about things.

Because from culture to culture, even from tribe to tribe, answers, when they exist, may differ, we are here concerned not with answers but with questions themselves. By having the students write poems in which they ask questions, we let them know that through language they may find expression for the things they wonder about.

In this writing exercise, the students are asked to select something that is not human (wind, cloud, star, sun, stream, rain, snow, fog, sand, rock, mountain, or a specific animal or object), and write a poem or paragraph in which they ask as many questions of their selection as they can think of.

A variation on this is to have the students write another parallelism in which every line is a question beginning with "I wonder why. . . " or simply, "Why. . . "

6. Similes

In a fifth grade class of Crow students, I asked the children what tribal activities they enjoyed the most. Their list included the annual Crow Fair, the competitive hand games and arrow games, and inter-tribal powwows. While discussing the hand games, I asked what about them they liked the most. One boy said he liked seeing all the women dressed in their shawls. I asked him, "What do they look like?" After a moment, he answered, "They look like prairie chickens." "That," I said enthusiastically, "is a *simile*. You can use it in your poem."

Comparing two things by using "like" or "as" can be challenging and fun for students when they get the knack for it. After giving them a number of examples, have the students begin to compile their own lists of similes. They then may draw similes from these lists to use in their poems and stories.

I always point out that the two compared things should not be *too* similar. Nor should the students, in general, compare natural things to man-made things. Thus, "The coyote ran as fast as a wolf," or "The hawk soared like a jumbo jet," do not make good similes. "The coyote ran as fast as a wind-swept cloud" or "The hawk soared like my own emotions" are better.

7. Alliteration

Alliteration is a wonderful alternative to the end rhymes children sometimes tend to overuse. It is a technique (a kind of rhyme) that students find easy to learn, and its effect on their writing is more sophisticated than the predictable echoes of simple end rhymes. Alliteration, or "head rhyme," is simply the use of words in a line or lines that begin with the same sound. Thus, "The *f*eather *f*loated *f*rom the sky" is alliterative.

The songs and oratory of many tribes often rely heavily on alliteration, so a great number of Indian children are at least subconsciously aware of it. By developing their control of this type of rhyme, students will discover that their writing takes an enormous leap toward sounding more adult-like.

Students can be encouraged to include alliteration in their poetry *and* prose writing. When used effectively, alliteration is subtle; the average reader is usually not aware of its presence but senses a pleasing quality of sound. This echoing quality, I tell students, makes alliteration the "sneaky rhyme." I warn that it should never be overdone, that two or three alliterative words within a line or two are enough, unless you intend to write them as tongue twisters.

Subjects That Inspire Writing

While the suggestions above teach several basic writing techniques, the following suggestions offer writing opportunities that relate to the students as individuals and as members of an Indian tribe.

1. Solitary Activities

Have the students write a poem or story about doing something alone. Stress activities that give the children time to be meditative and perceptive of their environment. An initial discussion period can be held during which the students talk about the various activities they engage in all by themselves. From this discussion a list can be drawn up and written on the chalkboard. Possibilities include walking; running; riding a horse; hunting; fishing; craft work such as beading or basket making; gathering nuts or berries; herding cattle or sheep.

2. Tribal Activities

Have the students write a poem or story about a particular tribal activity. Again, a discussion can be held about the tribal activities the students participate in. Depending on the students' tribe, some of the following may be appropriate: tribal or inter-tribal powwows; tribal ceremonies; round dances; squaw dances; giveaways; sweat baths; tribal games such as hand games, arrow games, ball games ; tribal or inter-tribal fairs; tribal parades.

Students who actively participate in any of these (some students may be grass dancers or jingle dress dancers, for instance) can be encouraged to write from that point of view.

Note: Students should *never* be asked to write about a tribal activity or ceremony that by tribal custom should not be discussed or written about openly.

3. Ancestors

Hold discussions about the students' tribal heritage and their ancestors. In multi-tribal classes, include all represented tribes. In classes where students of other backgrounds are present (ie., African-American, German, Irish, Mexican), include those as well.

Points of discussion, as well as topics for individual poems and stories, can include their ancestors' form of shelter (Plains children would write about tipis, Apaches about wickiups, Navajos about hogans, etc.); what they ate and how they got food; the means by which they traveled; the kind of clothing they wore; the kinds of ceremonies they held; the games they played; the things they did in the evenings; how life was different for children then; how their ancestors might have thought about their own ancestors; when the ancestors thought about the future, what they might have wanted for the students, their descendants; some of the tribe's great leaders and what made them great.

Additionally, the students can write poems or stories about a single, fictional ancestor, either a man or a woman, giving a physical description and detailing an activity he or she is involved in; a single ancestral family—mother, father, children, and perhaps the extended family, again with physical descriptions and activities; or a large group of ancestors and what they are doing.

4. Elders

Most children experience a deep love and concern for their grandparents. Indian children, perhaps more than children of other heritages, are often uncommonly bound to their grandparents as a reflection of the importance of the extended family. Not all tribes continue the traditions of clan or extended family life, yet almost all Indian children hold their grandmothers and grandfathers in the highest esteem. The value of this bonding between generations, if not understood objectively, is profoundly felt at a subjective level by most young Indians. Writing about grandparents, and other elders, then, comes naturally and is enjoyable to Indian students.

After discussing grandparents and other elders, have the students write a poem or story about a grandparent, or about both a grandmother and grandfather. Students may write about deceased grandparents. Those who have never known their grandparents should be encouraged to write about an older person with whom they share a loving relationship, perhaps an aunt or an uncle, an older cousin, a family friend, or a respected tribal elder.

The students can write poems or stories about being alone with and engaged in an activity with a grandparent; a grandparent involved in an activity he or she enjoys; or a grandparent engaged in teaching them something important.

5. The Reservation

Have the students write a poem or story about being at a favorite location on their reservation, such as by a river, in a forested area, on a hill or mountain. They can describe how they got there (walked, jogged, rode a horse, etc.); the place itself; why they like this place; or any tribal significance the place may have. This piece of writing can end with the students contemplating the people of their reservation and making a wish for the future of their tribe.

Other good ideas for creative writing are offered in "Inspiring Creative Writing," by Perie Longo, a chapter that appeared in earlier editions of this book.

Anthologies of Native American Literature

Brant, Beth. *A Gathering of Spirit: A Collection by North American Indian Women.* Firebrand Books, 1988.

Bruchac, Joseph. *Songs from this Earth on Turtle's Back: Contemporary American Indian Poetry.* Greenfield Review Press, 1983.

Foss, Phillip. *The Clouds Threw This Light: Contemporary Native American Poetry.* Institute of American Indian Arts Press, 1983.

Hershfelder, Arlene, and Beverly Singer. *Rising Voices: Writings by Young Native Americans.* Charles Scribner's Sons, 1992.

Highwater, Jamake. *Words in the Blood.* Meridian, 1984.

Hobson, Geary. *The Remembered Earth: An Anthology of Contemporary Native American Literature.* University of New Mexico Press, 1980.

Lesley, Craig. *Talking Leaves: Contemporary Native American Short Stories.* Dell, 1991.

Lourie, Dick. *Come to Power: Eleven Contemporary American Indian Poets.* The Crossing Press, 1974.

Niatum, Duane. *Harper's Anthology of 20th Century Native American Poetry.* Harper & Row, 1988.

Oritz, Simon J. *Earth Power Coming: Short Fiction in Native American Literature.* Navajo Community College Press, 1983.

Rosen, Kenneth. *The Man to Send Rain Clouds: Contemporary Stories by American Indians.* Vintage Books, 1975.

Rosen, Kenneth. *Voices of the Rainbow: Contemporary Poetry by American Indians.* Seaver-Arbor House, 1975.

Velie, Alan R. *American Indian Literature: An Anthology.* University of Oklahoma Press, 1979.

Chapter 14
Teaching English to the Native American Student
by Rachel Schaffer

Many Native American students speak dialects of English which are nonstandard, differing from Standard American English in grammar and pronunciation. The differences may stem from native language influences on bilingual speakers for whom English is their second language and/or from linguistic isolation of the speakers. Native American students may therefore have special problems and needs when they study English grammar, composition, and speech that require special sensitivity and teaching methods. This chapter is meant to offer practical suggestions for becoming aware of your students' special needs in order to teach them English as effectively as possible.

General Recommendations

1. Learn Some Basic Linguistics

Taking an introductory linguistics course is important for all teachers of English, but especially for teachers of minority students, who often speak differently from what we are used to thinking of as "proper English." A basic linguistics course is valuable because it will show you how language structure is analyzed objectively and scientifically, and because it will tell you about certain judgmental attitudes toward language varieties, attitudes which have nothing to do with the varieties themselves, but rather with the social status of their speakers.

Linguists talk about Standard American English (SAE), the dialect used by people educated in the dominant culture in formal writing and speaking, and about nonstandard (never *substan-dard*) dialects (regional, rural, or ethnic varieties of English), which may differ slightly or greatly from SAE. Linguists also talk about the attitudes SAE speakers have toward the nonstandard dialects, which usually are *prescriptive* ones: nonstandard speech or writing is "bad," "wrong," or "incorrect." Too often, these attitudes also extend to the speakers themselves. Madelon Heatherington (1980, p. 216) describes this feeling: "A child who uses correct language is presumably neat, polite, well groomed, and a paragon of virtue, whereas a child who uses incorrect language probably falls asleep in church, plays hooky from school, dissects cats, and takes dope."

When you know more about how languages are structured, you realize that every variety of language, every dialect, has rules of its own. They may be different from SAE, but it is impossible to claim that they are better or worse (that would be like claiming that "plural" is better than "singular" or that addition is better than subtraction); each system meets the needs of its speakers equally well. Linguists therefore prefer to take an objective, *descriptive* attitude to all language varieties, one where you make no value judgments, but appreciate each variety on its own terms. Once you accept this attitude toward language variation, you can appreciate language differences in your students without condemning them, and your classroom will be an open, accepting, and constructive place for language learning. By understanding language structure, you can help reverse negative attitudes toward native languages and encourage Native Americans to become more enthusiastic about learning English by being enthusiastic yourself about their own languages and dialects.

2. *Learn Something about Your Students' Languages*

I also recommend, if possible, that you learn something about your students' first language(s). I don't mean that you should become fluent (although that would be a valuable learning experience for its own sake), but if you know what kinds of word endings the language has, or what features in general are very different from English, you will be in a better position to explain areas of English (pronunciation, sentence structure, vocabulary) that students have trouble with. It should be possible to find out about your students' language by reading articles or books written about it or by asking native speakers who are familiar with how to describe their language structure. You could even ask your students, comparing how their language does something with how English does it.

3. *Learn Something about Your Students' Native Culture*

It's also very important to learn as much as possible about your students' home culture, a point made over and over again throughout this book. In a language class it is even more important to encourage students to participate and practice their speaking skills than in other subject areas, since the goal of the class is improvement in all language skills. The cultural differences in the use of silence and leadership roles, or competition vs. cooperation, can affect the entire atmosphere of a language class. If you understand those aspects of your students' cultures that can affect their willingness to speak or write in class, then you can help increase their willingness to do so.

Many Native American cultures, for example, make use of a silent learning period during which children observe and listen, but do not speak. For students used to such a learning method, the Natural Approach, with its built-in silent period, may feel like the most comfortable (and indeed, natural) method of learning English (see the chapter on bilingual education in this book for a discussion of Krashen and Terrell's Natural Approach). The Natural Approach also stresses the importance of a low-anxiety classroom atmosphere where language mistakes are easily tolerated. For cultures where learners wait until they are ready before demonstrating skill (rather than go through the learning process and mistakes in public), this atmosphere will be friendlier and less intimidating to beginning speakers and writers.

4. Use a Variety of Teaching Methods

Once you know something about your students' native language, culture, and learning styles (see Chapter 6 of this book for discussion of learning styles), you will have a better idea of the teaching techniques that will be most effective for your class. But every class and every student is different in how material is most effectively learned. Lois A. Hirst and Christy Slavik (1990, p. 135) point out that "research indicates a higher learning rate and greater retention of learning when information is processed through multiple senses." Thus, using a variety of methods and approaches will ensure that information is presented in different ways, and perhaps encourage greater student involvement. Above all, according to Jack C. Richards (1990, pp. 48–49), "Relevant concerns for the teacher . . . focus not on the search for the best method, but rather on the circumstances and conditions under which more effective teaching and learning are accomplished." In order to discover those effective "circumstances and conditions," you should feel free to experiment and to let the students know that you are trying something new. Teaching techniques that I have found to be effective for Native American students in composition classes (and for most of my students, in fact) involve the use of written and spoken models, culturally relevant examples and topics, group work, and individual tutorials outside of class.

5. Use Culturally Relevant Models

Most people feel more comfortable learning by example, rather than being asked to try something totally new with no model to follow. For many Native cultures, especially, this is one of the primary learning strategies. I therefore give my composition students several written models of each kind of assignment I ask them to write, whether grammar exercises, one-paragraph essays, or full-length essays. We do written examples on the blackboard; for oral exercises, I do some examples first or ask for a group response from the entire class so that students who are not quite sure what is expected can see others do the task. We discuss the models in terms of both strong and weak points, avoiding excessively negative terms like "bad" or "wrong," and I make a special effort to make my expectations for each task very clear before we begin.

Many of my Native American students have been surprised that they can actually write an acceptable essay about topics from their everyday lives and cultural backgrounds. They often think that they should write only about suitably academic (technological? mainstream American?) topics, rather than about topics closer to their own experiences, such as family, hometown life, and cultural events, or about differences they have noticed between Indians and non-Indians, or benefits or problems of being Indian. If students have trouble thinking of essay topics, I help them focus on possible areas by asking them about home, friends, family, hobbies, interests, knowledge of their culture and first language, and other personal topics. Students who write about subjects they know and like will write longer, more interesting compositions.

I also try to use culturally relevant topics in my writing examples and grammar exercises. I use student essays as samples as much as possible, and I have a sentence combining exercise based on a Navajo short story ("Chee's Daughter," by Juanita Platero and Siyowin Miller), a part-of-speech exercise taken from a biography of a warrior (*Crazy Horse, the Strange Man of the Oglalas,* by Mari Sandoz), and sentences that describe activities familiar to my students (riding horses, going to school) or that use their names as examples of various grammar points or even test questions. An unlimited source of other adaptable materials for many different grade levels is provided by the publications of the Council for Indian Education.

6. Give Group Assignments

For students whose cultures encourage cooperation over individual competition, class activities and assignments that use group work may be especially effective and enjoyable learning experiences. In teaching grammar and writing, I have students work in pairs or in groups of three or four to help each other edit and proofread work, produce short pieces of writing, or do exercises, sometimes with the same grade assigned to each member of the group. In teaching students to do research writing, I use the group activities to prepare and practice various skills such as paraphrasing or quoting, and follow the class activities with an individual take-home assignment. Most of my students have liked the variety in activities and have appreciated the extra feedback from another person. Students weak in one area receive help from someone other than the teacher, and usually are able to help their partners in a different area, a good way to build confidence and self-esteem. Strong students who don't need help still receive valuable experience in teaching others and in clarifying their own knowledge. Above all, students accustomed to cooperative living can work together in their own way, without needing to make one student "group leader."

Group work is also valuable in encouraging participation from otherwise quiet or passive students. Shy or insecure students usually feel more comfortable speaking in small groups rather than in front of the whole class; lazy students are usually forced to contribute something by other group members or by their own pride, and you can thus rely on peer pressure to save you from playing the role of overseer. I you assign the group one grade for all members, you encourage cooperation even more, since all members then work toward a common reward.

7. Offer Individual Assistance

As part of the course requirements, many college-level ESL programs have weekly *tutorials* individual meetings outside of class between teachers and students ranging from 15 minutes to an hour. These meetings are used to discuss the students' particular problem areas, explain comments on papers in more detail, and find out how students feel about their class progress. In large classes, students can be paired for slightly longer tutorials, each listening to the other's session, but for teachers who have several large classes, scheduling occasional individual conferences may be the best they can do.

For elementary and secondary school classes, where there may be very little free time during the day for outside tutorials, it may be possible to work some individual time with your students into the English class itself, or into a study hall or free period. I realize that this sounds like a tremendous burden, but the potential benefits from improved rapport with students and warmer class atmosphere may be worth taking the time.

8. Make Your Expectations Clear

For some students (and not just minority students, by any means), each new teacher is a mystery. What a teacher considers to be good or bad class work, satisfactory progress, appropriate behavior, effective evaluation measures for assignments or progress—in general, everything a teacher expects from the students—will vary from teacher to teacher and class to class. If you treat your students as partners in the learning process rather than adversaries, you can help to diminish the mystery—and the anxiety that can accompany it—by making your expectations very clear at the beginning of the course and by remaining consistent from then on. This includes explaining the usefulness of course requirements, whether content-related or grade-related, and explaining the methods of evaluation to be used—letter grades vs. point values vs. checkmarks—and criteria for evaluation—what is considered to be a serious problem (in writing or participation, for example) and what doesn't matter. As much as possible, students need to know how your mind works so that they know what you will expect from them.

Students also need feedback from you on their performance in the form of honest but diplomatic comments, written or oral. Comments should be both positive and negative, with emphasis on the former. It is easy to see mistakes and correct them, but it seems harder for people to realize that good points also can and should be noticed and praised. When I write comments on students' papers, I use two columns, one marked + and one marked −, and I try to make the + column as long as I can. It may never be as long as the minus column (it usually takes longer to explain how to fix a problem than to explain why something is done well), but it should *always* have several items and words of encouragement.

9. Encourage Exposure to English

When children acquire a first language fluently and naturally, they do so simply by being exposed to native speakers of that language. It is useless try to to teach children to speak by teaching them formal grammar rules: no native speakers stop to think about a particular rule before they speak. The same principle of natural language learning is true for less fluent speakers of English: they need constant contact with native English speakers, interacting in normal conversations where they can both speak and listen. It is therefore extremely important that, if possible, you arrange extra social contacts with native English speakers, perhaps through field trips, regular social events, or guests for one-on-one conversations in the classroom.

10. Address Problems Created by Different Language Structures

Bilingual students most often have problems with those second language areas that differ most greatly from their first language structure—and such differences can be extreme. Some areas of greatest difference occur only rarely in English, so spending a lot of time on problems in these areas will not help students' fluency very much. Problem areas should be covered in detail when they interfere with the student's communication of ideas or when they appear often enough in the student's speech or writing to be distracting (which in itself can impair communication).

Two major areas of English that cause problems for second language learners are idioms and word endings, especially inflectional (grammatical) endings. Idioms are difficult because they are essentially multi-word vocabulary items: phrases of two or more words that have a completely arbitrary meaning rather than the literal meaning found by combining the meanings of each of the words in them. Thus, the idiom "you're *pulling my leg*" has nothing whatsoever to do with pulling legs, but instead has the special idiomatic meaning "you're *joking.*" Students therefore have to memorize sometimes very long strings of words with only one short, arbitrary meaning, and sometimes when they want to use an idiom from their first language, they will translate it *literally,* word for word, into English. Since most languages have completely different idioms for the same idea (where they even *have* idioms for the same idea), the results may be unsatisfactory, frustrating, and frequently humorous (but at the speaker's expense).

Idioms must therefore be taught in the same way as single-word vocabulary items, with careful explanation that *all* of the words in the expression go to make up one completely different meaning. Using vocabulary-building exercises, working idioms into class and informal discussions, and giving examples of the appropriate use of idioms can all help students become familiar with the most common ones in English.

Word endings in English also cause a great many problems for speakers of other languages because morphology (which deals with words, prefixes and suffixes, and how they are arranged) is the most variable level of language structure, differing tremendously from language to language in terms of which grammatical features languages mark with morphemes (affixes of some kind) and which they ignore. Among others, English has affixes that mark nouns as plural or possessive (-s, -'s) and verbs as singular, past tense, perfect, or progressive (-s, -ed, -ed or -en, -ing); and other affixes can change the meaning and/or part of speech of a word (pre-, un-, -ive, -ment, to mention a few). Many Native American languages handle verbs and nouns in an entirely different way, so that the distinctions marked in English are not at all natural or intuitive to second language learners, or the arrangement of morphemes seems strange. Furthermore, English has many words that take irregular endings that must be memorized separately as special cases (for example, *children, spoken,* etc.). You will therefore find it necessary to explain these endings carefully and often, giving your students frequent practice before their usage becomes clear, and it will probably be years before the errors in your students' speech and writing are reduced to a significant degree.

One area of strong difference between language endings is illustrated by Crow, a Montana Indian language which has one ending for singular verbs (with singular subjects) and another for plural verbs (Kates, 1980, pp. 30–31). English, on the other hand, marks singular verbs only in the present tense and only for third person verbs, as in *she walks, he sleeps, it looks rainy;* there are no separate singular/plural endings for any other tenses or persons (*I walk* vs. *we walk, he walked* vs. *they walked*). If you taught Crow students, you could therefore expect them to frequently omit the -s ending on third person singular present tense verbs in English, or to add -s to other persons of singular verbs in the present tense, in an effort to make the English verb forms more regular (as in *he go* or *they sits*). Crow also does not mark verbs for tense (past, present, future), as English does, and Crow speakers therefore frequently shift tense in writing or omit the -ed, -en, or -ing endings.

Other Indian languages also mark grammatical distinctions different from those in English. Hopi has different forms of the plural marker for concrete concepts such as ''10 men'' vs. cyclical concepts (repetitions of the same event) such as ''10 days'' or ''10 strokes on a bell'' (Whorf, 1956, p. 139). Navajo has verb stems which differ depending on the physical shape (flat sheet, cylinder, wire-shaped, etc.) of the subject or object. (Hale, 1973, pp. 207–208). Speakers trying to learn a second language do not usually try to impose their first language's distinctions on the second language, adding markers where there are none, but they do omit markers in the second language for which their first language lacks distinctions. These areas in particular will require you to offer much discussion, frequent practice, many examples, and where possible, direct comparison to the students' first language.

Conclusion

Because the classroom environment and interaction with the teacher have such a strong effect on students' willingness to speak and write, they can play a major role in the success and progress of students' language learning. The more you know about sources of influence on your students' learning process, the better prepared you will be to meet your students' needs. Students will learn under virtually any circumstances *if the motivation is there,* and a true understanding of the students' culture, language, and learning styles will help you to encourage and bring out your students' natural love of learning.

References for Further Reading

Cantoni-Harvey, Gina. *Content-Area Language Instruction: Approaches and Strategies.* Reading, MA: Addison-Wesley Publishing Company, 1987.

Cazden, Courtney B., Vera P. John, & Dell Hymes (eds.). *Functions of Language in the Classroom.* New York: Teachers College Press, 1972.

Celce-Murcia, Marianne, & Lois McIntosh (eds.). *Teaching English as a Second or Foreign Language.* Rowley, MA: Newbury House Publishers, Inc., 1979.

Fromkin, Victoria, & Robert Rodman. *An Introduction to Language.* 4th ed. New York: Holt, Rinehart and Winston, 1988.

Hale, Kenneth. The Role of American Indian Linguistics in Bilingual Education. In *Bilingualism in the Southwest,* Paul R. Turner, ed. Tucson, AZ: The University of Arizona Press, 1973.

Heatherington, Madelon. *How Language Works.* Cambridge, MA: Winthrop Publishers, Inc., 1980.

Hirst, Lois A., and Christy Slavik. Cooperative Approaches to Language Learning. In *Effective Language Education Practices and Native Language Survival: Proceedings of the 9th Annual International NALI Institute,* Jon Reyhner, ed. Choctaw, OK: Native American Language Issues, 1990.

Kates, Edith C., and Hu Matthews. *Crow Language Learning Guide.* Crow Agency, MT: Bilingual Materials Development Center, 1980.

Krashen, Stephen, & Tracy D. Terrell. *The Natural Approach: Language Acquisition in the Classroom.* Hayward, CA: Alemany Press, 1983.

McCarty, T. L., & Rachel Schaffer. Language and Literacy Development. In *Teaching the Indian Child: A Bilingual/Multicultural Approach,* 3rd ed. Jon Reyhner, ed. University of Oklahoma Press. In press.

Ohannessian, Sirarpi. The Language Problems of American Indian Children. In *The Language Education of Minority Children.* Bernard Spolsky, ed. Rowley, MA: Newbury House Publishers, Inc. 1972, pp. 13–24.

Oxford-Carpenter, Rebecca. Second Language Learning Strategies: What the Research Has to Say. *ERIC/CLL News Bulletin, 9*(1), 1985, 1, 3, 4.

Richards, Jack C. *The Language Teaching Matrix.* Cambridge: Cambridge University Press, 1990.

Schaffer, Rachel. English as a Second Language for the Native Student. In *Teaching the Indian Child: A Bilingual/Multicultural Approach,* 2nd ed. Jon Reyhner, ed. Eastern Montana College, Billings, Montana, 1988, pp. 97–116.

Schooling and Language Minority Students: A Theoretical Framework. Los Angeles: Evaluation, Dissemination and Assessment Center, California State University, Los Angeles, 1981.

Shaughnessy, Mina P. *Errors and Expectations.* NY: Oxford University Press, 1977.

Stewner-Manzanares, Gloria, et al. *Learning strategies in English as a Second Language Instruction: A Teacher's Guide.* Rosslyn, VA: National Clearinghouse for Bilingual Education, 1985.

Whorf, Benjamin Lee. *Language, Thought, and Reality,* ed. by John B. Carroll. Cambridge: The M.I.T. Press, 1956.

Williams, James D., and Grace Capizzi Snipper. *Literacy and Bilingualism.* New York: Longman, 1990.

Other Resources for Further Information

Organizations and Journals

Teachers of English to Speakers of Other Languages (TESOL), TESOL Central Office, 201 D.C. Transit Building, Georgetown University, Washington, D.C. 20057. Has an annual meeting and Summer Institute. Publishes the *TESOL Quarterly* and *TESOL Newsletter.*

National Council of Teachers of English (NCTE), 1111 Kenyon Road, Urbana, Illinois 61801. Has regional and national meetings annually.

Publishes *College Composition and Communication, College English, English Journal* (secondary level), and *Language Arts* (primary level), and offers special member discounts on books and other publications.

Clearinghouses:

Educational Resources Information Center/Clearinghouse on Languages and Linguistics (ERIC/CLL), Center for Applied Linguistics, 3520 Prospect St. NW, Washington, D.C. 20007. Publishes the *ERIC/CLL News Bulletin* and a wide variety of monographs and specialized bibliographies.

Bibliographies of ESL Materials:

Aronis, Christine. *Annotated Bibliography of ESL Materials.* TESOL, Washington, DC., 1983.

LeCertua, Patrick J., Carolyn M. Reeves, and Keith Groff (eds.). *ESL Source Book: A Selective Bibliography for Second Language Teachers.* Department of Education, Idaho, 1986.

Reich, William P., and Jennifer C. Gage (compilers). *Guide to Materials for English as a Second Language.* National Clearinghouse for Bilingual Education, 1981.

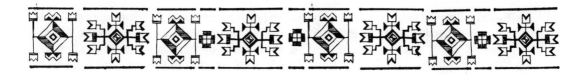

Chapter 15
Eliminating Language Barriers: Figurative English for Native Students
By Mick Fedullo

While there continues to be a need to develop educational curricula that are relevant to the Indian student's perspective and identity as an Indian, there also exists the need for educators of Indians to examine current curricula and textbooks already in use, and to adjust these to the specific and unique needs of Indian children. At most Indian schools, the English language texts remain those that were designed for mainstream, non-Indian students. *What* is taught is based upon the needs of middle-class white students.

In my years as a language development consultant working on twenty-five reservations in the United States and Canada, I have repeatedly observed ways in which existing English texts fail the Indian child. One of these is a lack of extensive teaching of American English idioms. The need to teach idioms as multi-word vocabulary items is discussed in this book by Rachel Schaffer. In this chapter I will discuss this need further, connect it to the teaching of general figurative English, and offer suggestions on how to incorporate this language dimension into the classroom. In so doing, I am proposing that figurative mannerisms are identifiable, teachable, and should be taught to the Indian student at all grade levels with the same emphasis with which vocabulary is taught.

Types of Figurative Language

By figurative English, I mean any verbal or written expression whose meaning is different from what a literal rendering of the words would suggest. Some figurative expressions can be communicated in writing, while others are communicated in speech by shifts in pitch, emphasis, or tone. Seven basic categories of figurative English, and their definitions, are:

1. **Idiom:** An expression whose meaning cannot be derived from its individual elements. Example: "What's the matter, cat got your tongue?" This idiom means, "Can't talk?" and has nothing to do with cats. Because they represent a major segment of American English, and because there are so many of them in use, an emphasis will be placed on the teaching of idioms.

2. **Euphemism:** A mild, indirect, or vague expression substituted for one thought to be offensive, harsh, or blunt. Example: "The old man passed away last week." Here, "passed away" is substituted for "died." Many euphemisms are also idiomatic: "Charlie got the pink slip." Here, "pink slip" is substituted for "dismissed" or "fired."

3. **Metaphor and simile:** A word, phrase, or extended expression applied to an object or concept it does not literally denote, in order to suggest comparison with another object or concept. Example: "Her project soared like an eagle until she overspent her budget; then it lost its feathers and crashed to the ground."

4. **Pun:** A word or combination of words used humorously so as to emphasize different meanings or applications, or the use of words that are alike or nearly alike in sound but different in meaning. Also called a *play on words*. Example:

   "This coffee tastes like mud."

   "It was only ground this morning."

   or

   "Goblin your food is bad for your elf."

5. **Irony:** A figure of speech in which the intended meaning is the direct opposite of the meaning of the words used. Irony in speech is often indicated by a sarcastic tone of voice. Example: "On a day of particularly bad weather, he mumbled, 'What a nice afternoon.' "

6. **Overstatement (or hyperbole):** A word or words used to exaggerate. Example: "If I don't get my homework done, my teacher will kill me."

7. **Understatement:** A word or words used to represent something less strongly or strikingly than the facts would bear out. Example:

   "I heard on the news that you had a bad earthquake in your area."

   "Well, yes, we had a little roller."

   Doctors often use understatement with the phrase, "This won't hurt."

Causes of Problems

Most English curricula tend to teach literal English, with an emphasis on vocabulary building. But, in truth, non-Indians communicate with an almost equal use of figurative English. Figurative usage is so widespread that mainstream children learn it from everyday discourse, not from their English lessons. Beyond relatively few and small units, there is not a *need* to teach figurative English to mainstream students. Vocabulary acquisition of single word items is prioritized over the teaching of idioms, euphemisms, and the other figures of speech. For Indian children, however, we must re-prioritize, or adjust, the English curriculum to address the lack of extensive figurative English usage among them. We must consider both literal and figurative English as equally important, and teach them with equal emphasis.

What has caused this insufficiency of figurative English among American Indians? First, it must be recognized that Indian children are educationally different; that is, the history of formal education for Indians radically differs from the history of white mainstream education. For a hundred years the Bureau of Indian Affairs (and a large number of religious schools) controlled Indian education, and their major goal was direct and unrelenting: assimilation of their Indian charges. This goal could never have been fully achieved, since resistance among Indians endured from generation to generation. Thus, many Indians had, and still have, a negative attitude toward "white" education, and attended school in "body" but not in "spirit."

It must also be recognized that Indian children are linguistically different from mainstream children. Whether they are English-first or ESL students, the English they use is colored by distinct influences and mannerisms of a specific native language. Teachers often subconsciously assume that if an Indian student speaks English, the child must share with mainstream students a common linguistic background. This is simply not true.

Historically, Indian students learned a composite English, which included the standard usage in their textbooks, the colloquial usage of their teachers, and the slang and vulgarisms of employees at the boarding schools and the agencies. The ordinary distinctions between these different dictions that non-Indian children learn through discourse were inadequately taught to Indian students.

Today, most reservation children do not have regular contact with non-Indians outside of school, so dimensions of the English language, such as figurative expressions, often strike the Indian child as unfamiliar and even bizarre.

Several years ago, I learned of a situation in which a class of sixth grade Navajo students had just begun taking a test. One boy, distracted as youngsters so often are by some flight of childhood fancy, did not go immediately on task. His teacher said to him, "Come on, now, let's get the ball rolling." Unfamiliar with the idiom, the boy spent the next several minutes trying to figure out why the teacher had told him to roll a ball. What ball? Roll it where? What did this have to do with the test? Valuable time was lost, and the boy, not finishing the test, scored low, primarily because the teacher was unaware that she had mis-communicated with the boy.

Such mis-communications are not the exception in many Indian classrooms—rather, they occur on a daily basis and contribute to the difficulties Indian students have in learning English. Further, as in the case above, it is usually the Indian student who is penalized as a result of such mis-communications.

In another case, a teacher at a Tohono O'odham school in Arizona caught herself in just such a situation the day after attending a workshop on this issue. She stopped me in the hallway and related the events of that morning: During the third period, she taught only one boy who had been selected for her gifted and talented program. After that morning's session, as the boy walked toward the door, she said to him, "You know, you're fifteen going on thirty." She then noticed the puzzled look on the boy's face, and she asked him if he knew what she meant. He did not. He had never heard the phrase. She explained that it meant he was very mature for his young age. Thus the encounter ended. But the teacher, in telling me this story, was astonished. She said, "In all my years of teaching here, I never considered that these students would not understand such phrases."

She also understood the possible negative consequences of such a mis-communication. Had she not caught the fact that the boy was confused by what she had said, and had she not explained the idiomatic phrase, what might the boy have gone away thinking? A number of negative interpretations were clearly possible. He could have concluded that she was telling him that he looked much older than he really was, and this would be distressing to any teenager. On the other hand, he might even have thought that she was making an advance toward him. In any event, a situation in which a teacher believed she was enhancing a student's self-esteem could have ended with the opposite effect, and she would have been completely unaware of it.

The preceding are but two of the many examples I have documented over the last few years, and they should alert us to the fact that if, in any given classroom, the probability of figurative English mis-communications exists, then we had better begin addressing the problem as soon as possible.

Recommendations for the Classroom

Such mis-communications are not restricted to the misunderstanding of idioms. They arise, as well, out of misunderstandings of the other figurative mannerisms described above. Metaphorical expressions, puns, irony, overstatements and understatements may confuse the Indian child, and therefore should be discussed frequently. These mannerisms tend to be spontaneous and usually original, so teaching them is best done within the contexts in which students encounter them, such as verbal exchanges, books, magazines, recordings, video tapes, and films.

There are, however, thousands of idioms and euphemisms that have become a fixed part of American English. These common expressions represent an extension of vocabulary, and should be taught as multi-word vocabulary items.

In the classroom, the teacher can:

1. Provide a Dictionary of Idioms

There are several very good idiom dictionaries on the market. The problem with most of them is that they include vulgarisms that are inappropriate in school. Perhaps the most thorough idiom dictionary that *does not* contain vulgarisms is *NTC's American Idioms Dictionary*. Teachers can use this book to build lists of idioms they will teach, as well as make it available to the students.

There are also books for children that teach idioms, such as *101 American English Idioms* by Harry Collis. These are certainly useful, though the number of idioms they offer is clearly inadequate.

Unfortunately, there are very few dictionaries of euphemisms. One of the most complete is *The Faber Dictionary of Euphemisms* by R. W. Holder. One quickly discovers, glancing through a volume like this, that most euphemisms refer to violent or sexual acts, or to death. This is not surprising, given the very definition that a euphemism is a substitute for something thought to be offensive, harsh, or blunt. Many euphemisms are certainly not meant for children's eyes, but the "Faber" is a useful resource for teachers.

2. Increase Self-awareness

It is often difficult for us to hear ourselves using figurative rather than literal English, yet making this distinction in our own speech is the first step in being able to effectively teach the figurative mannerisms Indian children need to learn.

We must hear ourselves as we speak to our students; we must learn to monitor our words as we utter them. When we catch ourselves using a figurative expression, we should stop and ask the students if they know what we mean by the expression. If an immediate answer is not forthcoming, we should offer the expression's meaning. Repeating the expression and its meaning several times, and then repeating them in the context of what we have said, will place the figurative expression in the light of understanding.

"Okay, class, let's get the ball rolling. . . . Do you all know what 'get the ball rolling' means? It's another idiom. It means, 'get started.' When someone tells you to 'get the ball rolling,' they are telling you to 'get started.' They are telling you to 'begin.' I just asked the class to get the ball rolling. What do I want you to do?"

3. Create Posters

Students can create weekly, biweekly, or monthly posters of idioms and euphemisms, to be hung in the classroom. Each poster displays a figurative phrase and the student's illustration of what a literal meaning might be. (For "cat got your tongue?", a student might draw a cat grabbing a person's tongue.) The actual meaning of the expression would also appear on the poster.

4. Keep Journals

Have the students keep their own individual idiom journals, into which they enter the idioms and euphemisms they learn throughout the school year. The journals can be used as continually expanding reference books. The students could write in their journals sentences using the expressions. They could also illustrate their own journals.

> *Catch forty winks:* take a short nap. I'm tired today. When I get home, I'm going to catch forty winks.

5. Make Checklists

A master checklist can be made. Students check off idioms whose meanings they have learned. Students should be able to use an idiom in an appropriate context.

6. Conduct Searches

Students keep with them a notebook into which they write down suspected idioms or other figurative expressions that they come across in books, magazines, newspapers, videos, films, presentations, conversations. One evening a week may be assigned for the students to search for figurative language, no matter what they are going to do that night (watch television, go to a move, attend a sports event, etc.).

Time is set aside in the classroom for the students to offer their suspected idioms, and every offering should be considered thoroughly—is it an idiom, or is it perhaps another form of figurative language? Each phrase should be classified, defined, and, if it is not already there, added to the appropriate figurative category. True idioms can be immediately added to displays, journals, and checklists, even if they are not on the current teaching list.

Schoolwide Possibilities

School-wide, teachers and administrators can:

1. Include Idioms in Announcements

If your school has regular morning or afternoon announcements broadcast over an intercom system, include in the announcements one or two idioms. Students in the classroom can then identify the idioms and discuss their meanings.

2. Use Idioms in School Newsletters/Newspapers

If your school published a newsletter or newspaper, include in each issue several idiomatic expressions that the students can search for, identity, and define. This could serve as the basis for a lively school-wide contest.

3. Put Idioms on Banners and Fliers

Idiomatic expressions can be used on sports banners ("The Sky's the Limit!") as well as on fliers and posters announcing activities and events ("A Student Performance That Will Knock Your Socks Off!").

References for Further Reading

Collis, Harry. *101 American English Idioms: Understanding and Speaking English Like an American.* National Textbook Company, 1990.

Collis, Harry. *101 American English Idioms: Teacher's Manual and Resource Book.* National Textbook Company, 1990.

Spears, Richard A. *Essential American Idioms.* Nation Textbook Company, 1990.

Spears, Richard A. *NTC's American Idioms Dictionary.* National Textbook Company, 1991.

Rogers, James. *The Dictionary of Cliches.* Ballantine Books, 1989.

Terban, Marvin. *Mad as a Wet Hen! and Other Funny Idioms.* Clarion Books, 1987.

Terban, Marvin. *Punching the Clock: Funny Action Idioms.* Clarion Books, 1990.

Three Blackfeet Bilingual Education teachers plan together.

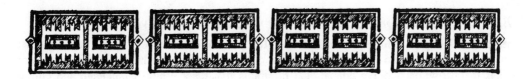

Chapter 16
Teaching the Native Language
by Jon Reyhner

Why Bilingual Education?

Many Indians see the loss of their language as "one of the most critical problems" facing Indian people today. They consider it essential that their children be taught in two languages, their own and that of the dominant society.

The opportunity to become fluent and be educated in both languages is important for four reasons.

1. The Native Language Is Essential to the Maintenance of the Culture

Although facts and information can be stated in any language, the beliefs, feelings, and way of looking at the world of a culture are diluted or lost when put into another language. Language and culture develop together. The words and structure of a language express the feelings of a people and their culture. Supposedly parallel words in another language do not accurately portray those feelings. Therefore changing to a different language necessarily results in a loss of part of the culture.

2. The Loss of Language Leads to a Breakdown in Communication Between Children and Their Grandparents and Denies Children Their Heritage

Tribal heritage provides a sense of group membership and belonging that is badly needed in an overly individualistic and materialistic modern society. In the words of John Collier, modern society has lost the "passion and reverence for human personality and for the web of life and the earth which the American Indians have tended as a central sacred fire."

3. Repression of the Native Language Is Destructive to Self-Concept

Forcing Indian children to suddenly give up their language and speak only English reinforces the idea prevalent in many schools that the native language and culture are of little or no value, thus effectively destroying the self-concept of many students.

4. Bilingual Instruction Results in Higher Academic Achievement

Research on bilingual education substantiates the conclusion that subtractive educational programs that seek to replace native language and culture with English language and culture cause students to fail, while additive educational programs that teach English language and culture in addition to the native language and culture create the conditions for students to succeed in their schoolwork.

In a review of the research on bilingual education, Cummins (1981) found a lot of studies reporting "that bilingual children are more cognitively flexible in certain respects and better able to analyze linguistic meaning than monolingual children." The U.S. Secretary of Education's Indian Nations at Risk Task Force found that "bilingual and multilingual children have a greater opportunity to develop their analytical and conceptual skills than monolingual children" and "schools that respect and support a student's language and culture are significantly more successful in educating those students" (Indian, pp. 14 and 16).

Many Indian parents, believing it will help their students in school, encourage their children to speak only English. Bernadine Featherly (1985), after research on Crow Indian students and an extensive review of the research, concluded that native language speaking parents should not try to "teach" their children to speak English. If the parents are not fluent in English, the children cannot become fluent by listening to them, so if they do not learn the Native language, they will start school without fluency in any language for the type of thought and expression school requires. Children who are fluent in one language have no difficulty learning a second or a third language, but children who do not become fluent in a language before entering school are usually handicapped throughout their lives. A well-planned maintenance bilingual program as described below can teach native language-speaking children the English language skills they need to live and work in the dominant English speaking society, if they so desire, on an equal basis with native English speakers.

Types of Bilingual Programs

There are four basic types of programs for bilingual students: (1) submersion, (2) immersion, (3) transitional, and (4) maintenance.

Submersion-type programs have historically been used with Indian students. They are placed in regular all-English classrooms with little or no special attention and left to "sink or swim." The result of traditional English-only "submersion programs" for Indian students is that their achievement in schools falls further behind whites as they progress through their school years. The whole history of Indian education is proof of the ineffectiveness of this system.

Immersion bilingual programs use the second language extensively to give students an environment where they are "immersed" in the second language. Immersion teachers speak to the children only in the language to be learned but, unlike in the "submersion" classroom, students are exposed to special second language teaching methods.

This type of program has been found to be very effective in teaching French and Spanish to middle-class English speaking students with no long term negative effects on children's skills in using English. However, such programs are not intended to replace the home language. English language instruction is continued in school or is brought back after an initial period of all second language instruction. This could be an effective means of teaching native language fluency to Indian students who are not fluent in their own language, or to non-Indian students in Indian communities. It has been effective in teaching their own languages to Native people in New Zealand and Hawaii. However, such programs used to teach English to Indian students lack the advantage of the students' own languages being the accepted language of society as is true for English speakers, nor do students revert back to their native languages as the main language of instruction. Therefore they tend to lose their first language skills.

For Indians, immersion programs can reinforce feelings of inferiority and worthlessness by ignoring the home language and culture of the child. Dominated minorities such as Indians do better in school if their language and culture are a part of the school's curriculum.

Transitional bilingual programs are designed to teach English to language minority students as quickly as possible. While children are taught extensively in their native language during their first year of school, instruction in English is quickly phased in so that by about fourth grade all instruction is in English. Transitional programs do little to promote native language skills. Even though they are the most common form of bilingual programs in the United States, Cummins, who reviewed a great deal of research on bilingual education, found no educational justification for transitional bilingual programs. He also found that quick exiting of students from transitional bilingual programs to the regular English-only program had negative effects.

Maintenance bilingual programs place the most emphasis on developing children's native as well as English language abilities. They are designed to teach reading, writing, and some other subjects in the native language of the child while adding English language skills and instruction in some subjects. Begun in 1967, the maintenance bilingual program at Rock Point Community School on the Navajo Reservation in Arizona graduates students who can read and write in Navajo and who also test out on English language standardized achievement tests superior to comparable Indian students who have not had a bilingual education. At Rock Point most students enter school speaking mostly or only Navajo, and they are taught to read first in Navajo. Students add English reading instruction starting in the middle of the second grade. In kindergarten seventy percent of the instruction is in Navajo with the rest of the time spent teaching students oral English. By second grade students are receiving half their instruction in English and half in Navajo. In the upper grades fifteen to twenty percent of the instruction is in Navajo with the rest in English. In the early grades, mathematics are taught first in Navajo and then the specialized English vocabulary is taught later. By teaching content area subjects in the early grades in Navajo, Rock Point students are not held back in those subjects until they learn English. The concepts they learn in Navajo are retained and usable by the student later in either language, and almost all basic reading skills learned in the Navajo reading program transfer into the English reading program.

In 1983 Rock Point students by eighth grade outperformed Navajo students in neighboring public schools, other Navajo speaking students throughout the reservation, and other Arizona Indian students in Reading on the California Achievement Test. On the grammar (written English) portion of the test the results were much the same. In mathematics, the Rock Point students did even better, outperforming the comparison groups and approaching or exceeding national averages. It is important to remember these excellent results did not appear right away; they were the result of 16 years of bilingual curriculum development at Rock Point.

Bernard Spolsky of the University of New Mexico summed up the results of the Rock Point School's education program:

> In a community that respects its own language but wishes its children to learn another, a good bilingual program that starts with the bulk of instruction in the child's native language and moves

systematically toward the standard language will achieve better results in standard language competence than a program that refuses to recognize the existence of the native language. (Rosier & Holm, 1980, p. vi)

The Natural Approach to Language Acquisition

Linguists and educators warn against a translation approach to teaching any language. Krashen and Terrell (1983) have developed what they call "The Natural Approach to Learning Languages." This method is equally effective in teaching English to Native language speakers and in teaching an Indian language to students more fluent in English.

The first principle of this approach is that *"comprehension precedes production."*

This implies,

1. The instructor always uses the target language (the language to be learned).
2. The focus of the communication is on a topic of interest to the student.
3. The instructor strives at all times to help the student understand.

The second principle is that *language production,* whether oral or written, *is allowed to emerge in stages,* first nonverbal communication, second by single words such as yes or no, third by combinations of two or three words, fourth by phrases, fifth by sentences, and finally by more complex discourse. In the beginning students use a lot of incorrect grammar and pronunciation. Krashen and Terrell emphasize in their method that "the students are not forced to speak before they are ready" and that "speech errors which do not interfere with communication are not corrected."

The third principle is that *the goal of language acquisition is communication.* Each classroom activity or lesson is organized around a topic rather than a grammatical structure. Topics include field trips students are taking, classroom science activities students are doing, or games students are playing. Students need to do more than just talk about a topic; they need to participate in associated activities. Children learn from their own experiences, not other people's.

Krashen and Terrell's fourth principle is that classroom activities must not put any kind of stress on the students to perform beyond their capabilities:

An environment which is conducive to acquisition must be created by the instructor—low anxiety level, good rapport with the teacher, friendly relationship with other students—otherwise acquisition will be impossible. Such an atmosphere is not a luxury but a necessity. (p. 21)

By not focusing on vocabulary, such as memorizing the names of numbers and colors, or grammar, students acquire language skills they can use. Only if students use the language skills they acquire will they remember them. It is important that an environment both inside and outside of school be provided where a student can use newly acquired language skills. The home is an obvious place to use the native language, but some tribes have also started radio and television stations with native language programming.

Students must also have environments where they can use the language they are learning in conversation. One of the important factors in the success of the Rock Point Community School curriculum is that students are encouraged and required to talk and write a lot in both languages. One Cheyenne family whose children never spoke the Cheyenne language set aside two days each week, Friday and Saturday, in which no English would be spoken in the home. If any family members spoke English, they were ignored as if they were not heard. It became an enjoyable activity for the children and parents together, and the children soon became relaxed in the use of their native language.

Teaching Materials for Bilingual Programs

A spoken language can be taught without written materials, but the attempt is seldom successful in the school setting. However, it is pointless to teach reading in an Indian language if only a few books are available in that language. The degree to which teaching reading and writing is stressed will depend upon the amount of printed material available in the language. Commercial publishers are not interested in the small markets which even the largest tribes represent. However, you may find some material available from missionary organizations and the Wycliffe Bible Translators, both of which have a long history of missionary interest in translating religious works into Indian languages.

Bilingual Materials Development Centers were funded in the 1990s by Title VII of the Bilingual Education Act to produce materials that were not available through commercial sources. These Centers have printed materials in many Indian languages. However, the amount of native language materials is hardly adequate for real bilingual teaching even for the Navajos, who are by far the largest tribe in the United States and have a history of concern for the preservation of their language. Even less material is available in the native languages of other tribes.

Even when Native language material is available, it seldom has the controlled vocabulary needed to make beginning reading easier for students. Stories transcribed from elders may contain words with which Indian children are unfamiliar. An excellent method for avoiding inappropriate vocabulary in beginning reading is the "language experience" approach to teaching reading, discussed in more detail in the chapters on Whole Language and developing reading skills. The methods discussed there are equally applicable to either English or the Native language.

Examples of Materials Development at the Local Level

As a director of a bilingual program on the Blackfeet Reservation, I arranged for the taping of some elders telling traditional and historical stories in the Blackfeet language. These stories were then transcribed by a Blackfeet linguist working with the Blackfeet Dictionary Project at the University of Lethbridge. A selection was then made from these stories to make up a booklet, *Stories of Our Blackfeet Grandmothers,* for use with intermediate grade students (published by the Council for Indian Education in 1984).

Students can draw pictures and have their teacher write down stories they tell about their pictures or photographs can be taken of the community and made into a book with student supplied text from what they answer when asked, "Tell me about this picture." Two examples of materials that can be produced with the help of younger students are *Heart Butte: A Blackfeet Indian Community* (1984) and *We Live on an Indian Reservation* (1981), both of which are available from the Council for Indian Education. Older students can take pictures, interview elders and other community members, and write their own book. An example that includes work of older students at Rock Point Community School is *Between Sacred Mountains* (published by The University of Arizona Press in 1984).

The poet Mick Fedullo has edited a number of booklets of expressive poetry by Indian students. Some of the students' teachers believed that their students had no ability to write expressive poetry in English until they observed the enthusiasm for writing under Mick Fedullo and saw the results. While this poetry is in English, the same expressive language activities can be done in the native language. A good example is the booklet, *Hman Qaj Gwe Inuudja,* done in Havasupai at Havasupai Elementary School in 1985 with the assistance of Akira Yamamoto, a Yuman language linguist.

For primary grade children, self-made books, hand printed and student illustrated, work fine and are appreciated by parents. For older children, more elaborate books are also useful. Only a few years ago, to publish such language experience books would have required expensive professional typesetting and printing. The special characters required by most Indian language orthographies added to that expense. Today with micro-computers and laser printers, good quality material can be produced in school at a fraction of the former costs, and, using photocopying machines, an unlimited number of copies can be made relatively inexpensively.

A note of caution needs to be given to teachers who want to publish native language material with cultural content. Some tribes require prior approval of such material by a tribal cultural committee before it can be printed. In all cases, local people should be involved in producing and editing traditional stories.

The Role of Linguists

A full fledged bilingual program requires teaching reading in the native language. There are over two hundred Indian languages still in use in the United States. A writing system (orthography) has to be developed for each of these languages if it is to be written. Robert St. Clair (1982) feels that while professional linguists tend to develop sophisticated orthographies that reflect the grammatical structure of the language, literacy programs for elementary schools need simple, practical writing systems similar to the Initial Teaching Alphabet (i.t.a.). A linguist with an educational background is to be preferred in developing a simplified orthography suitable for use with children. Sources of linguistic help for schools and tribes include universities, the Wycliffe Bible Translators who are found on many reservations, and a number of Indian linguists who have been trained at the Massachusetts Institute of Technology, University of Arizona, and other schools with linguistic departments that have shown an interest in Indian languages.

In addition to simple, practical phonetic orthographies, St. Clair sees the need for simple classroom dictionaries of frequently used words, an "experience based dictionary," which only includes common definitions of words and uses them in sample sentences. With the help of Indian people, missionaries have researched and published dictionaries such as the Franciscan Fathers' *An Ethnologic Dictionary of the Navajo Language* (St. Michael's Press, St. Michael's, AZ, 1910) and the English-Cheyenne Dictionary (Council for Indian Education, Billings, MT, 1976) produced with the help of the Wycliffe Bible Translators. Competing tribal dialects should not be a problem since the same orthography can be used with different dialects.

Robert St. Clair feels that tribal elders have an important role to play in a bilingual program:

> If there are any tribal members who can really save the program [of language renewal], they are the elders. These are people who may be in the sixty- to eighty-year-old range who have actually spoken the language fluently as children and who fully participated in the ways of the tribe. They still know the ceremonies and are the most valuable elements in any language renewal program. The secret is to get them to work with young children. They can teach them to speak the language and, if circumstances permit, the children can teach them how to read and write in the new system. This program, then, requires parental as well as communal support. (1982, p. 8)

In New Zealand, Maori grandparents are running a volunteer program of day care centers which feature an immersion program in the Maori language. A similar program with university help is being run in Hawaii.

Conclusion

Partly in response to the "English-only" movement that is currently promoting a constitutional amendment to make English the official language of the United States, today there is a renewed interest in American Indian languages. A number of tribal governments, including the Navajo, Northern Ute, and Pascua Yaqui, have passed tribal language policies. In 1990, as a result of lobbying by Indian people, President Bush signed into law the Native American Languages Act (Title 1 of Public Law 101–477). In this act the U.S. government finds that "the status of the cultures and languages of Native Americans is unique and the United States has the responsibility to act together with Native Americans to ensure the survival of these unique cultures and languages." The act declares that there is "convincing evidence" that student achievement, community pride, and educational opportunity are "clearly and directly tied to respect for, and support of, the first language of the child."

The act goes on to declare it the policy of the United States to "preserve, protect, and promote the rights and freedom of Native Americans to use, practice, and develop Native American languages" and to "recognize the right of Indian tribes and other Native American governing bodies to use the Native American languages as a medium of instruction in all schools funded by the Secretary of the Interior." In addition, the act affirms "the right of Native Americans to express themselves through the use of Native American languages shall not be restricted in any public proceeding, including publicly supported education programs."

In 1991, the U.S. Secretary of Education's Indian Nations at Risk Task Force issued its final report, giving strong support for bilingual/bicultural Indian education. The second of the ten goals for Indian education set by the Task Force states that "by the year 2000 all schools will offer Native students the opportunity to maintain and develop their tribal languages and will create a multicultural environment that enhances the many cultures represented in the school." In 1992, President Bush and the Congress of the United States convened a White House Conference on Indian Education with representatives of both reservation and urban Indians. This White House Conference again gave strong support to keeping American Indian languages and cultures alive. Kenji Hakuta concluded a historical study of bilingual education with the thought that,

> Perhaps the rosiest future for bilingual education in the United States can be attained by dissolving the paradoxical attitude of admiration and pride for school-attained bilingualism on the one hand and scorn and shame for home-brewed immigrant [and Indian] bilingualism on the other. The goals of the educational system could be seen as the development of all students as functional bilinguals, including monolingual English-speakers. The motive is linguistic, cognitive, and cultural enrichment. . . . (1986, p. 229)

I am not recommending native language instruction as a substitute for English language instruction or English as a substitute for the Native language, but the development of truly bilingual students, at home in two languages. In seeking to preserve their languages and cultural heritage, tribes are not rejecting the importance of English language instruction for their children. No tribe has recommended that restoration of their language outrank the importance of teaching English (Leap, 1982).

Assimilation is not a one-way street to progress and Native Americans can learn to participate successfully in white society *and,* at the same time, retain their language and traditional Indian values to become what Malcolm McFee (1968) has described as the 150% man. This 150% person is the goal of bilingual education.

Northern Cheyenne educator Dick Littlebear (1990, p. 8) sees "our native languages nurturing our spirits and hearts and the English language as sustenance for our bodies."

Other Resources for Further Information

Evans, G. E., K. Abbey, and D. Reed. *Bibliography of Language Arts Materials for Native North Americans: Bilingual, English as a Second Language and Native Language Materials 1965-1976.* Los Angeles, CA: American Indian Studies Center, UCLA. 1977.

Evans, G. E., and K. Abbey. *Bibliography of Language Arts Materials for Native North Americans: Bilingual, English as a Second Language and Native Language Material, 1975- 1976: With Supplemental Entries for 1965- 1976.* Los Angeles, CA: American Indian Studies Center, UCLA. 1979.

National Association for Bilingual Education (NABE), 1201 16th St., N.W., Room 407, Washington, D.C. 20036, Phone 202 822 7870. Has annual meetings with workshops for teachers. Publishes *NABE News* and *NABE Journal.* Has state affiliates.

References for Further Reading

Cummins, Jim. *Bilingualism and Special Education: Issues in Assessment and Pedagogy.* San Diego: CA: College-Hill Press, 1984.

Cummins, Jim. "Empowering Minority Students: A Framework for Intervention." *Harvard Educational Review,* 56 1986, pp. 18–36.

Cummins, Jim. "The Role of Primary Language Development in Promoting Educational Success for Minority Students." In California State Department of Education, *Schooling and Language Minority Students.* Los Angeles, California State University at Los Angeles, 1981.

Collier, John. *The Indians of the Americas.* New York: W. W. Norton, 1947.

Featherly, Bernadine. "The Relation between the Oral Language Proficiency and Reading Achievement of First Grade Crow Children." *Dissertation Abstracts International,* 46, 2903A.

Fuchs, Estelle, and Robert J. Havighurst. *To Live on This Earth: American Indian Education.* Garden City, NY: Anchor Books, 1973. (Reprinted by the University of New Mexico Press, 1983).

Hakuta, Kenji. *Mirror of Language: The Debate on Bilingualism.* New York: Basic Books, 1986.

Indian Nations at Risk Task Force. *Indian Nations at Risk: An Educational Strategy for Action.* Washington, D.C.: U.S. Department of Education, 1991. (Final Report of the Indian Nations at Risk Task Force)

Krashen, Stephen. *Inquiries and Insights.* Hayward, CA: Alemany Press, 1985.

Krashen, Stephen, and T. C. Tracy. *The Natural Approach: Acquisition in the Classroom.* Hayward, CA: Alemany Press, 1983.

Leap, William. "Roles for the Linguist in Indian Bilingual Education." In *Language Renewal among American Indian Tribes,* edited by R. St. Clair and W. Leap, pp. 19–30. Rosslyn, VI: National Clearinghouse for Bilingual Education, 1982.

Littlebear, Dick. "Keynote Address: Effective Language Education Practices and Native Language Survival." In Jon Reyhner (Ed.), *Effective Language Education Practices and Native Language Survival* (pp. 1–8). Choctaw, OK: Native American Language Issues, 1990.

McFee, Malcolm. "The 150% Man, A Product of Blackfeet Acculturation." *American Anthropologist,* 70–6, 1968, pp. 1096–1107.

Ovando, Carlos J. and Virginia P. Collier. *Bilingual and ESL Classrooms.* New York: McGraw-Hill, 1985.

Reyhner, Jon. "Maintaining and Renewing Native Languages in the Schools." In *Survival and Renewal: Native American Values.* Sault Sainte Marie, MI: Lake Superior State University, in press.

Reyhner, Jon. (Ed.). *Teaching American Indian Students.* Norman, OK: University of Oklahoma Press, 1992.

Rosier, Paul, and Wayne Holm. *The Rock Point Experience.* Washington, D.C.: Center for Applied Linguistics, 1980.

St. Clair, Robert. "What Is Language Renewal." In *Language Renewal among American Indian Tribes: Issues, Problems, and Prospects,* edited by Robert St. Clair and William Leap.

Rosslyn, VI: National Clearinghouse for Bilingual Education, 1982.

Studies on Immersion Education: A Collection for United States Educators. Sacramento, CA: California State Department of Education, 1984.

Trueba, Henry T., and Carol Barnett-Mizrahi, (Eds.). *Bilingual and Multicultural Education and the Professional: From Theory to Practice.* Rowley, MA: Newbury House, 1979.

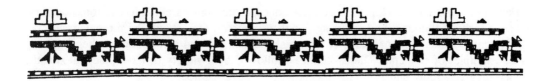

Chapter 17
Science for Native Americans

"Science is what we do at two o'clock." That is the feeling of many Native American students, a reflection of science instruction that is mostly learning from books and memorization of facts which students don't consider important for themselves. Students should, instead, find science class fun and exciting, a time when they can experiment, discuss, and try out new ideas that relate to their interests and that are important in their daily lives. It should be a time when both the newest ideas from the TV news and the wisdom of their grandfathers can combine to solve their own problems and those of their communities. Science should not be only "at two o'clock." It should relate to many things throughout the day, particularly social studies, literature, and math. It will be important to the students if, beginning in the primary grades, science is problem solving, experimentation, and an opportunity for students to learn exciting things about the world around them. Teachers should model the excitement of science; let the students see that it is something that is fun for everyone.

As Taylor (1988) points outs, "Currently, most contemporary scientific knowledge is passed on via textbooks and rote memorization. In contrast, ancient Indian science was practical, involved a working knowledge of the environment, and was passed on to new generations via stories, games, and the experiences of daily life." Isn't that also the most effective way of teaching science in the classroom?

Integrate Science; Don't Neglect It

Too often, especially in the reservation school or the Alaskan Native village, science has been largely ignored, pushed aside by the pressure of trying to teach reading skills and language improvement. But these skills are learned best through reading, writing, and talking *about* something, and what better than through the science that affects the students' daily lives.

Few students develop a real interest in science in high school unless they have been inspired by their experiences in elementary school. Primary grade children are anxious to learn about the world around them. Every branch of science is exciting to them. Build on that interest. By the fourth grade, students love to experiment, to draw their own conclusions. All they need is some science problems that can be solved through experimentation with locally available materials, some instruction in scientific methods, and a relaxed, positive approach.

Help your students develop their science concepts through careful observation, comparing, organizing, critical thinking, and inferring. As they progress, they should be presented with challenging, complex situations of real life, with realistic projects and simulations, rather than single isolated examples of concepts. These should be followed by a variety of local practical situations in which they can apply and reinforce the skills they have learned.

Textbooks and curriculum guides are a necessary source. They guide teachers, reminding them of concepts that must be taught, but those concepts should be developed by the students themselves, as they observe in both natural and classroom settings. They should be challenged to obtain data from their homes and communities and compare those data. Then they are ready to verify their conclusions through reading, and to learn to record and analyze their data through graphing, tabulating, and through the arts.

Teach the Language of Science

Often, when students have not completed their assignments, teachers assume it is because they didn't make the necessary effort. Or teachers believe that their students' lack of understanding of a concept was due to not paying close attention. However, the real problem may be that the students are unable to comprehend the material because of the terminology used. The vocabulary of science is very different from "village English." There may be many words that are completely unfamiliar to the students. More often, the students recognize all the words and think they know their meanings. Then neither they nor the teacher can understand why the material doesn't make sense to the students, not realizing that the meanings the students have learned have little relationship to the meanings of the words as used in the textbooks or by the teacher. A word may have a dozen meanings; the student may know only one.

Teachers should carefully read text material with the vocabulary of the community in mind; then before the students read, they should discuss thoroughly with the students any possibly misunderstood words, using examples to clarify meanings.

Begin with Native American Science

Indian students should know that at the time of the European invasion of America, American and European natives were approximately equal in scientific knowledge, and that much of the Indians' traditional knowledge is still useful today. Teach your students about the Mayas' advanced knowledge of astronomy, the Aztecs' study of genetics, the Incas' technical approach to architecture and their intricate use of brain surgery, the fact that although their approach was different, most North American tribes were more knowledgeable than their European peers in zoology and in the use of herbal medicines. Let them know that their own ancestors contributed more different food plants to our present diets and the rest of the world than their European counterparts did. Then ask parents and local elders to accompany your classes on field trips to teach them where to find edible wild plants and material for weaving and other projects, and have them teach the students about the local animal life.

Bring in local scientists and other knowledgeable adults to explain concepts in the classroom and to show the application of classroom experiments to modern life. Many tribes have forestry, energy, or soil conservation departments that could provide speakers.

Teach the students the Native American skills of careful observation of all of nature. If they live where there is snow, take them outdoors after a fresh snowfall and show them that they can gain as much knowledge of the ways of animals through the Native skill of reading their tracks as they could through reading books. A helpful source of information is the book *Mystery Tracks in the Snow* (Gilliland, 1990). It provides information on all the North American mammals and ways of learning about them through observation. For interest, and to relate the modern to the traditional, the names of each animal are given in the usual English and Latin, and also in the languages of some of the Indian tribes in the areas in which each animal lives.

The study of animal life, the use of Indian legends, even the study of the earth itself, involves not only knowledge but moral and spiritual values. When students bring these up, don't avoid them or pretend they are not important, much less use a preaching or know-it-all attitude. Let students discuss the issues openly, and let them know that they all have a right to their own opinions, but that they also have an obligation to listen openly to others' opinions before making judgments. The book *Brother Eagle, Sister Sky, A Message by Chief Seattle* (1991) is a great way to introduce the subject of conservation through the words of a great Native American chief.

Science can even be tied to Native literature in ways that most people never realize. An excellent book that should be in the hands of every elementary teacher is *Keepers of the Earth* (Caduto and Bruchac, 1988). This book contains 27 Native American legends representing all areas of North America. After each story are detailed plans for several science experiences that relate specifically to that story. What better way to start a science lesson than by the telling of one of the children's own cultural stories!

Teach Science Through Group Problem Solving

As brought out in Chapter 5 on cooperative learning, group problem solving is part of Native American culture. Bring to the classroom many things from nature and let the students work in groups to learn about them through hands-on experiments. Let them plant beans in mason jars with paper towels wrapped around the inside. Plant the beans between the towel and the glass so students can observe them sprouting and see the growth of roots and leaves. Then let them experiment with different soils, different amounts of water and sunshine, and discuss together the possible causes of their observations, drawing their own conclusions.

Through guidance in conducting their own experiments, students can learn the scientific method of making educated guesses ("hypotheses"), controlling variables, collecting and systematically recording information, then drawing logical conclusions. They can do all this in small groups, learning to work together to verify their opinions.

As Caduto (p. 10) suggests, "If the lesson is about trees, take them to a tree. . . . If you are studying water, visit a pond. Avoid prolonged discussion. To see it, smell it, hear it, touch it or taste it is to know it better."

On an early spring day, students in a Montana reservation elementary school went to an area along a nearby river where they spent a half day studying the environment. They hiked the area, observing the geology, the plants, the mammals, birds, and insects. Then they divided into small study groups. Each group measured and marked off a one square meter of ground which they studied in detail, describing the kind of soil and ground cover, identifying and counting every plant, every insect. Then they studied a larger area, identifying trees, birds, etc. In late May, they returned and did the same study of the same spot, thus recognizing the great changes that had taken place in two months' time.

Nets were used to catch a variety of small fish from a nearby lake. These were placed in aquariums in the classroom so the students could learn to identify all of them and study their habits. At the end of their study, the students themselves returned to the spot where they had found the fish and other things they had gathered, thus assuring themselves that nothing was harmed and the processes of nature were not disturbed.

This kind of approach to science will encourage all students, but is especially important to those who feel a relationship to nature and the natural way of life.

Don't Ignore the Taboos

There are many things that can be done in the classroom, especially in the study of biology, that are taboo to many Native American students. Before you begin your experiments, be aware of local cultural beliefs that may make your particular experiments offensive to some students. The killing of any animal, including an insect, or even a plant, simply so that it can be studied is a sacrilege to many Native Americans. Some may expect it to bring illness or even death to them or a loved one.

Owls and spiders have special powers. To some Indians of the Southwest, discussion of the owl or even the writing of the word could bring great harm. Amphibians, reptiles, and turtles have special significance to many groups. Coyotes have a special place in the lore of all tribes.

Before you begin your biological experiments, discuss your plans with knowledgeable students, or even with parents or knowledgeable Native friends. Know what is acceptable and what is not. In many cases, if your class consists mostly of non-Native students and you consider an experiment important, it may be that a Native student who cannot actively participate in an experiment, or even touch the thing being studied, can be the recorder for the group, learning and participating in that way.

What about Modern Problems and Technology?

Native students usually quickly see the relationship of the biological sciences to the old culture, but they seldom take much interest in the physical sciences. Yet all Native people rely on some type of lighting and heating, on modern medicine, and are in contact with telephones, TV, automobiles, and appliances. Most of my Native students have thought of these things as being from the non-Indian world that you accept and use, but that you don't try to understand or even think much about. Once they are made aware that they can actually find out what makes these technologies work, they may become interested in the scientific principles behind them. These technologies are a practical lead-in to the physical sciences.

The life of every Native student has been affected by alcohol, drugs, or tobacco. A study of their effects should be included in the science program at every level, not as moralizing, but as a scientific study.

Summary

If we want Native American students to become interested in science and become skillful in its use, we have to show them its application in their everyday lives, relate it to their culture and their goals, and let them experience the thrill, the excitement of discovering facts for themselves. Students who look on science as "play for a purpose" learn rapidly and remember what they were taught. They will reach this point sooner if we relate our instruction to the knowledge and skills of the old culture and let them solve practical scientific problems through group effort.

References for Further Reading

Burgoyne, Paul C. "Native American Problems in Biology Classes." *Teacher to Teacher*, p 315.

Caduto, Michael J., and Joseph Bruchac. *Keepers of the Earth: Native American Stories and Environmental Activities for Children*. Fulcrum. 1988.

Chief Seattle. *Brother Eagle, Sister Sky*, with paintings by Susan Jeffers. Dial Books. 1991.

Cole, K. C. "Things Your Teachers Never Told You About Science: Nine Shocking Revelations." *Kui Tatk*, Vol. 2–2, Fall 1986. pp 4–5.

Deloria, Vine Jr. "Traditional Technology." *Winds of Change*. Vol. 5–2, Spring 1990. pp 12–17.

Dick, A. *Village Science*. Iditarod Area School District, Iditarod, Alaska. 1990.

Gilliland, Hap. *Mystery Tracks in the Snow: A Guide to Animal Tracks and Tracking*. Naturegraph. 1990. 142 pp.

Kid Science. Science Activity Magazine for Elementary Teachers.

Kipohtakaw Education Centre. *Teacher's Guide: "Walking with Grandfather," and "Great Wolf" and "Little Mouse Sister."* Lethbridge University Alberta. 1984.

Richau, Deborah. *Introduce Science to Students Using the Environment: A Guide for Teachers of Native American Students*. Native American Science Education Assoc. 1981.

Snively, Gloria. "Traditional Native Indian Beliefs, Cultural Values, and Science Instruction." *Canadian Journal of Native Education*. Vol. 17–1. 1990. pp. 44–59.

Taylor, Gene. *Hands on Science*. EDRS 1988.

Watahomogie, L. M. Powskey, and J. Bender. *Ethnobotany of the Hualapai*. Hualapai Bilingual Program, Peach Springs, AZ.

Chapter 18
Mathematics for the Native Student
by David M. Davison

A classroom of Indian students is working on problems based on data collected from an arrow throwing contest. The students are graphing distances arrows are thrown by different individuals. They are involved in discussions about comparing the distances the arrows were thrown. The idea for these problems did not come from a mathematics textbook or typical teachers' guide. This teacher is answering the challenge to make her classroom responsive to the mathematics learning needs of her students.

American Indian students are typically not culturally in tune with the mainstream Anglo system of learning. Traditionally the history of mathematics serves to illustrate how people have interacted with their environment in a quantitative way. For example, early American mathematics history is rich with situations such as the Aztec calendar and Mayan numeration that can be used to motivate classroom learning. However, only Western mathematics history is treated in the classroom.

The respect of Native students for their past, and their understanding of how mathematics can influence their present and their future, calls for more serious attention to presenting classroom mathematics in more appropriate ways.

Three Ways of Increasing Mathematics Learning

Native students will learn more mathematics if the concepts presented in the classroom are culturally relevant, are responsive to their preferred learning styles, and emphasize the learning of English language mathematics terms.

1. Use Culturally Relevant Materials

As Hap Gilliland pointed out in the first chapter of this book, a culturally relevant curriculum should value the students' heritage and build on ideas that are meaningful to them. One way a teacher can make mathematics meaningful is by using culturally relevant materials. The use of such material is advantageous for two reasons. First, the students see mathematics applied to *their* real world. All too often Indian students see no relation between school mathematics and reality and therefore have little motivation to apply themselves to the study of mathematics. Through the use of examples like the one described above, the teacher is able to stimulate the interest of the students in mathematics. Second, students have a strong interest in learning about their own culture. The use of culture-based mathematical illustrations provides the students with the opportunity to learn about their culture while studying mathematics.

In the arrow throwing contest, the Crow Indian students were actively involved in the learning because the situation described is a regular part of the tribal culture. Other events that have strong cultural significance can also be used as a basis for teaching mathematics to American Indian students in a more motivating manner. Phenomena such as bead frame loomwork, hand games, and sand paintings can be used to teach many mathematical ideas.

In a unit involving a study of buffalo, for example, many mathematics-related activities are possible. Some sample activities include comparing the size of buffalo herds at different periods, estimating the amount of grazing land needed to support these buffalo, calculating the number of people that can be fed from a large buffalo, discussing ways of estimating size and weight of buffalo, and estimating the distance a herd can travel in a given time period.

A collection of culturally relevant materials, whether Indian or non-Indian, cannot be substituted for a coordinated mathematics curriculum. It behooves the curriculum planner to begin with a well-integrated mathematics program and to explore as many ways as possible to make the curriculum meaningful. Meaningful examples could describe situations in which Indians might be involved, such as one dealing with horses. We have found that Indian students regard school mathematics as meaningless, as having no bearing on their lives. The way mathematics is presented in textbooks only serves to reinforce this belief. If the students are to learn the mathematics that they need, the concepts will need to be presented in a more appealing manner. The use of culturally relevant stimulus material to illustrate the application of these concepts will help to attain this objective.

2. Adapt to Native Learning Styles

The Native students' learning of mathematics is also influenced by differences in their learning styles. The Native student is more typically a visual/kinesthetic learner than an auditory learner. Most school instruction is more auditory/abstract in its emphasis and does not respond to the Native student's preferred style of learning. Native students process mathematics in a less abstract way because their view of the world is more practical.

Typical mathematics learning materials are prepared on the assumption that all students learn mathematics in the same way. An examination of such materials indicates that the dominant mode of presentation of mathematics is abstract. Available evidence indicates that most Native students do not process mathematics in an abstract way, but depend on tactile and visual stimuli to facilitate learning. In a society where most curriculum is abstract in focus, the student whose focus is more visual will have difficulty dealing with the material.

The elementary mathematics curriculum emphasizes competence in work with number and its operations. Geometry assumes a less prominent place. Chapters in geometry are usually near the end of the book and may possibly be treated in a superficial manner. Geometry is the one branch of mathematics that can stress Indian rather than non-Indian approaches to mathematics. Success in geometry is related to a kinesthetic processing of the environment. For example, we found that when given the geometric attribute pieces containing the primary colors, four shapes, and two sizes, non-Indians classify primarily by color first. Indian students, on the other hand, mostly classify by shape first. This observation supports the notion that these Indian students' preferred style of mathematical processing is essentially kinesthetic.

Few curricular efforts have been devoted to addressing different learning styles in mathematics. Perhaps the best known approach to primary mathematics stressing tactile methods is found in Mary Baretta-Lorton's *Mathematics Their Way*. This program is activity-oriented; students learn mathematical ideas by working with familiar objects. While the program is intended to help all primary students learn mathematics, its emphasis is such that minority students now have a chance to learn mathematics in an understandable way.

Many people, in the Anglo as well as in the American Indian culture, find mathematics devoid of meaning—nothing more than jargon and symbol manipulation. The result is mathematics underachievement, anxiety, and aversion. Many of the people who do succeed in post-school mathematics use sensory perception, models and imagery. This is very different from the views of school mathematics described above. Family Math stresses the use of manipulatives and activity methods in the middle grades as well as in the primary grades. Certainly, an emphasis on a hands-on approach to mathematics learning would help Indian students make more sense of the way mathematics is presented.

Curriculum designers are being made aware that not all students learn mathematics in the same way. Materials that place emphasis on the use of hands-on activities will help students whose primary learning mode is kinesthetic, not abstract. The use of an activity-centered approach in working with Native students is one way of responding to their different learning style.

3. Emphasize the Learning of Mathematical Language

A third way in which the Native student relates differently to the mathematics curriculum is in the use of language. In the mathematics classroom many terms are used in ways that differ from normal English usage. For example, the word 'product' in mathematics refers to the result of multiplying two numbers, whereas in conventional English it connotes something that has been completed. Students who come from homes where the English language is not used extensively are less likely to be aware of the varied meanings of such terms. Further, the student whose first language is not English is not accustomed to hearing the mathematics vocabulary outside of the mathematics classroom.

Bilingual education programs stress the use of the native language to help teach English language concepts. This is true in mathematics as well as in other subject areas. We would expect, then, that competence in the mathematics terms in the native language would help the students learn these terms in the English language. However, in our work with Crow Indian children we found that the knowledge of Crow counting number names was limited. The students knew Crow names only for the fractions one-half and one-fourth, they did not differentiate between the cardinal and ordinal uses of number even though the terms exist in the Crow language, and, apart from the words for circle, square, and triangle, names for geometrical figures were not known. This led us to conclude that some of the expected benefits of bilingual education are not occurring insofar as the mathematics vocabulary is not being mastered.

In his work with the Navajo Indians, Douglas Garbe found that the students were not getting enough appropriate instruction in mathematics vocabulary. He recommended that vocabulary to be mastered be clearly identified, and that information on each student's performance in vocabulary be passed on to the teacher of the next grade. This teacher should try to use the student's past experience with each term to help give the term meaning in a mathematical context. The introduction of new terms should be carefully orchestrated. A term should be used in context over and over—students should show that they can pronounce the word, spell it, and use it in a correct context. Attention needs to be paid to the interference caused by 'sound alike' words, those that differ in spelling, pronunciation, and meaning, for example, sum, some, sun. Important vocabulary should be reviewed regularly. Mastery of this mathematical vocabulary should be taught, not as an end in itself, but as a means of mastering more mathematics.

David Davison and Daniel Pearce observed that students' lack of mastery of the English language adversely affected their mathematics achievement. In work with disadvantaged Crow Indian students, they found that having the students keep math journals improved both their writing and mathematics skills.

Even students who are no longer bilingual, or who have only residual vestiges of their native language, still have trouble processing English language mathematics. Bill Leap (1982) speaks of "residual cultural processing." The students use the English language but they do not understand the nuances of English language thinking with facility. Accordingly, they need more experience speaking and writing mathematics in context to improve their grasp of English language mathematics.

Summary

We have seen that three factors influence the Native student's ability to learn mathematics. While these factors to some extent affect the mathematics learning of all students, the consequences can be quite serious where minority students are concerned. American Indian students view mathematics differently, and their mastery of the English language is less sophisticated. If we are to succeed in teaching more mathematics to Native students, we should consider three ways of adapting the way mathematics is typically taught.

First, culturally relevant stimulus material should be used wherever appropriate to stimulate the interest of the students. This is particularly critical as most Native students see little relevance for their lives in the mathematics they study. Second, different students have varying preferred styles of learning. The conventional curriculum stresses mathematics as an abstract discipline and, therefore, excludes from the attainment of success those who process mathematics in a more visual/kinesthetic manner. Third, the Native student, whether bilingual or not, experiences difficulty with the subtleties of the English mathematics terminology. Deliberate instruction in English language mathematics vocabulary is needed to overcome this difficulty.

It is assumed by many that the Native student should not be expected to do well with mathematical concepts. I suggest that this assertion is unfounded, that Native students will experience success in mathematics if appropriate strategies are used to present the concepts to them.

References for Further Reading

Baretta-Lorton, Mary. *Mathematics Their Way.* Menlo Park, CA: Addison-Wesley, 1976.

Bradley, Claudette. "Issues in Mathematics Education for Native Americans and Directions for Research." *Journal for Research in Mathematics Education,* 15, 1984, pp. 96–106.

Davison, David M. "Mathematics." In *Teaching American Indian Students,* edited by Jon Reyhner, pp. 241–250. Norman, OK: University of Oklahoma Press, 1992.

Davison, David M., and Daniel L. Pearce. "The Influence of Writing Activities on the Mathematics Learning of Native American Students." *Journal of Educational Issues of Language Minority Students,* in press.

De Avila, Edward A. "Bilingualism, Cognitive Function, and Language Minority Group Membership." In Rodney R. Cocking and Jose P. Mestre, eds. *Linguistic and Cultural Influences on Learning Mathematics.* Hillsdale, NJ: Erlbaum. 1988. pp. 101–121.

Garbe, Douglas G. "Mathematics Vocabulary and the Culturally Different Student." *Arithmetic Teacher,* 33–2, 1985, pp. 39–42.

Green, Rayna, and Janet Welsh Brown. *Recommendations for the Improvement of Science and Mathematics Education for American Indians.* Washington, DC: American Association for the Advancement of Science. ED 149 896, 1976.

Leap, William L. "Assumptions and Strategies Guiding Mathematics Problem Solving by Ute Indian Students." In Rodney R. Cocking and Jose P. Mestre (Eds.). *Linguistic and Cultural Influences on Learning Mathematics.* Hillsdale, NJ: Erlbaum. 1988. pp. 161–186.

Schindler, Duane E., and David M. Davison. "Language, Culture and the Mathematical Concepts of American Indian Learners." *Journal of American Indian Education,* 24–3, 1958, pp. 27–34.

Stenmark, Jean Kerr, Virginia Thompson, and Ruth Cossey. *Family Math.* Berkeley, CA: Regents, University of California, 1986.

Chapter 19
Technology in the Classroom
By David Spencer

The use of technology in the schools has been called "the revolution that failed" or "fizzled." Some writers have even stated that there are few technological solutions to education's problems. (Olson, 1992, p. 2) Salomon (1990) writes that even the computer lab, now sanctified in American education, is a bad idea.

Perhaps the problem is that computers have been used for their own sake, and not as the best way to teach a subject. Computers should not be the curriculum or an addition to the curriculum, but a powerful tool to help in the teaching of many subjects, not only social studies, sciences, and languages, but all subjects, even art, math, and music. They should be recognized as such by both educators and students.

An Arab proverb states, "Each child is a precious jewel, born without inscription." It is our job as educators to inscribe upon this jewel of a child. By school age much inscription has already been accomplished by parents and community. What we inscribe must match what the culture has already inscribed. Indian students often do not see the application of most school learning, especially computers, to life outside of school. It is therefore especially important that we introduce technology to them as a better way of learning the concepts which are valuable to them in their own lives.

This chapter will focus on three areas of technology: the telephone, telecomputing, and multimedia.

The Telephone

The first and easiest technology to use is the telephone. Every classroom should have access to a telephone. Is it logical to advocate 21st century technology (the computer) when most teachers don't have access to the telephone, a 20th century technology? Telephone projects can teach many things from telephone manners to using "800" numbers to request information. In a recent unit on the A.I.D.S. epidemic a teacher spent time after class on the phone to the A.I.D.S. hotline. Why not have the students make these calls? Other "800" numbers will work well with geography and social studies: call those tourist bureaus for colorful brochures and maps containing information about cities, states, and countries.

Telecomputing

My interest in computer assisted language learning begins with this observation on computer use at the elementary school level: the students are not using the computer for creative, interactive activities. Instead, they are playing games and doing simulations. Too many computers are used as electronic flashcards. "I have been dismayed that so much computer use in the schools has been limited to skill-and-drill, the old wine of textbooks in the new bottle of electronics." (Tchudi, 1988, p. 26) Hopefully, the role of skill and drill in writing and reading instruction is diminishing with a more sophisticated understanding of the nature of language acquisition. The search for more culturally appropriate software led me to investigate word-processing. Word-processing is an effective use of computers with Native American students, and is clearly enhanced when the student is writing for a reason other than to please the teacher. Telecomputing can provide this reason.

One computer application which weaves together the whole-language philosophy with the world of information age technology is telecomputing. A modem-equipped computer can communicate with other modem-equipped computers over ordinary telephone lines. This form of communication, called telecomputing, has special implications for promoting language development with Indian students.

Writing and reading "on-line," using telecomputing, can be one of the elements of an innovative curriculum design for all students. Limited English proficient students can benefit from this blend of technology and language called by one author "the perfect fit for the bilingual student." (Sayers, 1987, pp. 23–24)

As a tool for writing, telecomputing provides three characteristics of authentic writing programs. (1) It is functional and serves a real purpose. (2) It uses all aspects of language and does not focus on isolated symbols. (3) The students in their writing are addressing a real audience other than the teacher. (Brisk, 1989, p. 537)

As a tool for reading, telecomputing is also functional. It involves a real response from an authentic contact. The writer of the message can be a fellow student, a tutor, or an expert in the area of research. The message (authentic context) can be a response to a question, a challenge to play a game, or an investigation of a particular topic. The student uses all aspects of the language and gets an excellent opportunity to understand the importance of mechanics, spelling, and conventional form. This form of verbal exchange becomes a dialogue. When using telecomputing, the product of this dialogue is not centered on speaking and listening; it is centered on writing and reading. Telecomputing is an opportunity to gain insights on the pragmatics of language: how we use writing and reading to "speak and listen" across time and over great distances.

Above all, the networking format brings purpose to writing, provides an audience, and helps to bridge the gap between the classroom and the real world. Telecomputing can help to motivate students; it is new, exciting, and fun.

The current focus in language arts instruction is on interactive communicative activities which are integrated with subject matter. Reading and writing are closely related skills best taught together, not as separate entities. The key is wholeness. Knowledge is received by the learner through listening and reading, then shared with others through speaking and writing. An integrated approach calls for using language to solve problems related to themes or units. Language is the tool used to learn the subject matter rather than an end in itself. In a comprehension-centered curriculum, the motivation for literacy must be based on personal and social language functions. First, the students explore an intrinsically interesting, culturally relevant theme or unit. They use all the skills of language during this process. Then, with telecomputing, the product which results from this process can be "up-loaded" onto the network to be sent to a sister class. The "sister class" receives the material and responds with requests for more information, reactions to the product, or with a product of its own. These responses are then "downloaded," saved, and printed for class use.

The work is divided into three stages: pre-computer work, computer work, and post-computer work. (Hardisty, 1989, p. 76) The portable Franklin Electronic products, including dictionaries and encyclopedias, are hand-held computers that can be used at all three stages of the computer work, even in the computer lab. These computers are the size of a calculator; they are portable and can be used anywhere that learning takes place. Work done before using the computer includes selection of topic and planning for resources. This stage could involve small, cooperative group discussions on what to do and how to do it. The Franklin Electronic Dictionary allows the student to search for a word without initial mastery of dictionary skills. Called by one language arts teacher the students' dictionary of choice, this small computer is ideal for cooperative learning situations. If an item is misspelled, the student can choose from a list of close approximations in English. A new Franklin product is the hand-held encyclopedia. This computer allows the learner to search for more information with the help of electronic cross-referencing. While using the computer word-processing programs, the students are encouraged to use the built in dictionary and thesaurus to check spelling and investigate new vocabulary words. From the students' own writing they can generate appropriate vocabulary and spelling lists. The follow-up stage includes responding to a sister class or doing a project to apply knowledge to new situations.

For the bilingual classroom, networking is an ideal way to support first language literacy. In a bilingual tele-networking project called "Orillas," the students used both the first language (Spanish) and the second language (English) to complete language activities. The students became international news reporters, writing, editing, and producing a newspaper which was sent to the sister class. "The most successful projects have been those which have a life of their own away from the computer and can be amplified by the participation of the 'sister class.' " (Sayers, 1987, p. 24) The "Orillas" project met the goal of involving the community in the literacy effort by recording the wisdom of the extended family. The students interviewed family members about favorite proverbs. These proverbs were recorded, compared, sent to a sister class and then compiled in a data base for further comparison and editing. The product, a book of proverbs, was more than an exchange between two highly motivated classes linked through tele-networking. The book was the product of a community effort.

Parental involvement has always been a difficult but vital element in bilingual education. By taking advantage of the cultural resources of the community, through the vehicle of tele-networking, the "Orillas" project helped to empower the community and develop literacy. (Cummins, 1989, p. 82) For communities with a local language the scope of the exchange can be slightly different, but equally powerful. Using a microcomputer as the server, a local BBS (Bulletin Board System) can be an ideal communications tool. One computer, with a dedicated phone line, can be the hub of communications with all the computers in the community. The community then gives the systems operator (sysop) the directions for establishing conferences of local importance. The local BBS, using the language of the community, is an ideal way to enhance language development and to empower the community.

As we attempt to bridge the gap from computer as drill instructor to computer as a tool for learning, we will find fellow educators who ask where all of this fits into the curriculum. In his visionary article "Invisible Thinking and the Hypertext," Stephen Tchudi describes the need to teach using an integrated approach: "The . . . curriculum . . . may, at first glance, appear to be in opposition to the demands of the public and press for education in fundamentals. However, I would argue that such a curriculum deals fully with the basics, both the basics of initial skill mastery and the 'higher literacies' of learning. Further, it is 'disciplined,' both in presenting the knowledge and information traditionally contained in disciplines, and in requiring (or better, encouraging) . . . sustained, systematic, disciplined inquiry." (Tchudi, 1988, p. 10) The Montana Office of Public Instruction (1990, p. 3) says: "Integration in eduction is basic to helping people survive and succeed." Telecomputing offers a vehicle for transmission of products that are the result of an integrated process.

A BBS (Bulletin Board System) available to Montana educators is Big Sky Telegraph. Like a conventional bulletin board, messages are categorized in conferences which reflect common interests. For example, one conference, "Kidsnet," is dedicated to electronic pen-pals. In another conference, "Native Net," students and teachers meet to share ideas in both the files and message areas.

Another BBS (Russell Country BBS) offers Native American computer graphics for sale through phone lines, modem, and computer. The NAPLPS (North American Presentation Level Protocol) software is designed to enhance Native American self-esteem by promoting and selling computer graphics as "share-ware." It can be examined for free, like browsing in a book store, but once it is "down-loaded," it must be purchased. "The expansion of use of this medium, with its combination of text and artwork, could have a significant influence in the Native American classroom." (Denton, 1992, p. 2)

Multimedia

For years one tool of the ESL (English as a Second Language) teacher has been the picture file. These files are difficult to prepare and more difficult to manage. Although the computerized picture file is an improvement, the future of computer assisted language learning is found in interactive multimedia. Using HyperCard on the Macintosh computer, the teacher can present a multidimensional lesson integrating visuals, sound, and text. While the combination of word-processing and telecomputing is important, the real potential for the Macintosh lies in multimedia. (Ambron, 1992, p. 71) This blend of language input using video/hypermedia applications offers this opportunity to Native American students. The programs are relatively simple and the potential is enormous. We can make our own culturally appropriate software. The students can learn to mix language (oral and written) with images to create simple and complex routines. These routines lead to more complex and expressive language. Through this use of technology, we no longer treat language or computers as the subject. They are both tools we use to discover this world and others.

> The printing press is an instrument that mechanizes human writing, itself a technology that mechanized human memory. Computers, roughly speaking, mechanize and amplify not only memory but also another aspect of the human mind, which is reasoning. (McCorduck, 1985, p. 28)

Multimedia can provide the environment to move beyond computer as writing master and well beyond computer as drill master. Combine the creative, reasoning mind with the ultimate tool of education, the computer. We now have the opportunity to blend art, sound, and languages. The benefits can be powerful for all students. This could be the means of encouraging

Native American students to explore their own languages, to examine their own cultures. "This learning and training can increase their sense of individuality, self-esteem, and self-expression." (Denton, p. 2)

It is time to investigate innovative curricular applications using telephones, telecomputing, and hypermedia. Once the students discover these uses of the computer as a tool for learning, they will begin to teach the other students. Perhaps they will even teach the teachers.

References and Other Resources

Ambron, Sueann, and Hooper, Kristina. *Learning with Interactive Multimedia. Developing and Using Multimedia Tools in Education.* Microsoft Press. 1990.

Big Sky Telegraph. Western Montana College of the University of Montana. Dillon, Montana. 59725. Voice—(406) 683–7338. Modem—(406) 683–7680.

Brisk, Maria. Book Notices. *Writing in a Bilingual Program: Habia una Vez.* Ablex Publishing Corporation, 1986. Carole Edelsky. TESOL QUARTERLY. 23, 3. 1989.

Cummins, James. *Empowering Minority Students.* California Association for Bilingual Education. 1989.

Denton, Cynthia. "ShareArt. The American Indian Share-Art Gallery." *Big Sky Telegraph.* NativeNet. Files. "NativeArt."

Franklin Learning Resources. 122 Burrs Road. Mt. Holly, New Jersey. 08060. 1 800 525 9673.

Hardisty, David, and Wideat, Scott. *CALL. Computer Assisted Language Learning.* Oxford University Press. 1989.

McCorduck, Pamela. *The Universal Machine: The Confessions of a Technological Optimist.* Harcourt Brace Jovanovich. 1985.

Montana Office of Public Instruction. "Integration," *Montana State Communications Art Curriculum.* 1990.

Olson, Lynn. "Contrary to Predictions, Use of Technology in Schools Elusive." *Education Week.* January 8, 1992.

Russell Country BBS. P.O. Box 359. Hobson, Montana. 59452. Voice—(406) 423–5433. Modem—(406) 423–5505.

Salomon, Gavriel. *Education Technology,* October, 1990. Captured on Big Sky Telegraph. University of Montana. Western Montana College. Dillon, Montana. hrn. BUED Conference.

Sayers, Dennis, and Brown, Kristin. "Bilingual Education and Telecommunications: A Perfect Fit." *THE COMPUTING TEACHER.* April, 1987.

Tchudi, Stephen. "Invisible Thinking and the Hypertext." *ENGLISH JOURNAL.* January, 1988.

Waggoner, Michael. *Empowering Networks: Computer Conferencing in Education.* 1992. Educational Technology Publications.

Indian drummers at a pow-wow.

Chapter 20
Music and Movement for the Native American Student
by Deborah Reinhardt

As the music teacher at a Native American school, I found that my students were very receptive to music and eager to participate in musical activities such as singing, playing instruments, creating original music, and listening for specific musical elements. It was when I first attended a pow-wow and watched some of my students dance that I realized how important the link between movement and music was for these children. A student who could not play the drum with a steady beat during class was able to time each of his steps perfectly with the changing beat of the dance chant.

At this point, I began to include movement as a regular part of the music classes. Movement activities allowed all students to be completely involved in the musical experience and to express their individual musical understandings in a non-verbal fashion. The students were able to demonstrate what they had learned about any music concept with greater ease. They were also better able to apply what they had learned to other musical behaviors such as singing, playing instruments, and listening.

Recommendations for Including Movement in the Music Program
Music lends itself to active involvement for the student. When music is combined with movement, the learning becomes even more active and individual. The following sections provide suggestions for including movement with musical activities.

1. Planning for Successful Movement Experiences
Movement activities require space that is clean, open, and free of obstacles. Desks and other equipment may need to be moved to provide this space. The clean or carpeted floor should be free of rough areas that might cause the students harm.

Before beginning any movement activity, have the students find individual space in the room. Individual space is an area in which the student can move freely without making physical contact with another student. If inappropriate physical contact such as bumping or hitting occurs during the movement activity, stop the activity and ask each student to find an individual space.

Begin each movement activity by introducing the students to a start and stop signal. If problems occur during the movement activity, stop the activity until the problem is solved and the students are ready to begin again. These signals can be as simple as "move when the music starts and stop when the music stops." Other choices for signals include the use of a specific instrument such as the gong or a single word such as "pause."

It is important to monitor the students' energy level. Fatigue during an extremely active movement activity can lead to carelessness and injury. If the students appear to be tiring, stop the music and try a few moments of stretching and deep breathing. Resume the activity when the students appear to be breathing normally and evenly.

2. Selecting Music

Movement activities can be performed with recorded music. By using recorded music, you have the chance to introduce the students to many types of music, including traditional Native American music. When you use a recording, you have the choice to observe the class or join in the activity with the class. Many of the basal music text recordings include compositions that are suitable for movement activities. A list of some of these texts and other record sets suitable for movement activities are given in the reference list at the end of this chapter.

Music for movement can also be provided by playing an instrument. You need to decide if your ability and skill with the instrument are sufficient for the activity. An advantage to playing music on an instrument is that you can change and adapt the music to the students' movement. Piano and simple percussion instruments work well with these types of activities as these instruments allow the option of giving vocal instructions and encouragement during the activity.

When selecting music, it is important to listen to the selection and try the activity that the students will perform. There is no substitute for this step. It is during this process that you discover whether or not the proposed movement activity is appropriate with the specific music composition. For example, if the movement activity is to alternate different styles of walking with the sections of music, and the tempo of the music is very slow, you may want to change the activity to different styles of swaying and sliding.

3. Plan For and Encourage Student Success

If we expect our students to succeed and to learn from an academic activity, the students *will* succeed and learn. It is no different with movement activities. If movement activities are approached with a positive attitude and the expectation that they are worthwhile, the students will experience success and they will learn.

Begin a movement activity by asking the students to focus their listening on the music. After the students have heard the music, encourage the students to move to the music. The students may respond with a specific movement that has been previously introduced, or they may use a new creative movement. Discuss and work with these responses by asking the students for feedback about their movement. The students will evaluate the appropriateness of their response if they are given the opportunity for evaluation. Follow up this discussion with another opportunity to move to the music using the new ideas or to improve the previous movement.

The teacher should be prepared to move during the presentation of a movement activity. When the students discuss the appropriateness of their movement or suggest new movements for the music, you can help clarify and work with the ideas by trying and working with the students on the suggested changes. Adults often feel insecure about using movement activities as a teaching technique because they are not comfortable with movement. Movement is not part of most programs of teacher training, yet some students have strong learning ability in the kinesthetic and tactile modes. As teachers, we need to feel comfortable with all of the teaching techniques which might help our students to learn.

To feel comfortable with using movement in the classroom, try doing a movement activity in private. Find some recorded music and select one of the suggested activities in this chapter. Initially, adults may feel awkward trying a movement activity, but with patience and perseverance, a sense of ease and poise will soon result.

4. Build a Repertoire of Movement Responses

There are two basic types of movement responses which are usually developed gradually over time. Nonlocomotor movements are done in place and include bending, stretching, swaying, swinging, turning, twisting, and rocking. Locomotor movements such as walking, running, marching, hopping, jumping, skipping, galloping, leaping and sliding result in moving from one place to another. It is possible to work with the two basic types of movement at the same time.

Begin by having the students experiment with nonlocomotor movements. Nonlocomotor movements can be suggested by asking the student to imitate ordinary everyday actions. Ask the students to stretch as if they had just awakened, to bend down and pick up a pencil, to sway like the grass in the breeze, to swing a baseball bat, to turn like a door on its hinges, or to rock like a baby.

Vary each of these motions by changing the suggestion: bend down and pick up a heavy rock, bend down and pick up a cat. Encourage the students to use their whole body, all levels of space (high, medium, low), and all areas of space (front, back, side). These movements can be accompanied with simple percussion instruments such as the hand drum, tambourine, maracas, triangle, wood block, guiro, cymbals, or xylophone. Students also enjoy providing the accompaniment for the rest of the class with these instruments.

Locomotor movements require much more space than nonlocomotor activities. As most school-age students can already perform many of these locomotor movements, it might be necessary to begin with variations on the basic movements. For example, ask the students to walk as if they are walking on ice, uphill, downhill, or in slow motion. Encourage the students to move in different directions and to use all levels of space. Students can be very creative in their movement responses to these simple suggestions. You should encourage this creativity.

Simple percussion instruments can be used to accompany these activities. The hand drum is particularly effective with locomotor activities. Recorded materials can be used, but be sure to listen to the selection to make sure that the tempo is appropriate to the suggested movement.

5. Movement Activities for Music Learning

It is fairly easy to begin using movement by asking the students to move to the beat. Choose a song with a steady beat or play a simple accompaniment with a steady beat. Vary the activity by having the students step in one direction until you say "change," at which time they will step in a new direction. Once the students can move to a steady beat, add meter to this exercise. Ask the students to move only on the stronger beats. The movement will be two, three or four times as slow as the beat. After this has been done successfully, suggest that the students find partners:

one person will step the beat while the other steps the meter. Another variation which requires more coordination is to have each individual step the beat and clap on the stronger beat. This activity can help in learning and understanding the relationship between beat and meter in music.

Rhythms naturally occur in all language, and it is not uncommon to use the rhythm of speech to learn about rhythm in music. Try using some of the speech patterns from the native language of your students. For example, the Northern Cheyenne word for night, "taa' eva," is the rhythm pattern long-short, while the word for pepper, "mehme menótse," is the rhythm pattern short-long. My students stepped the rhythm for night, the rhythm for pepper, and then combinations of these two rhythms. These rhythms are quite common in music, so a natural follow up to this activity was to ask the students to identify these rhythms in a song which they then learned.

Movement activities working with changes in tempo and dynamics are fairly easy to present. Tempo changes result in changes in the speed at which the movement is being performed. Select a song with tempo changes such as the "Hall of the Mountain King" from the *Peer Gynt Suite* No. 1 by Edvard Grieg, or "Little Train of the Capira" from *Bachianas Brasileiras* No. 2 by Heitor Villa-Lobos. Ask the students to begin with a specific locomotor movement such as walking. As the tempo of the song changes, the speed at which the movement is being performed should change. The type of movement that the students perform may change as the students react emotionally to the changes in the tempo.

When dynamics change, the amount of energy with which the physical gesture is being performed changes. Choose a composition with dynamic changes such as "Shaker Tune" from *Appalachian Spring Suite* by Aaron Copland, or "Baroque and Blue" from *Suite for Flute and Jazz Piano* by Claude Bolling. Both nonlocomotor and locomotor movements can be used for working with dynamics. Ask the students to vary their movement according to the loudness or softness of the piece. The students may change their movement from nonlocomotor to locomotor depending on the changes in the music.

Changes in the pitch of the song can be shown by changes in the level of the body. Select a simple song like "Twinkle, Twinkle, Little Star." When the pitch ascends, the natural tendency is for the student to stretch upwards. When the pitch descends, the tendency is to move downwards. Begin by having the students use their whole bodies to show the direction of the pitch using stretching and bending. Eventually, this movement can be reduced to using the arms to show differences in the pitch. This can eventually be combined with locomotor movements.

Melodies are made up of pitch and rhythms, and have a definite sense of direction or line. Most melodies are made up of several phrases, or shorter segments similar to a clause in speech. Select a song which the students have sung. You might try this activity with "Twinkle, Twinkle, Little Star" after the students have worked with the changes in pitch direction. Ask the students to step the beat while singing the song, and to step in one direction until they take a breath. With the new breath, the students should move in a new direction. The students are showing the phrases with this activity.

Most songs are made up of short sections with slightly different melodies. Select a song with a verse (A) and a refrain (B) such as the folk songs "Riding in the Buggy" or "Hop Up, My Ladies." Have the students select a movement for the verse and a different movement for the refrain. When the students use the different movements for the different sections. they are showing the form (AB) of the song.

Among the other combinations of sections frequently found in music is the three-part form (ABA) and the rondo (ABACA). Examples of three-part songs include "Nobody Knows the Trouble I've Seen," which is a spiritual, "Shoo, Fly" by Reeves and Campbell, "Carillon" from *L'Arlesianne Suite* No. 1 by Georges Bizet, or "Minuet" from *Eine Kleine Nachtmusik* (K. 525) by Wolfgang Amadeus Mozart. The rondo form can be heard in "Viennese Musical Clock" from the *Hary Janos* Suite by Zoltan Kodaly, "Fossils" from *Carnival of the Animals* by Camille Saint-Saens, or the *Gypsy Rondo* by Franz Josef Haydn. The same basic movement activity for the two-part form can easily be adapted to either of these forms. Observe the students while they move to see if their movements reflect the change in the sections found in the piece.

6. Movement Activities Using Native American Stories

To pull some of these activities together, it is important to think about ways to include several music concepts in a single learning activity. One way to accomplish this is to look for simple, short and easily remembered stories for the students to dramatize and accompany with their own music. Many of the stories and legends of the Native American people are suitable for this type of activity.

For example, the Northern Cheyenne folk tale "The Bear, the Coyote and the Skunk" can be used to give the students a chance to combine their movement, instrument playing and singing skills in a new setting. The text of the story follows.

> I will tell you a story.
> A long time ago, a bear was going along a path. A coyote was coming from the opposite direction. They met.
> The bear said to the coyote, "Get out of my way! This is my path!"
> "No, *you* get out of my way! This is *my* path," the coyote replied.
> While they were arguing, a skunk came slowly along. "Move out of the way! This is my path!" he said to them. He slowly turned around. He moved slowly backwards toward them.
> When they saw him they each ran off in his own direction. No one knows where they ran.
> (From *Cheyenne Short Stories*. 1977. Billings, Montana: Council for Indian Education. p. 14.)

After we had worked with tempo, dynamics and pitch, we used this story to combine these musical elements. The first time the students heard the story, we concentrated on learning the sequence of actions taken by the characters during the story. I asked all the students to move like all the characters in the story. As the animals moved at different speeds, the students concentrated on varying the tempo of their movement to fit the actions of the characters.

The students then selected and added instruments to accompany the movement of each animal. After we worked with movement and instruments, we performed the story. Some of the students acted as the animals while other children played instruments to accompany the character.

To further refine the story, we added dynamic changes and designated certain instruments to represent each animal. In addition to providing the students with the chance to be or accompany all of the characters, the additional performances allowed the students to experiment with their own movements and their own ways of playing the instruments while concentrating on adding a new musical element. During these sessions, the students began to experiment with singing the lines for their characters with improvised melodies.

These suggestions for using movement with music are not meant to replace an existing music curriculum, but they can be easily included in any existing music program. Try some of these ideas, and adapt, change and expand upon all of these suggestions. Enjoy exploring with your students. They will provide you with many ideas if you give them the opportunity for self-expression. I really enjoyed teaching Native American students partly because of the many wonderful ideas about the relationship between music and movement that we discovered together. I hope your experience is as enjoyable.

References for Further Reading

Aronoff, Frances Webber. *Music and Young Children.* New York: Turning Wheel Press. Expanded Edition, 1979.

Burnett, Millie, and Patti Schliestett Wiggins. *Today's Creative Children Sing, Play and Move.* Dubuque, IA: Kendall/Hunt.

Burnett, Millie. *Dance Down the Rain, Sing Up the Corn: American Indian Chants and Games for Children.* Allison Park, PA: Musik Innovations, 1975.

The Council for Indian Education (Box 31215, Billings, MT 59017). Booklets and publications of Native American stories.

Curtis, Natalie. *The Indians' Book: Songs and Legends of the American Indians.* New York: Dover, 1907. (Reprinted 1968).

Fichter, George. *American Indian Music and Musical Instruments; with Instructions for Making the Instruments.* New York: McKay, 1978.

Findlay, Elsa. *Rhythm and Movement: Applications of Dalcroze Eurhythmics.* Evanston, IL: Summy-Birchard, 1971.

Haselbach, Barbara. *Dance Education.* London: Schott, 1978.

My Music Reaches to the Sky: Native American Musical Instruments. New York: Ford Foundation, 1973.

Rubin, Janet, and Margaret Merrion. *Creative Drama and Music.* Needham Heights, MA: Ginn Press.

Weikart, Phyllis. *Movement Plus Rhymes, Songs and Singing Games.* Ypsilanti, MI: High/Scope, 1988.

Weikart, Phyllis. *Teaching Movement and Dance.* Ypsilanti, MI: High/Scope, 1982.

Recordings

Adventures in Music. New York: RCA Victor Record Division.

Authentic Music of the American Indian. Beverly Hills, CA: Legacy International.

Bowmar Orchestral Library. Glendale, CA: Bowmar Records, Inc.

Canyon Records (4143 North Sixteenth Street Phoenix, AZ 85016). Many recent releases.

Ethnic Folkways Library. New York: Folkways Records and Services. Many recordings featuring a specific tribe or tribes from the same geographical area. Currently distributed by The Smithsonian Institution (Constitution Avenue, Washington, DC 20560).

Folk Music of the United States from the Archive of Folk Song. Library of Congress (Music Division, Recording Library, Washington, DC 20540). Series which include many recordings from the collections of Frances Densmore and Willard Rhodes.

Indian House (Box 472, Taos, NM 87571). Recent recordings featuring specific tribes.

Powwow Songs. New York: New World Records.

Six Two-step Dance Songs; Six Skip Dance Songs; Four Double Time Songs. Phoenix, AZ: Canyon.

Songs and Dances of the Eastern Indians from Medicine Spring and Allegheny. New York: New World Records.

Songs of the Earth, Water, Fire and Sky. New York: New World Records.

Songs of the Love, Luck, and Animals. New York: New World Records.

Current Music Series

Holt Music. New York: Holt Rinehart and Winston. 1988.

Music and You. New York: Macmillan. 1988.

World of Music. Morristown, New Jersey: Silver Burdett and Ginn. 1988.

Chapter 21
Culture and Communication Through Art
by Connie Einfalt

Art is a language which every child speaks and one of the first media that children use to communicate. Children throughout the world have nearly identical stages of development in their art which transcend race or cultural background. While some cultures value these expressions more than others, children use these marks for emotional, intellectual, physical, and social growth. They should be guided knowledgeably in their artistic expression; their continued use of art for personal growth depends upon it.

The Alliance for Arts Education for the Bureau of Indian Affairs, B.I.A., administered an Arts Needs Assessment Questionnaire in 1976 in the schools of the B.I.A. to determine what was needed for a successful art program in Native American schools. They found that in the schools' communities:

1. 82.7% felt a culture-related art curriculum should be developed for American Indian children.
2. 79% stressed the importance of integrating art into the school curriculum.
3. 48% indicated a need for adequately trained art educators.

Recommendations for Art Experiences

Teachers, researchers, and consultants in the field of Native American Art Education recommend the following strategies for teaching art.

1. Create Culturally Relevant Experiences

Reinforcing the Native American student's tribal identity is a significant outcome of learning about art. "Art is an integral part of their cultural base," according to Leona M. Zastrow, a Native American art education consultant. It is important for educators to develop a working knowledge of how art was utilized by the specific culture they are teaching. Teachers should familiarize themselves with Native American Art and the culture of the students being taught, and develop a keen interest in the historical and contemporary idiosyncracies of the art of that tribe.

Of course, the best source of information about a specific tribe is the tribal elders, though it sometimes takes perseverance and a genuine interest to gain access to artistic cultural instruction. Linda Ganzel, a K–12 art instructor at Macy Public School in Macy Nebraska, told me that when she first came to the Omaha tribe, the community wanted her to teach culture, but she had trouble finding anyone willing to trust her enough to teach her the culture. She honestly admired the people's beadwork. Once when she was watching an older man do beadwork, he told her, "If you teach me to weave [for his dance costume], then I'll teach you to bead." He taught her to bead the peyote stitch; she practiced and practiced. Once she felt she had mastered several different beading techniques, she started to teach her students to bead—then the students came back and taught her new methods from their elders. The friendships which resulted laid a base for her for further study. Ganzel also found a source of support for her program from mothers and grandmothers who had a strong desire for their children to study Native arts.

Native Americans use art for power in a variety of ways. Experiences or projects should be sensitive to tribal beliefs and practices. An example of this is the creation of personal Kachina dolls. According to Okrent (1991), "Kachinas are regarded as intermediaries between the spirit world and man. It is looked on as a sacrilege for non-Indians to make three-dimensional representations." Other examples of sensitive areas are projects which depict the ghost dance or totem poles. Even Native Americans for other tribes understand the significance of these art objects and realize that creating them is offensive.

2. Invite Artists from the Tribe to Visit, or Take Field Trips to Studios and Museums

Learning from and employing the knowledge and skills of the tribal community to teach accurately is both relevant and beneficial. "Art values deteriorate at a rapid rate when cultural values are lost," according to Leo Bushman, who studied Eskimo art for the National Art Education Association. Whenever possible visits from Native American artists are positive experiences for several reasons, for example, as a positive role model for students and to show the future value/(fragment) of what the students are currently learning. In addition, visiting collections or museums can have a tremendous impact upon students, who can apply what they observe to their own work.

3. Be Cognizant of Reasons Students Should Learn Art

Art education should not be approached as a gifted and talented program; it is beneficial for all students, no matter what their skill level. Through visual art, the affective, cognitive, and psychomotor domains of students can be fully engaged. Studies by Howard Gardner, a cognitive psychologist from Harvard University, on the human mind confirm that art is a cognitive activity and is necessary for a child's cognitive development. He says, "Art cannot and should not be considered apart from the rest of the child's evolving capacities. There are intimate yet ignored links between the child's drawing and the rest of his burgeoning power."

Educators should realize the ramifications of artistic skill development. Those who work with early childhood education programs develop not only visual communication skills but also skills in other communication areas. Programs such as Head Start utilize art materials to enable children to progress more quickly to language systems. There has been some documentation on the relationship between early childhood experiences with art materials and later abilities to read and write. The earlier children are given and encouraged to use art materials, the more eye-hand coordination will develop. Their future reading and writing abilities depend upon the development of these skills. In turn, the child's visual perception heightens, allowing for a readiness for reading.

Art has also been proven to be effective in enhancing self-esteem. Ganzel feels that her students look at the art experience as an opportunity to be involved with something for which there is no right or wrong. It therefore is a place for a safe encounter in learning, sometimes an escape from the school environment. She uses the time in art to counsel her students—there is a predominance of individual instruction in her teaching style.

4. Become Familiar with the Stages of Development

Because art is not a required subject in many schools, teachers' backgrounds for teaching it vary greatly. In many states, art education classes are not required for elementary classroom teachers to become certified. However, it is worthwhile for educators to realize that the field of art education is a dynamic area of study which has been changing significantly, and to become familiar with the philosophies pertinent to the teaching of art. Two of these are summarized here.

The book, *Creative and Mental Growth,* by Viktor Lowenfeld, is an excellent reference for anyone teaching art. Lowenfeld believes that children should be allowed to grow and develop naturally without the imposition of adult symbols and perceptions. He felt the teacher's role was to stimulate, motivate, guide and evaluate, and the teacher's responsibility was to help the children become aware of their visual way of working. Appropriate art media should be noted for each stage to ensure success. Children's stages of development in art are approximate; in today's ever more visual world, sometimes the stages seem to be advancing more quickly than when Lowenfeld studied them.

The **Scribbling Stage** is the first stage, occurring from two to four years. During this stage, a child progresses from (a) disordered scribbling to (b) controlled scribbling and then to (c) the naming of scribbling. It is important in this stage to provide art materials which require no technical mastery. The teacher or parent merely provides a guiding hand, allowing the child to naturally progress from one stage to another.

During the **Pre-schematic Stage,** which occurs from four to seven years, children organize their scribbling to form representative images. They begin to develop unique and personal symbols to portray themselves and their world.

The **Schematic Stage,** which occurs from seven to nine years, is also a significant artistic stage. The development of the baseline, a universal symbol for the ground, is an indicator of children's awareness of themselves in their environment.

The stage of **Dawning Realism** extends from nine to eleven years. The child's work shows a greater awareness in portraying objects in a realistic way, using many details. It is very important for children to be guided in their drawing skills at this stage.

The **Pseudo-Naturalistic Stage** extends from eleven to thirteen. Research has shown that children at this age begin to abandon art as a form of expression if they become dissatisfied with their skills; therefore, much attention should be paid to successful and meaningful projects. The final product becomes very important to the child.

Adolescent Art is the final chapter in children's experiences forming the transition to adulthood. Relationships and the cultural tendencies of their peers become important subjects for students' work.

5. Include Art History, Aesthetics, and Criticism

An approach which varies from Lowenfeld's child-centered approach to teaching art has gained recognition lately: the Getty Center for the Arts' cultural approach to teaching. Discipline Based Art Education, or D.B.A.E., calls for the study of art history, aesthetics, and art criticism as components of teaching art, in addition to art production.

The approach the Getty Center advocates is a multi-cultural approach, utilizing the richly divergent history of art. The study of art history can give the students a knowledge of their past. The study of other cultures will give the students a wide base for comparing their own culture (Thorpe and Libhart, 1965).

Two key components advocated by the Getty Center are in the areas of aesthetics and art criticism. Aesthetics means to see, comprehend and appreciate the images that affect or please one. Art criticism is explained as the ability to analyze, interpret, and evaluate the qualities of visual images. Many art teachers devise teaching strategies for developing criticism and aesthetic abilities by using questioning and group discussion. It would be advantageous for teachers to do further reading on conducting art discussions.

There are some important thinking skills that can be practiced by engaging students in higher level thinking experiences. In an excellent article in *Art Education,* Wardle (1990) discusses the use of symbolism.

Because some Native American students are not comfortable in large, structured discussions, several teachers have developed alternative ways for students to lead students in aesthetic discussions. Linda Ganzel prefers for her students to use small group discussions. In this way, students can also critique each other's work in a safe group, where discussions become more positive and comfortable. Another method is employed by a teacher in Arizona, who has his students write personal papers about works of art. If a student is to view a particular landscape, he might have the student write a story based upon an experience that would remind the student of the place.

6. Develop Experiences Which Have Relevance to the Students' Lives and Backgrounds

For Linda Ganzel, the experiences she creates for her students need to have spiritual or meaningful connotations in order to motivate them. For instance, to give more meaning to a landscape study, she has taken her students to one of the places which have a special meaning to the tribe. She has observed that for her students, there is an inherent value to the study.

Even in the study of art history, if a teacher builds bridges of relevance, it seems to motivate students to learn not only about their own cultures, but also about cultures and artists from outside their own locale. M. C. Escher's drawings are naturally motivating for almost all students. Ganzel showed her students "Three Worlds," which fascinated them. One theme that she discussed when she introduced Escher's work was his use of repetitive patterns—which her Native American students were familiar with in their own artistic traditions. She had the students create their own symbols for an Escher style design. She also observed that her students were intrigued by Escher because his work used several different levels of meaning. For instance, the students discussed his work and realized that the trout swimming in the pond could represent the water world, the lily pads floating on top represented the earthly world, and the trees reflected in the water could either represent the world of the air or the world which is reflected or not completely seen. The students appreciated the symbolic references that Escher used.

Ganzel also noted that her students are highly motivated both personally and from the community to use their tribe's traditional symbols in their own work. The students receive much positive reinforcement from their elders for their usage of these symbols, according to Wardle (1990).

Meaning within Native American art is expressed through graphic symbolism of at least four types:

1. Symbols, such as people, spirits, corn, animals, water, etc.
2. Color, with each color having specific meaning and assigned properties.
3. Use of natural materials, stone, bone, feather, wool, clay or leather.
4. Materials from which, and techniques through which, the art work is made.

One project which could be highly successful at almost any level is for students to create a personal book. The students are invited to talk to their elders about a legend that they know. The students then write down the legend and create illustrations of it, using virtually any medium, drawing, painting, printmaking, or even sand-painting. The cover could be made of a natural material, or beaded or quilled. There are many valuable outcomes from this experience: it would promote seeing relationships between many different disciplines in the curriculum, it would use a variety of learning styles, and in some cases, it might be the first time that the story has ever been written.

Conclusion

The benefits of art experiences for Native American students, as for all students, are clear and worth the efforts required to make art instruction meaningful. The more teachers understand about their students' backgrounds and lives, the better they can help their students journey into culture and communication through art.

References for Further Reading

Books

Ambler, J. Richard. *The Anasazi, Prehistoric People of the Four Corners Region.* Museum of Norther Arizona, 1989.

Gardner, Howard. *Art, Mind, and Brain: A Cognitive Approach to Creativity.* Basic. 1982.

London, Peter. *No More Second-hand Art.* Boston, Mass.: 1989. Shambhala Publications.

Lowenfeld, Viktor. *Creative and Mental Growth.* N.Y: The Macmillan Company, 1964.

Sargent, Lori, and Jo Reid Smith, "Teaching the Indian Child Art." In Hap Gilliland, *Teaching the Native American,* first edition. Kendall/Hunt. 1988. pp. 173–176.

Thorpe and Libhart. *Craft Horizons.* 1965.

Walters, Anna Lee. *The Spirit of Native America, Beauty and Mysticism in American Indian Art.* Chronicle Books, 1989.

Magazines

Okrent, Inez. "Storyteller Dolls Express Tradition." *School Arts Magazine,* pp. 23–48, February 1991.

Saville-Troike, Muriel. "Navajo Art and Education." *Journal of Aesthetic Education,* Summer 1984, pp. 41–50.

Wardle, Barbra L. "Native American Symbolism in the Classroom." *Art Education,* pp. 13–24, September, 1990.

Resources

Zastrow, Leona M. *Resources for the Classroom Teacher, Southwest American Indians.* Roswell, N.M., 1981.

Zastrow, Leona M. *The American Indian Tradition and Transition Through Art.* Roswell, N.M., 1991. (Good lessons)

Zastrow, Leona M. *Learning Science by Studying Native American Pottery.* Roswell, N.M., 1991.

Chapter 22
Incorporating Native American Activities into the Physical Education Program

By Robert W. Grueninger

Frequent mention has been made in this reference to holistic learning, living in a multicultural society, developing a positive self-concept, recognizing the uniqueness of every child, adapting instruction to students' learning styles, and having a culturally relevant curriculum. Since physical education brings together the body, mind and spirit in a learning environment, it is, by its nature, holistic. Moreover, if, as has been suggested, the learning style of Indian children emphasizes observation, physical activity, and artistic and spatial skills, the physical education curriculum might offer a nearly ideal learning environment. Material learned in other areas might be reinforced through physical activity, such as by acting out stories, by playing games mentioned in history or English class, or by reinforcing native language instruction in the gymnasium. Ideas for integrating the curriculum are limited only by desire and imagination, so long as the special responsibilities of physical education toward physical fitness and motor skill development are not ignored and the needs of the child are met.

In this chapter, several suggestions will be given to maximize the effectiveness of physical education for the Native American child, to make education more relevant, successful, and culturally meaningful.

Teach Native American Games

Include units on traditional games and activities in the curriculum of the elementary, middle, and senior high school. Such efforts should be received with greater enthusiasm on the part of your Native American students.

At the elementary school level, activities rooted in Indian culture include Blind Man's Bluff, Prisoner's Base, Crack the Whip, Hide and Seek, and Follow the Leader. For the upper grades, lacrosse, field hockey, ice hockey, soccer, and football each has its place in Native American history.

Emphasize the History of Native American Games and Sports

It also supports the needs of Native Americans if you teach the history of the games and sports being introduced. Help the child to recognize that, in the past, the values and skills which a Native American needed for survival were perpetuated through games and sports. Thus, activities often simulated hunting, food gathering, tipi building, relaying vital messages, or fighting. Skills emphasized were those of throwing spears, shooting arrows, riding horses, and running. Games both developed and tested the strength, stamina, speed, pain tolerance, and courage required for life.

Try These Games for Elementary School Children

Blind Man's Bluff (Kindergarten–Primary Grades)

A blindfolded player stands in the center while all of the others skip around the perimeter of the circle. The ''blind man'' taps three times with a stick and everyone stops and stands still. Then, the ''blind man'' points at a player with the stick and asks that child to make an animal noise, e.g., ''Quack like a duck,'' or ''Whinny like a horse,'' etc. If the ''blind man'' correctly guesses the player's name, the two exchange places. If not, everyone starts skipping again. To allow more players the chance to take part and to avoid embarrassing the ''blind man,'' limit the number of unsuccessful attempts.

Corncob Darts (Primary Grades)

Darts made of shelled corncobs and feathers were tossed underhand at a circular target drawn on the ground at various distances. Twenty feet was common, although the target could be nearer or farther depending upon the skill level of the participants. A suitable dart may be improvised by tying a knot in a bandanna; tie a stone inside the knot to increase the weight, if necessary.

Fish Trap Game (Primary Grades)

Among Northwestern Coast Indians, a tag game was played in which somewhere between three or four and twelve children would hold hands and form a fisherman's net and three or four others would be the ''fish.'' The object was to trap the ''fish'' by touching them with any part of the net. Once caught, a ''fish'' became part of the net. The game continued until all of the ''fish'' were caught.

Hoop Race (Primary Grades)

The Beaver Clan of the Seneca Nation enjoyed a circle relay involving passing a 24 inch diameter hoop over the head, body, and legs of each player around the circle and back again in reverse sequence (step into the hoop, over the trunk, and off over the head). The first team to complete the hoop passing without missing a person or step was the winner.

Dodge Ball (Upper Elementary)

Mandan, Pawnee, and other prairie tribes played a form of dodge ball in which a batter would toss up and bat a rawhide ball with a four ft. hardwood stick. If any of the eight or so fielders encircling the batter caught the ball, that fielder would throw it from that spot at the batter. The batter had to dodge the ball while staying inside a four ft. diameter circle. If hit, the batter became the fielder, and the thrower, the batter. Design your variation, using a rubber playground ball.

Pin Guard (Upper Elementary)

In Louisiana and Arkansas, the Caddo Indians played an interesting team game, not unlike what is now known as "Pin Guard." A field about 30 ft. by 70 ft. was marked out, and six clay "Indian clubs" were placed side by side along each end line. Two teams of seven players each competed, each being confined to its own half of the field. The object was to bowl or throw a basketball-sized ball so that it would knock down the pins. When a team possessed the ball, the other defended its pins. Play continued until one team had knocked over all the pins on the other team's end line.

Hoop and Pole Games (Upper Elementary)

Sports implements often were derived from weapons used in hunting or in war. Thus, the shield became a hoop in the hoop and pole game, and the spear became the pole. Sometimes arrows or darts were thrown at the rolling hoop.

For physical education classes today, the "Buffalo Hunt" game of the Oklahoma area seems most adaptable. The objective is to throw a blunt spear through a 10 in. (i.d.) ring made of green branches wrapped with rawhide. Children are divided into groups according to available equipment, so as to allow maximum participation consistent with good safety practices. The groups may be further subdivided into two lines, throwers and retrievers. The last person in the throwers' line rolls the hoop, and the first throws the pole at it. Each child is given five trials. Throwers become retrievers, and retrievers join the throwing line as rollers, etc. Close supervision is advised, to prevent someone from being hit by a pole. Vary the throwing distance according to the players' skill.

Prisoner's Base (Upper Elementary)

Any number of players are divided into two teams, each team defending one half of the play field. Each team has an area designated as its prison, somewhere near its own end line. Within the prison are placed three blocks or balls. The object of the game is to steal the opponents' blocks without being caught in enemy territory and thrown into prison. Once caught, prisoners may be freed only by being tagged by a member of their own team.

Alaskan Native Games (Upper Elementary-High School)

Traditional Inuit and Dene games are included in the Arctic Winter Games (Jones, 1989). In the one-foot high kick, a player jumps off both feet and kicks a suspended cloth target with one foot. A running start may be used; the athlete must land and maintain balance on the kicking foot. With each successful kick, the target is raised. An accomplished adult may kick a target over eight feet high.

The two-foot high kick requires that the take-off and landing be made with the feet together and that the target be struck with both feet.

Other Alaskan Native games taught in the Anchorage School District include Indian leg wrestling, stick pull, seal hop, toe kick, and knee jump (Frey and Allen, 1989).

Include These Activities for Intermediate and High School

Archery

The following steps in learning archery have their historical precedents among Native Americans: (a) standing and shooting at a stationary target; (b) standing and shooting at a moving target, such as a ball of yucca (Navajo); (c) standing and shooting at a buffalo hide being dragged by rawhide; (d) trying to have more arrows in the air at one time than your opponent, in a rapid fire technique; and (e) launching a piece of straw into the air and trying to hit it with an arrow, similar to trap shooting (Crow). The Blackfeet had their own version of archery golf, consisting of shooting an arrow into the ground, shooting a second arrow at the first, and so on. The Pawnee variation consisted of shooting an arrow about 50 yards ahead to land flat; other archers then attempted to shoot so that their arrows would come to rest across the first.

Shinny and Ice Shinny

Shinny was the forerunner of both ice and field hockey, and was popular from Canada to Mexico, from the Atlantic to the Pacific. Teams competed by defending goals located at opposite ends of the field or by taking turns and counting the number of strokes that it took to score a goal by hitting the ball along the ground with the stick. The crooked sticks were similar to the ice hockey sticks of today, although skates were not used. Introduce shinny as a lead-up game to field hockey.

Lacrosse

While ancestral forms of bowling, hockey, baseball, wrestling, and football may be found in many parts of the world, lacrosse is uniquely American Indian. The Iroquois called the game "Tokonhon," the "little brother of war." But, French settlers thought that the curved sticks used by the Senecas resembled their bishop's staff, which was called, "la crossier." Therefore, they named the game "lacrosse."

Lacrosse was a violent sport, with much running and quick starts, and often involved injury. The rules have been refined through the years, first to teams of 30 or so per side, and eventually to the current 10-a-side for men, 12-a-side for women, and a field the size of a soccer pitch. Rules of safety and protective equipment have been added. Modern lacrosse is played widely in North America by both men and women. A variation, Box Lacrosse, is played in iceless hockey rinks, adopting rules from ice hockey, lacrosse, and "murder ball."

Foot Games

Games played with the feet include foot catch, soccer, and both kick ball and kick stick races.

Foot catch was played by tribeswomen, who balanced a small deerskin ball on top of the foot, kicked it into the air, and then caught it again on the foot. Among the Eskimo, the ball was 1-1/2 to 2 inches in diameter, made of buckskin, somewhat akin to the popular hackeysack. (Hackeysack is a trademark name.)

The World Footbag Association gives several tips on skills and drills using a small footbag. The primary volleying skill consists of lifting the ball up and towards the body gently with the top of the foot, not kicking it away as in soccer. The basic kicks consist of contacting the footbag (1) with the top of the foot near the toes, and (2) with the knee. After setting up the ball with these kicks, try the (3) inside kick, with the instep, (4) the outside kick, with the lateral border of the foot, and the (5) back kick, with the outside of the foot over your back or shoulder. Play begins with a courtesy hand toss from another player.

Kick Ball Races

Tek'mu Pu'ku means, in Moquelumnan tribal language, "to kick little dog," and was one of many kick ball and kick stick races. Two parallel lines were marked six inches apart, extending 50 to 100 yards or more; a post was placed at each end of the lines. The object was to keep the small buckskin ball between the lines while foot racing. If the ball went out of bounds, it was restarted from that point.

Running

For many tribes, running was and still is an important part of life. Pueblo children were told to "look to the mountain tops and the running (will) be easy." Hopi children and adults would get up before dawn and run many miles to the fields to cultivate and then back again by nightfall. Each session had its running races, e.g., for corn planting in the spring and harvesting in the fall. Then there were the "ceremonial runners," who ran messages from village to village.

The physical educator should feel confident in emphasizing running as a fitness activity which is part of the Native American heritage. Instruction in common track and field events, too, would be most appropriate. A similar overhand throwing pattern is used whether the implement is a spear, throwing arrow, or javelin.

Demonstrate Traditional Equipment

Of the many books on Native American sports and games, several describe the equipment used by different tribes, sometimes with detailed instructions on how to make it. Canoes, sleds, snowshoes, moccasins, hammocks, kayaks, ponchos, toboggans, parkas, stilts, swings, tops, and in fact, rubber balls are all equipment invented by Indians. Of course, equipment may be improvised with the use of newer materials. Since Indians continually made the best use of what they could find in their environment, such as by using metal for arrow tips and spear heads when iron became available, it would not seem impure to use synthetics, plastics, or even manufactured equipment in teaching and practicing traditional activities. For example, hoops made of plastic or of rubber hose joined with a wooden dowel and tape could substitute for the traditional wooden hoops in the hoop and spear game. Equipment for field hockey and lacrosse is available from many sporting goods companies that advertise regularly in *Scholastic Coach* or in the *Journal of Physical Education, Recreation, and Dance*. For retaining that important sense of history, however, show your students some authentic or homemade replicas of the equipment actually used.

Ten Suggestions for Physical Education

1. Incorporate activities with a cultural background of Native American participation in a way that promotes physical fitness through participation of every student—not with a few players actively involved and the rest standing around watching. Ease students into team sports, teach the skills required, drill them on the skills and their application, and then coach them so that they are all part of the action.

2. When introducing a game or sport, give background information that links current participation with that of the children's ancestors. In addition to giving interesting historical anecdotes, show some of the equipment used in the past.

3. Involve Native American students in planning, demonstrating, helping to teach, and officiating at activities.

4. Assign players to teams or use a method of choosing team members that will avoid possible embarrassment to students. Blackfeet women had an impartial way to choose teams for shinny. Each player would place her individually carved stick on a pile. A blindfolded person would pick up the sticks from the pile, two at a time, dividing them into two smaller piles which henceforth formed the teams (Whitney, 1977.). This way no one's feelings were hurt by being chosen last.

5. In evaluating student performance, use criterion referenced standards or use norms specific to the population being tested. This may mean establishing new norms from the test data at a particular school or area, which a student may find more meaningful than standards based on a larger population with little or no representation from Native Americans.

6. Recognize that successful performance in school depends upon a supportive home environment, good health, and proper nutrition. A child who has low self-esteem or who has chronic fatigue and depression will not perform well in school either academically or physically.

7. Help students build self-esteem these three ways:
    (a) Learn their names; recognize them as individuals. A name gives identity and pride, and is therefore a valuable personal possession.
    (b) Seek opportunities to commend children. Be positive. Research has shown that a 4:1 ratio of positive to negative feedback is most beneficial to student achievement in the elementary grades.
    (c) Lead through personal example and through teaching about successful Indian athletes who can serve as additional role models—Jim Thorpe, Billy Mills, Frank Hudson, Bart Starr, Johnny Bench. Further information on outstanding Indian athletes may be obtained by writing the American Indian Hall of Fame, Haskell Indian Junior College, Lawrence, KS 66044.

8. Choose activities that are inclusive rather than exclusive. Games such as dodgeball that have the objective of eliminating players from the inside of the circle may be modified so that players once hit become throwers rather than spectators.

9. Plan open houses, sports festivals or other such activities as part of your public relations efforts. These may help to increase parental participation and support for your school programs.

10. Teach for concomitant learnings of fair play, cooperation, skill in observation, courage, patience, humor and self-reliance. Traditionally, Indian games stressed endurance, perseverance, skill, brute force, and the ability to withstand pain. Games and sports, properly planned for and conducted, afford opportunities to teach fair competition, the desire to excel, sportsmanship and respect for self and others.

References for Further Study

A. Books and Articles

Blood, Charles. *Indian Games and Crafts*. New York: Franklin Watts Press, 1981. 32 pp. Tells the young reader how to make signs and symbols, a necklace, an apron, a dancing bustle, a breastplate, plus how to play the Indian games of arrow toss, a stick game, and shinny.

Culin, Stewart. *Games of the North American Indians*. New York: Dover Publications, Inc. 1975. (Originally published as "Games of the North American Indians," Twenty-Fourth annual Report of the Bureau of American Ethnology to the Smithsonian Institution, 1902–03, by W. H. Holmes, Chief. Wash., D.C.: U.S. Government Printing Office, 1907.) An excellent historical reference compiled around the turn of the century. Includes a tabular index of games played by various tribes, and describes numerous games played with implements.

Frey, Richard D., and Mike Allen. "Alaskan Native Games—A Cross-Cultural Addition to the Physical Education Curriculum." *Journal of Physical Education, Recreation, and Dance* (JOPERD), 60–9. Nov./Dec. 1989. pp. 21–24.

Grueninger, Robert. "Physical Education for the Indian Student." In Jon Rehyner (Ed.), *Teaching the Indian Child: A Bilingual/Multicultural Approach*. Second Edition. Billings, MT: Eastern Montana College. 1988. pp. 255–269.

Discusses additional Indian games to use in physical education.

IEA Resource and Evaluation Center One. *Indian Culture Unit: American Indians and Sports*. Available from NAR/ORBIS, Suite 200, 1411 K St. NW, Wash., D.C. 20005. 1986.

Jones, Robert A. "Arctic Winter Games—Untapped Potential." *Journal of Physical Education, Recreation, and Dance* (JOPERD), 60–8. Oct. 1989. pp. 62–64.

MacFarlan, Allan A. *Book of American Indian Games*. New York: Association Press. 1958. Describes how to play 150 different Indian games, grouped according to age suitability, with suggestions for adapting running, relay, kicking, hunting, tossing and catching, and challenge games and contests.

Nabokov, Peter. *Indian Running*. Santa Barbara, CA: Capra Press. 1981.

Oxendine, Joseph B. *American Indian Sports Heritage*. Champaign, IL: Human Kinetics Books. 1988.

Whitney, A. *Sports and Games the Indians Gave Us*. New York: David McKay. 1977.

Wolfe, Karleen. "Things to Do." In *Classroom Activities for the Middle Grades*. Olympia, WA: Office of the State Superintendent of Public Instruction. 1982.

B. Films and Videocassettes

Running Brave. (Videocassette.) 106 min. Popular release. Inspirational story of Billy Mills' distance running career, from the Pine Ridge Reservation in South Dakota to a gold medal at the 1964 Olympics in Tokyo.

The Honor of All. (Film.) 90 min. Available from the Indian Health Service. The incidence of

alcoholism on a British Columbia reservation was 100%, affecting every man, woman, and child. Now that same reservation, Alkali Lake, is completely dry of alcohol. A fascinating film showing how the destruction force of alcoholism can be overcome, allowing people to live happier, more fulfilling lives.

C. For Further Information

National Association of Girls' and Women's Sports (NAGWS). *Official Field Hockey-Lacrosse Guide*. Available from the AAHPERD, 1900 Association Drive, Reston, VA 22091.

National Collegiate Athletic Association (NCAA). *Lacrosse Rules and Interpretations*. Available from the NCAA, 6201 College Blvd. Overland Park, KS 66211–2422.

World Footbag Association. *Official Players' Manual*. Golden, CO: Author. 1985. Available from the World Footbag Association, 1317 Washington Ave., Suite 7, Golden, CO 80401. An introduction to footbag games, giving their history, basic kicks, tips, and rules.

Chapter 23
Learning from the History of Indian Education
by Jon Reyhner

What type of teaching has worked well with Native Americans in the past? Despite the fact that Indian education has been characterized in a congressional report as "a national tragedy'" (*Indian Education*, 1969), there have always been responsive teachers who have worked to meet the special needs of their Native American students. Also, Native Americans were becoming doctors, teachers, and ministers a century ago, and more and more of them are successfully attending universities and colleges today.

Traditional education for Native Americans began with the extended family and taught survival skills that allowed Indian children to learn how to procure food and shelter in an often adverse environment and how to live in harmony with nature and their fellow man (Morey & Gilliam, 1974). Native American education produced tribal members fit to survive and prosper in the North American environment. Apprenticeship provided a means of higher education for those seeking to become healers and religious leaders. With the coming of the Europeans, the living conditions of Native Americans changed rapidly through the introduction of guns, horses, Christianity, new diseases, and many other foreign developments.

Organization of Schools for Indians
The first Europeans, when they considered Indian education, saw it in religious terms. They felt Indians were uncivilized and needed to be saved by becoming Christians. Dedicated missionaries, both Catholic and Protestant, sought to convert Indians to Christianity. Many missionaries found that the quickest and most logical way to explain Christianity to Indians was to learn their languages and to translate the Bible into those languages, as it had been translated centuries before into the many languages of Europe. In 1663 John Eliot published an Algonquian translation of the Bible (Bowden, 1981). While he used the native language, Eliot did not try to draw any connection between Christianity and traditional culture. Instead he encouraged converts to come together in what proved to be unsuccessful "praying" towns where they were to dress and live like the colonists.

After the American Revolution, the new U.S. government felt it was necessary to civilize Indians living in the country so that they would live in harmony with the settlers who were moving in on their lands. The idea of Indian education was to make yeoman farmers of Indians, thus freeing up the vast Indian hunting grounds for White settlement. Many Indian missionaries combined their attempts to Christianize Indians with the effort to make them farmers.

By 1838, the federal government was operating six manual training schools with eight hundred students and eighty-seven boarding schools with about 2,900 students (*Indian Education,* 1969, p. 11). In 1839, Commissioner T. Hartley Crawford formalized development of manual labor schools to educate Indian children in farming and homemaking (*Report,* 1976, pp. 38–39). Pressure by settlers and the federal government led to treaty after treaty being signed with Indian tribes. In return for accepting reservations, tribes were offered annuities and education. An example of the promises made can be found in the Fort Laramie negotiations by President Grant's Peace Commissioners:

> Upon the reservation you select, we propose to build a house for your agent to live in, to build a mill to saw your timber, and a mill to grind your wheat and corn, when you raise any: a blacksmith shop and a house for your farmer, and such other buildings as may be necessary. We also propose to furnish to you homes and cattle, to enable you to begin to raise a supply of stock and with which to support your families when the game has disappeared. We desire to supply you with clothing to make you comfortable and all necessary farming implements so that you can make your living by farming. We will send you teachers for your children. (Prucha, 1985, p. 18)

Protestant missionaries translated religious and educational tracts into Sioux starting in 1834. In 1882, Stephen R. Riggs completed a *Grammar and Dictionary of the Dakota Language* (Wilson, 1983, p. 11). The Santee Normal School was started in 1870 to train Sioux teachers. It received government funding until 1901, when funding for sectarian schools was ended. Wilson reports that

> Although considered by many people at the time to be one of the best schools of Indian education, the institution received criticism for teaching Indians to read and write in their own language. (1983, p. 27)

Charles Eastman was one of the most famous students who attended Santee Normal School. Eastman, who graduated from Dartmouth and who became a medical doctor, is most famous for his autobiographies describing his transition from "the deep woods to civilization." Eastman, educated by missionaries, became convinced after observing the materialism of late nineteenth-century America that "Christianity and modern civilization are opposed and irreconcilable and that the spirit of Christianity and of our ancient [Sioux] religion is essentially the same" (Eastman, *Soul of the Indian* as quoted in Wilson, 1983, p. 87).

A teacher on the Warm Springs Reservation in Oregon reported in 1862:

> Indian children, situated as they are in this reservation, in commencing an education, are placed at a great disadvantage as compared with white children. They are unable to enunciate many of the sounds represented by the letters of the English alphabet, and being ignorant of the meaning of words which they learn and the sentences they read, the exercises do not naturally possess an equal interest to them as to white children. (Report, 1863, p. 295)

This teacher also declared that the textbooks he had were for "advanced scholars" and that more elementary ones were needed (p. 296). Another teacher on the Tulalip Reservation in Washington reported, "My scholars complain that they do not understand what they read in English, and, in order to aid them, I am compiling a Snohomish-English and English-Snohomish Dictionary" and that his students "must become as orphans, that is, they must forget their parents as far as possible in order to abandon the habits of the Indians with less difficulty" (*Report*, 1863, p. 406).

In the 1878 *Annual Report of the Commissioner of Indian Affairs,* "education of their children" was seen as the quickest way to civilize Indians and that education could only be given "to children removed from the examples of their parents and the influence of the camps and kept in boarding schools" (*Annual Report,* 1878, pp. xxv–xxvi). In the same report school children were described as "hostages for good behavior of [their] parents" by Lieutenant R. H. Pratt (p. 174).

In 1878 Pratt brought 17 Indian adult prisoners of war from Florida to Hampton Institute and recruited another 40 boys and nine girls from Dakota Territory (Eastman, 1935, pp. 63 and 67). The children were encourage to speak English, but were not punished if they did not (p. 68). Two years later Pratt opened the famous Carlisle Indian School in Carlisle, Pennsylvania, after obtaining support from the local community and Congress (pp. 77–78). Initially there were 136 students. Disturbed by the small food allowance provided by the Indian Bureau, Pratt insisted that the students be fed on army rations (p. 82). From then to 1903 Carlisle graduated 158 Indian students and had another 1,060 students who did not graduate (p. 71). The school provided an elementary education to older Indian students, who usually remained away from their families for three years. In the summers students were placed with area families under the "Outing System." The average age of new students at Carlisle was 15 (p. 216).

Pratt argued with missionaries who he felt did not "advocate the disintegration of the tribes, and giving to individual Indians rights and opportunities among civilized people" (p. 113). Pratt wanted his students to merge with the White population.

Carl Schurz, Secretary of Interior under President Rutherford B. Hayes, felt the alternatives for Indians were extermination or civilization. The object of Indian policy was "unquestionably the gradual absorption of the Indians in the great body American citizenship" (Prucha, 1973, pp. 14–15). Reservations were seen as "socialism" (p. 73), a charge repeated recently by James Watt, Secretary of the Interior during Ronald Reagan's first term as President.

Methods of Instruction

Under Schurz the Indian Bureau issued regulations in 1880 that "all instruction must be in English" (Prucha, 1973, p. 199) in both mission and government schools under threat of loss of government funding. It was felt by J. D. C. Atkins, Commissioner of Indian Affairs from 1885 to 1888, that "to teach Indian school children their native tongue is practically to exclude English, and to prevent them from acquiring it" (Prucha, 1973, p. 203). The ethnocentric attitude of the late nineteenth century is evident in Atkins' 1887 report:

> Every nation is jealous of its own language, and no nation ought to be more so than ours, which approaches nearer than any other nationality to the perfect protection of its people. True Americans all feel that the Constitution, laws, and institutions of the United States, in their adaptation to the wants and requirements of man, are superior to those of any other country; and they should understand that by the spread of the English language will these laws and institutions be more firmly established and widely disseminate. Nothing so surely and perfectly stamps upon an individual a national characteristic as language. (Prucha, 1975, p. 175)

Despite patriotic announcements like the one above, observers in the field like General Oliver O. Howard reported that successful missionary teachers learned the tribal language so that they could understand them (1907, pp. 139–140 and 320).

A number of Indian Service employees who worked in Indian boarding and day schools at the turn of the century have written autobiographies. They reported good and bad experiences. Janette Woodruff (1939), hired as a matron, found Crow children in 1900 to be "restrained and orderly and never given to outbursts of any kind" (p. 26). She found that to teach the children, "There always had to be a concrete, and objective way of presenting an idea" (p. 65). She observed that teachers who did not demonstrate their lessons found attempts to teach "utterly futile" (p. 97).

Gertrude Golden (1954), who started teaching in Oregon, found her students "excelled in those subjects which required observation, imitation and memory and were more backward in those demanding reasoning and imagination" (p. 8). She found many teachers worked in Indian schools only for the money and had no respect for the "lousy Indians" they taught (p. 10). Estelle Brown (1952), working at Leupp Boarding School, found "no employee was here because of an interest in Indians and their welfare. We were here to make a living" (p. 153).

School principals and inspectors were often more interested in the attractiveness of the bulletin boards than the quality of teaching (Golden, p. 13). Brown (1952) reported that if the students sat quietly with shoes shined and noses wiped, the inspector would send a good report back to Washington about the teacher (p. 88).

In one school Golden worked in she found the educated Indians working in the school segregated from the white employees (p. 70). She found among all the tribes she worked with a universal aversion to learning English, "the language of the despised conquerors" (p. 83). Albert H. Kneale (1950) concluded after a long career in the Indian service which started as a teacher with Sioux in 1899 that

> Every tribe with which I have associated is imbued with the idea that it is superior to all other peoples. Its members are thoroughly convinced of their superiority not alone over members of all other tribes but over the whites as well . . . I have never known an Indian who would consent to being changed into a white man even were he convinced that such a change would readily be accomplished. (p. 105)

On being transferred to a school in Oklahoma, Kneale found the discipline "notoriously bad." To keep students from running away, windows were barred and doors padlocked, a common practice. An attempt to restore discipline by force by a "hard-bitten army sergeant" ended with the sergeant being beaten and sent to the hospital. Kneale refused to follow recommendations to continue the old policies, and through interpreters secured the cooperation of the boys by organizing them into companies and letting them choose their own officers:

> These officers, with myself, formed a group to enact such rules and regulations as it was deemed wise to enforce, to pass judgment on all infractions of these rules and outline proper punishments for infractions. Every boy in school pledged obedience to the rule of this group.
>   It worked! (p. 86)

Estelle Brown replaced a teacher who took one look at the Crow Creek School in 1897 and left. She found the living and working conditions harsh, crude, and discouraging and requiring lots of patience (1952, pp. 36 and 42). "Instinctively, [she] felt that, in teaching Indian children to like and want the things we liked and wanted, we were heading in the wrong direction" (p. 42). The Indian service bureaucracy was preoccupied with paperwork and staff morals rather than the first-hand views of their field workers or the Indians they supposedly served (p. 173). "A knowledge of the pupil's environment was not considered necessary since their education aimed to make the environment unsuitable to them'' (p. 204).

Brown found her students to be underfed, forever scrubbing the school, and housed in unheated dormitories. Corporal punishment was discouraged in favor of depriving students of playtime or making them work longer hours. Hoke Denetesosie, a Navajo, found as a boarding school student early in this century that

> Conditions at the School were terrible. . . . Food and other supplies were not too plentiful. We were underfed; so we were constantly hungry. Clothing was not good, and, in winter months, there were epidemics of sickness. Sometimes students died, and the school would close the rest of the term.
>
> It was run in a military fashion, and rules were very strict. A typical day went like this: Early in the morning at 6 o'clock we rose at the sound of bugles. We washed and dressed; then we lined up in military formation and drilled in the yard. For breakfast, companies formed, and we marched to the dining room, where we all stood at attention with long tables before us. We recited grace aloud, and, after being seated, we proceeded with our meal. . . .
>
> Some teachers and other workers weren't very friendly. When students made mistakes they often were slapped or whipped by the disciplinarian who usually carried a piece of rope in his hip pocket.
>
> At the end of the term in May parents and other visitors would come to the school. (Johnson, 1977, pp. 83–85)

Education in white ways was seen as a way to destroy Indian tribal life and to rid the government of its trust and treaty responsibilities. The General Allotment (Dawes) Act passed by Congress in 1887 was designed to break up Indian reservations by giving Indian families small 160 acre farms and allowing the remaining reservation land to be sold to whites.

The Dawes Act did not lead to assimilation of Indians into the dominant society as planned. Instead, it eroded their land base by 140 million acres and made them more dependent on the federal government. The Meriam Report of 1928 condemned the allotment policy and the poor quality of services provided by the Bureau of Indian Affairs. In discussing education, it pointed out shocking conditions in boarding schools, recommended not sending elementary age children to them, and urged an increase in the number of day (non-boarding) schools.

After Franklin D. Roosevelt was elected president in 1932, he appointed John Collier Commissioner of Indian Affairs. Collier helped reverse the assimilationist policies of the Bureau of Indian Affairs. The Indian Reorganization (Wheeler-Howard) Act of 1934 ended allotment of Indian lands and provided for Indian religious freedom and a measure of tribal self-government. Collier also encouraged the teaching of Indian culture and languages in government schools. After World War II the assimilationist trend again gained strength. Under President Dwight D. Eisenhower, several Indian reservations were terminated. However, the new policy to terminate reservations was quickly reversed, and a new policy of Indian tribal self-determination was started that continues to this day.

Conclusion

In this chapter a brief look at how Indians have been taught in the past is given. Perceptive teachers of Indian students saw the advantages of using Indian languages and recognized the gap between what Indians wanted and what was forced upon them in mission and government schools. In the last thirty years the civil rights movement has focused attention on the rights of

Native Americans. Reports like *Indian Education: A National Tragedy, A National Challenge* (1969) focused attention on schools serving Indian students. Schools serving Indian students were also examined from an anthropological perspective (King, 1967; Wolcott, 1967) and found to be destructive to the identity of the children they served. The cultural discontinuity between home and school (Spindler, 1987) and the fact Indian schools often do not recognize and build upon the heritage of their minority students made them ineffective. The lack of culturally appropriate teaching methods and materials, including instruction and materials in their native language, for cultural minority students in most schools is still acute.

Today there are clear and present dangers on several fronts to culturally appropriate curriculum for minority group children in the United States. The "English Only" movement, as promoted by groups such as *U.S. English,* by advocating the adoption of English as an official language (presumably to be used as the sole language in all official government activities including public schools) jeopardized the early education of non-English speaking American children. The "cultural literacy" movement that has received a lot of media attention with E. D. Hirsch, Jr.'s new book *Cultural Literacy: What Every American Needs to Know* (1987) jeopardizes the teaching of non-Western, non-European and non-Judeo-Christian, heritages in our schools.

In 1990, Indian people responded to the "English-Only" movement by getting Congress to pass the Native American Languages Act. The same year the Secretary of Education established an Indian Nations at Risk Task Force. After holding hearings and gathering testimony from Indian people across the country, the Task Force came out strongly in favor of native language use in schools in their final report. In 1992, Indian people gathered from around the country in Washington, D.C., for the first ever White House Conference on Indian Education. Conference delegates passed resolutions expressing strong support for teaching of Native languages and cultures in the schools and getting better trained teachers to teach Indian students.

Throughout history, teachers who were responsive to their Indian students have been more successful than those who have slavishly taught from textbooks and curriculums that do not reflect the cultures of their students. Today more than ever teachers must become advocates for their minority students, protecting them from culturally insensitive textbooks, curriculums, teaching methods, and tests. The late nineteenth and early twentieth century ethnocentrism, cultural chauvinism, and insensitivity to students' needs described in this chapter still exist. Students' lives can be changed for the better by individual teachers learning from their students as well as teaching them.

References for Further Reading

Annual Report of the Commissioner of Indian Affairs to the Secretary of the Interior for the Year 1878. Washington: Government Printing Office, 1878.

Bowden, Henry Warner. *American Indians and Christian Missions.* Chicago: University of Chicago Press, 1981.

Brown, Estelle Aubrey. *Stubborn Fool: A Narrative.* Caldwell, ID: Caxton, 1952.

Eastman, Charles A. (Ohiyesa). *From the Deep Woods to Civilization: Chapters in the Autobiography of an Indian.* Lincoln: University of Nebraska Press, 1977. (First published in 1916).

Eastman, Elaine Goodale. *Pratt: The Red Man's Moses.* Norman: University of Oklahoma Press, 1935.

Golden, Gertrude. *Red Moon Called Me: Memoirs of a School Teacher in the Government Indian Service,* edited by Cecil Dryden. San Antonio, TX: Naylor, 1954.

Hirsch, Jr., E. D. *Cultural Literacy: What Every American Needs to Know.* Boston: Houghton Mifflin, 1987.

Howard, Oliver O. *My Life and Experiences among our Hostile Indians*. Hartford, CT: A. T. Worthington, 1907. (Reprinted by DeCapo, New York, 1972).

Indian Education: A National Tragedy, A National Challenge (The Kennedy Report). Washington, D.C.: U.S. Government Printing Office, 1969.

Johnson, Brodrick H. (Ed.). *Stories of Traditional Navajo Life and Culture by Twenty-two Navajo Men and Women*. Tsaile, AZ: Navajo Community College Press, 1977.

King, A. Richard. *The School at Mopass: A Problem of Identity*. New York: Holt, Rinehart and Winston, 1967.

Kleinfeld, Judith S. *Eskimo School on the Adreafsky: A Study in Effective Bicultural Education*. New York: Praeger, 1979.

Kneale, Albert H. *Indian Agent*. Caldwell, ID: Caxton, 1950.

Meriam, Lewis (Ed.). *The Problem of Indian Administration*. Baltimore: John Hopkins.

Morey, Sylvester M., & Gilliam, Olivia L. (Eds.). *Respect for Life: The Traditional Upbringing of American Indian Children*. Garden City, NY: Waldorf Press, 1974.

Prucha, Francis Paul (Ed.). *Americanizing the American Indians*. Cambridge, MA: Harvard University Press, 1973.

Prucha, Francis Paul. *Documents of United States Indian Policy*. Lincoln: University of Nebraska Press, 1975.

Report of the Commissioner of Indian Affairs for the year 1862. Washington: Government Printing Office, 1863.

Spindler, George D. "Why Have Minority Groups in North America Been Disadvantaged in their Schools?" In *Education and Cultural Process: Anthropological Approaches,* edited by George D. Spindler. Prospect Heights, IL: Waveland, 1987.

Wilson, Raymond. *Ohiyesa—Charles Eastman, Santee Sioux*. Urbana, IL: University of Illinois Press, 1983.

Wolcott, Harry F. *A Kwakiutl Village and School*. Prospect Heights, IL: Waveland, 1967.

Woodruff, Janette. *Indian Oasis*. Caldwell, ID: Caxton, 1939.

The Authors

Dr. Hap Gilliland (Editor, and author of Chapters 1–7, 9, 10, 12 and 17), Professor of Education at Eastern Montana College and president of the Council for Indian Education, has devoted more than twenty-five years to the Education of Native American people. He has taught Indian, Eskimo, and Aleut students at every level from second grade through university graduate school in Montana, Alaska, California, and Washington. He is known for his training sessions for teachers of Native American students in most of the western states, Alaska, and Canada, as well as his work with teachers of the Native children of New Zealand, Australia, Venezuela, Hawaii, and the Philippines. His interests in teaching, exploration, backpacking, photography, and Native cultures have led to the publication of five college texts, sixteen children's books, and one novel. He has also edited over one hundred children's books on Native American life.

Dr. Rachel Schaffer (Co-editor, and author of Chapter 14, English) is a specialist in sociolinguistics. As Associate Professor of English at Eastern Montana College, she teaches a variety of linguistics and composition courses to undergraduate students. She takes special interest in the problems and needs of Native American students.

Lori Sargent (Artist) is a professional artist whose studio is in Riverton Wyoming, on the Wind River Reservation. She exhibits in galleries throughout the country. She has taught art at the elementary school through university graduate levels.

Dr. Sandra K. Streeter (Ch. 8, Parents) is Associate Professor of Education at Eastern Montana College. She has worked with Indian Schools in South Dakota, Minnesota, Oklahoma, Montana, Arizona, and Mississippi.

Dr. Jon Reyhner (Ch. 9, Social Studies, Ch. 16, Native Language, and Ch. 23, Indian Education) is Associate Professor of Education at Eastern Montana College. He and his Navajo wife have lived on reservations throughout the West during his years as teacher and administrator in Indian schools.

Dr. Adrian Heindenreich (Ch. 9, Social Studies), Professor of Native American Studies at Eastern Montana College, has devoted his life to the teaching of Indian students.

Dr. Sandra J. Fox (Ch. 11, Whole Language), Oglala Sioux, has twenty-five years experience in Indian Education. Her emphasis has been the teaching of reading and language arts in BIA schools and in IEA programs.

Mick Fedullo (Ch. 13, Creative Writing, and Ch. 15, Language Barriers) is a language development consultant in American Indian Education. He has taken his writing and language programs to schools on twenty-five reservations across the United States and in Canada. He is co-founder of the non-profit organization ArtsReach: Educational Arts Programs for American Indian Students, and has served as an advisor to the National Education Association-sponsored program, "Solutions That Work." His program, "It's Like My Heart Pounding: Imaginative Writing for American Indian Students," has been selected by the National Education Association as a national exemplary program. He is author of the non-fiction book *Light of the Feather: Pathways through Contemporary Indian America* (Morrow, 1992).

Dr. David M. Davison (Ch. 18, Math), originally from Australia, is Professor of Education at Eastern Montana College and has had broad experience teaching mathematics in varied cultural settings, including experimental work with Crow Indian students.

David Spencer (Ch. 19, Technology) is the ESL (English as a Second Language) specialist for the Hardin, Montana Schools. David is interested in language development issues and is active in TESOL (Teachers of English to Speakers of Other Languages) and MABE (Montana Association for Bilingual Education). He lived and taught English in Tunisia and the Kingdom of Saudi Arabia. David and his wife and daughter live on the Crow Indian Reservation.

Dr. Deborah Reinhardt (Ch. 20, Music and Movement) is Assistant Professor of Music Education at Ball State University in Muncie, Indiana. She taught choral, instrumental, and general music in the public schools for twelve years, including the Busby School of the Northern Cheyenne. As a holder of the Certificate Jacques-Dalcroze, M. M. in Dalcroze Eurhythmics, and a Ph.D. in Music Education, she is an active clinician and workshop presenter on the use of movement in the music curriculum.

Constance L Einfalt (Ch. 21, Communication through Art) Connie is a high school art teacher who is currently a teacher on special assignment for the Thompson School District in Loveland, Colorado. She has taught secondary art for fifteen years in both the Thompson School District and the Jefferson County School District in Lakewood, Colorado. As a Subject Area Leader in Art for her district, she has focused on developing a new art curriculum for her district which will create meaningful experiences in art for children. Her students have been given national exposure for their metalsmithing work, which is based upon the student self-concepts. Her students' work is often based on metaphorical thinking; the work is often used to create self-awareness. Connie is a second-generation art educator. Her mother taught high school art and not only used Viktor Lowenfeld's philosophies on her students but also on her daughters. Connie's belief that children's own experiences and backgrounds should drive the curriculum were undoubtedly derived from a life steeped in art education.

Dr. Robert W. Grueninger (Ch. 22, Physical Education) enjoyed his affiliations with Indian students and colleagues in Montana for ten years before returning to the Midwest to become Chair of Health, Physical Education, and Recreation at Morehead State University in Kentucky.

Index